PLAY ON

Also by Mick Fleetwood

Fleetwood: My Life and Adventures in Fleetwood Mac

Also by Anthony Bozza

Crash and Burn
(by Artie Lange with Anthony Bozza)

Purpose: An Immigrant's Story
(by Wyclef Jean and Anthony Bozza)

I Am the New Black
(by Tracy Morgan and Anthony Bozza)

Why AC/DC Matters

Too Fat to Fish
(by Artie Lange with Anthony Bozza)

*Slash: It Seems Excessive ... But That Doesn't Mean
It Didn't Happen* (by Slash with Anthony Bozza)

INXS: Story to Story: The Official Autobiography
(by INXS with Anthony Bozza)

Tommyland
(by Tommy Lee with Anthony Bozza)

Whatever You Say I Am: The Life and Times of Eminem

MICK FLEETWOOD

& Anthony Bozza

PLAY ON

Now, Then & Fleetwood Mac

The Autobiography

LITTLE, BROWN AND COMPANY

NEW YORK   BOSTON   LONDON

Little, Brown and Company
Hachette Book Group
1290 Avenue of the Americas, New York, NY 10104
littlebrown.com

First Edition: October 2014
Published simultaneously in Great Britain by Hodder & Stoughton

Little, Brown and Company is a division of Hachette Book Group, Inc. The Little, Brown name and logo are trademarks of Hachette Book Group, Inc.

The publisher is not responsible for websites (or their content) that are not owned by the publisher.

The Hachette Speakers Bureau provides a wide range of authors for speaking events. To find out more, go to hachettespeakersbureau.com or call (866) 376-6591.

The poem "Start Close In" by David Whyte is from the collection *River Flow*, published by Many Rivers Press. Copyright ©David Whyte 2007. Photograph credits appear on page 328.

ISBN 978-0-316-40342-9 (hc) / 978-0-316-40357-3 (large print)
LCCN 2014950489

10 9 8 7 6 5 4 3 2 1

RRD-C

Printed in the United States of America

For my children, Tessa, Lucy, Ruby and Amelia

START CLOSE IN

Start close in,
don't take the second step
or the third,
start with the first
thing
close in,
the step
you don't want to take.

Start with
the ground
you know,
the pale ground
beneath your feet,
your own
way of starting
the conversation.

Start with your own
question,
give up on other
people's questions,
don't let them
smother something
simple.

To find
another's voice,
follow
your own voice,

wait until
that voice
becomes a
private ear
listening
to another.

Start right now
take a small step
you can call your own
don't follow
someone else's
heroics, be humble
and focused,
start close in,
don't mistake
that other
for your own.

Start close in,
don't take
the second step
or the third,
start with the first
thing
close in,
the step
you don't want to take

David Whyte

CONTENTS

IF MUSIC BE THE FOOD OF LOVE . . .

Play on. Two words, no more, but they've said it all to me.

They've been, at different times, a simple direct order, a call to action, a mantra and a comforting concept that promised rebirth. I first read them in the most beautiful and romantic couplet in *Twelfth Night,* my favourite of Shakespeare's works. I've never forgotten it; in fact I took it to heart immediately because it spoke to me. When things have moved me so profoundly in this life, be they people, places or things, no matter how they've come to me, I've made them forever a part of me. I've signed countless autographs with the phrase 'Play on'. I've said it to many people in many contexts. As I've made my way through life, as intricate and difficult as it has often been, as ecstatic and debauched as it has too often been, those words have always been with me. What they've come to mean to me has been a rock when the rest of my world was set adrift.

The entire couplet is the inspiration behind the title of Fleetwood Mac's fourth studio album, *Then Play On*, released in 1969, which I still count as my favourite record. My second favourite is easy to choose: it's *Tusk*, released ten years later by a very different incarnation of the band – the only one that many of our fans are familiar with. To those fans reading these words, please do stick around, you'll be amazed to learn how many roads we travelled before we met you.

On the surface, *Then Play On* and *Tusk* have little in common sonically, but listen deeper and you'll hear a band with its back against the creative wall, recording music at the brink of its existence. Both of those albums were made when we would either play on or cease to be, and when the idea of overcoming the insurmountable through creating anew was the only way out for us. I can't say that I saw it as a solution, but I felt it as my faith, and I preached to my compatriots to play on – and that's what we did.

I'm still here, lucky enough to be partnered with the greatest musical comrades I could ever hope to have. We have been through so many ups and downs, and though I denied it for years, particularly to my loved ones, I know now that since this band began, I have devoted my entire life to it. In every incarnation Fleetwood Mac has brought me so much joy that I hope whatever our fans have taken from the music is a fraction of what I've got from it. I've also realised, through trial, lots of error, growing older and hopefully wiser, how much that choice has weighed on my family. It's hard to devote yourself to a musical family of our magnitude while trying to nurture one of your own; it's an unfair tug-of-war I am still working out.

Music is a beautiful language, one that anyone with a beating heart can understand, no matter where they're from. We need to share that, we need to honour that; it's one of the only things that defies the boundaries humans love to erect. Music has seen me through everything – because when all else failed me, it remained the one thing I could rely on. It was, literally, the only thing I knew I could do with some degree of skill.

More than that, it has always brought me joy and allowed me to find my centre. When I've felt lost in life, if I've lost myself in music, I've always found my way again.

I am sixty-five years old at the time of this writing, looking back at forty years in rock and roll. My first gig as a drummer took place in London in the 1960s when I was still a teenager too young to be legally drinking, even in England. I had no proper training, just a desire to be a part of the culture I saw evolving, combined with an innate attraction to rhythm. I went after a dream and found it backing some of the best English blues players of my generation during a time that changed history. I didn't plan any of it, but I did believe that if I stayed true to my muse, I would find my way. And I have – though it's never been easy.

On my farm in Maui, Hawaii, an island that I've been visiting regularly since the 1970s, and of which I've been a full-time resident for over a decade, I have a weather-sealed barn full of memorabilia: photographs, journals, clothes, cars, endless video tapes, concert recordings, all of it bits of Fleetwood Mac and my life. As much as I've always been driven creatively to move forward toward something bigger, brighter and unknown, I'm also a deeply-rooted nostalgic. I adore photos, mementoes, all bits of ephemera that represent each and every time and space I traverse. I'm a hoarder when it comes to these things. I love to document the moment, as much as I realise how much that moment is transient, nothing but a stop on the road.

I am thankful for that preservationist instinct because, having moved houses so many times, across continents, from the UK to Australia to Europe and the States, it's a minor miracle that so much of this stuff is still in my possession. I'm not sure how to accurately convey what it's like to open a photo album and find a Polaroid of a friend who has passed away, or pages of handwritten lyrics of songs, all of them with edits by my bandmates, from decades previous. A flood of memories wash over me when I find these treasures, all of them new again, focused by the perspective I've gained in the years since. It's a beautiful kind of limbo, seeing yourself, your past alongside your present, through a new set of eyes.

I share this by way of an explanation of how this book began. My co-writer and collaborator, Anthony Bozza, interviewed me on my farm in Maui for *Playboy* magazine in March 2012, at a time when I'd just unearthed over fifty hours of footage of Fleetwood Mac touring Japan in 1977; the culmination of the *Rumours* tour. We were in our prime and it was the finale of the band's highest high to date, so I hired a film crew to travel with us, giving them free rein to capture us both on stage and off. My intention was to edit the film and release it as a feature to run in cinemas the year after we wrapped the tour. That never happened; so many things got in the way, and I forgot about that little film for *thirty years*. I wasn't even looking for it when I found it: I was trying to locate home movies my parents had shot of my siblings and me when we were kids. Instead I found a pile of tins in a box that had somehow made its way intact through the various storage units I've had over the years.

I had all of it converted to digital, preserving the saturated colours of the original work as much as possible, then I hired an editor and set about doing an organisational rough cut of what I decided would be a film, a DVD, who knew – I just knew it had to be shared. I was reviewing the first edit of those forty hours of history when Anthony arrived. It was wonderful to relive those all-but-forgotten moments with Anthony, a life long Fleetwood Mac fan. It refreshed my zeal and excitement and so began our journey. Over the course of the next two years, during trips to Maui, and time on the road during our 2013 tour, he and I relived the past. The result is what you now hold in your hand.

This book will not be a definitive history of Fleetwood Mac; you can find the facts and figures and plenty of rumours elsewhere. This is much more personal. It is the story of all that has ever mattered to me, the moments, the people, the time. It's the story of my life in rock and roll and the blues and how the band that has meant everything to me came to define me. I used to say that wasn't the case, but I know now that it's true.

I see things with wonder each and every day. Sometimes I wonder how the hell I got here. I love drumming and I know I've never been suited to do much else, but truth be told, I regard myself as a guy who happens to drum, not as a guy who is a drummer. It's a strange and subtle contradiction, but it's part and parcel of how I see things and how I'm just now learning who I am. I've always valued progress over reflection, and romanticised drama and chaos more than I should have. I don't feel that way anymore. I'm taking the time to look inside now. I'm still a student. I'm still 'in process'.

It reminds me of another philosophy of mine that I rely on when the going gets tough. When it all becomes too much, pick yourself up and go somewhere. Go somewhere you've never been, somewhere you've dreamed of going, somewhere romantic and mysterious. Go anywhere you can, because a journey is an adventure and adventures are how we learn who we really are. Writing this memoir has been a journey for me and I invite you to join in my adventure. It's time now and I'm ready, so if you're coming with me, off we go.

CHAPTER I

THE OLD MILL

Windmill, Norfolk, 1939 (an excerpt):

*We stayed a week and awoke each dawning to the mournful cry of
the curlew.*
The old mill echoed to our youthful laughter
And we lived, oh how we lived.
Every minute was savoured as something special, something rare,
As if we knew the sand was running out
And each second should be cherished with infinite care.

My sweetheart looked at me with fear in her eyes,
'That telegram that arrived today,
'Tell me my darling, what did it say?'
It said, 'Rejoin squadron without delay'.

Wing Commander Fleetwood

I come from a very warm family. My father, John Joseph Kells
Fleetwood, my mother Bridget Maureen, and my sisters Susan
and Sally, and me, we were always close. We were the type of

family that did everything together and always had dinner together, usually my mum's homemade healthy food: lots of soup and roasted chickens, green beans and potatoes. There was always an abundance of huge belly laughs round the Fleetwood dinner table all our lives.

My parents moved house nearly every three years because of my father's career as a wing commander in the Royal Air Force, so for most of my early childhood we were freshly arrived in a new country. Our family unit was the only thing that was familiar and constant, and I believe the ever-changing backdrop and the feeling that we were strangers bound us even closer. I can recall the wonder of it all quite easily, because as a young boy I was fascinated, as were my sisters, by the exotic places where we lived. Norway and Egypt were wonderlands quite different from the UK, which we considered our true home. They instilled within me the idea that the world was a vast place full of amazing and very different people. It was also a great rock-and-roll training camp for me because I became used to travel and being a stranger just passing through. Both sets of my children travelled a lot as kids and inherited the same comfort with moving around.

My earliest memories are of learning to fit in wherever I was, which served me in ways I had yet to understand in my future life as a musician. I have a few vivid memories of those days before my teens. I remember nearly drowning in Egypt; I'm not sure how or why I got into water too deep for my abilities, but I was pulled out by a man in a flowing blue cloak and when I looked up at him I thought he was a magician. He was very much another type of being, which is how my time in Egypt and in Norway left me feeling overall. This was a good thing: I realised, even at my age, that there was something special about their culture and that I should learn from the people who lived there. It was the proper way to do things, which was how my parents taught us.

My parents had a warm and wonderful relationship with each other and seeing that throughout my formative years affected my concept of love and what a romantic relationship should be. They cherished each other; they were best friends, always laughing together and completely in love and, aside from us children, they valued their time alone together above all. My mother was an anchor for my dad and supported all of his pipe dreams. He pursued his writing for three years after he left the Royal Air Force and before he rejoined civilian working life. Mum supported him by moving the family onto a sailing barge to cut costs and to allow him a sanctuary in which to create. She didn't for one minute question him nor complain about living on this odd little boat. Dad did his thing and though it didn't work out, there was no resentment or love lost between them.

My mum had a knack for both keeping my dad's feet on the ground and finding a way to make his dreams a reality. They'd planned, well ahead, how they would spend their later years, blissfully on their own in the South of France after we kids had flown the coop and Dad had retired from the RAF. The problem was that Dad didn't have the money to buy a house in the south of France, so the two of them came up with a plan they could afford. They leased a small parcel of land in Le Muy in the Provence region, near some farmland just a short ride from the Mediterranean coast. They put a caravan on it, the non-motorised camper type that gypsies would live in, and installed plumbing, and every summer they would go down there and have their time to themselves. Later on, when I had the means, I bought a parcel of land next to theirs and a second caravan to go with it so that my sisters and I might visit them. It was a gorgeous piece of land with a view of the ocean and I hoped to build them a house on it eventually. It was such fun to live there like gypsies. My parents loved it and planned to live out their years there.

Dad was always well turned out. It was a holdover from his military days, because that expression meant your appearance was impeccable: a perfect spit and polish on your shoes, down to the soles, and with your hair and collar perfect. He had been in the Household Cavalry in addition to the RAF so he knew how to present himself properly. He had style and I really liked that. My mother did too, she loved to dress up and they always checked themselves in the mirror before they went out to a cocktail party. We weren't brought up surrounded by wealth and luxury, but my parents did a lot with a little and they always looked great. They also had fun up until the very end. I'd bought Dad his dream car, a red convertible Mercedes, and the two of them talked about driving it to their place in the South of France with the wind in their hair.

Unfortunately my father was taken from us too early, well before he and Mum had time to properly enjoy their golden years. When he became ill, at the age of sixty-two, I endeavoured to get them down there for at least one more week, but sadly that wasn't to be.

My father was an Irish storyteller and a wonderful, generous soul; the type that still believed he hadn't done enough at the end of his life, even though his list of achievements outshines most. He was a gentleman and a dreamer and I've done my best to live my life as I imagine he would have, because he was a true role model. I know that I'm very lucky in this regard, because so many people go through life without a guide, and without parents who led by example. My father flew planes, he led men in wartime, and along with Mum he taught my sisters and me how to live and how to love, and I'm proud that I truly knew him. So many men never know their fathers as men, but not me. As adults, before he passed away, we really got to know each other.

I attended quite a few schools in my youth, not only because we moved frequently but also because I was a terrible student. It wasn't that I didn't want to learn, I did and still do. I have a curious mind and I enjoy all manner of history, science and philosophy. I'm also fascinated by what would be considered 'fringe' subjects – the occult, conspiracy theories, and so on – as much as I am by traditional fields of study. The desire was there, but it was disproportionate to my abilities. I have what would be diagnosed easily today as severe dyslexia, so reading, reading comprehension, and most of the basic skills required to stay afloat in school without major assistance are absent in me. Back then, particularly in the UK, learning disabilities weren't understood or even accepted, so students like me were simply left behind. My parents only knew I had problems at school.

Not once did they make me feel that I was disappointing them or that I'd failed them. Nor did they ever beat me up and tell me I needed to go to college. I just have a sense that they understood, as I did, that school wasn't for me. They didn't know the shame I felt at being so unable to succeed. It wasn't easy to show them tests where I'd scored zero per cent, nor did I want to tell them that the times when I had got some paltry per cent right, I'd had to cheat. I found cheating to be worse than failing because it's so exhausting, constantly trying to cover your bases. Dyslexia is very hard; you spend hours going in circles because you don't know how to go in a straight line.

My days at school were nothing short of torture. I developed what I've come to call, since it has followed me through my life, the 'Blackboard Syndrome'. It is a form of paralysis that I can trace back to the very first time I was asked to go to the chalkboard to answer a question. I can't remember the subject – perhaps it was maths – but it wouldn't have mattered; I was done for the moment my name was called. The anxiety of performing something I didn't understand before my class was more than I could bear. If the teacher had handed me a piece of paper with the answer just before calling me, it would have made no difference. The act of walking to the front of the room and attempting to reason through anything at all in front of my peers was just too much for me.

I've suffered from the Blackboard Syndrome for years, so now I understand that it is a lethal combination of performance anxiety and my dyslexia, a duo of traits that renders me useless under pressure given certain conditions. If I feel the pressure to produce or to get something 'right', added to the fact that I know myself well enough to distrust my interpretation of 'the facts' and 'the answer', and I have no one close by who can help me reason my way through it, I find myself in a bind. You'll see how it has played out in my life and how I've learned to live with it, but as a young man in school there could have been nothing worse. Absorbing knowledge in the traditional schoolbook and classroom setting is the antithesis of how I'm able to learn things. I was a fish out of water in an organised educational institution, no matter how liberal or progressive it may have been – and believe me, my parents tried everything under the sun.

School was a matter of survival for me each and every day. I did what I could; whenever I felt that a teacher might call on me, I'd raise my hand first and ask to go to the bathroom.

Some of them figured this out and waited for my return to call me up front. This made things even worse, knowing that a trial awaited me upon my return to the classroom. When they got me up there, I would stand, taller than anyone else in my grade class (I'd shot up past them all by the time I was ten, suffering the bone-wrenching aches of growing pains in my legs every summer) and I'd go mute. I'd just stand there and say nothing. I'd do my best to waste time while appearing to work out the answer, which essentially consisted of doodling on the board. I wished that I could draw better, because I was crap at that too, thinking that maybe if I drew something clever at least I'd get a laugh and perhaps a benevolent pass from the teacher.

It never worked out that way. Instead I was too shy and too paralysed, which made those moments at the board last forever, until the teacher realised just how little I knew and just how poor a student I was and finally had mercy on me. What I needed was a sense of humour and a form of expression. Alas that came much, much later, after I'd abandoned school altogether.

I'm quite convinced that the brain I have comes from my mum's side, because my mother and her kin have a very different, very wonderful way of thinking – one that's not suited to stereo-typical 'straight' thought. My sister Susan had the same issue that I do, and like me, she found a way to turn it into something positive and creative. She became an actress and made it a part of her art.

What I didn't know was that my dyslexia would later serve me well once I turned to playing drums. It wasn't clear to me until years later, when I really began to *think* about drumming, which was something I found myself doing quite naturally. After I'd become known for drumming, and had a 'style' that people talked about, I began to ponder, wonder what exactly that style was. By nature what we drummers do is manage a series of spinning plates, but I realised quite quickly when I found myself talking shop with other plate-spinners that my methods of keeping my plates spinning are entirely my own. When I tried to explain it, they thought I was having a laugh at their expense or entirely mad.

That made it all crystal clear to me – my drumming was an extension of the Blackboard Syndrome. I really had no idea, nor the ability to explain in musical terms, what I was ever doing in a particular song. Upon further reflection, I've realised that all of this stems from my learning disability, and now that I've made something out of my irregular way of processing information, I'm damn glad. Dyslexia has absolutely tempered the way I think about rhythm and the way I've played my instrument, or any other for that matter, and that's the long and short of it.

In the late 1970s Boz Scaggs opened up for us on tour and he had the incredibly gifted Jeff Porcaro on drums. Jeff was still a teenager, and a couple of years away from getting together with his brother to form Toto, who went on to great success in the 1980s. Jeff, may he rest in peace, died at just thirty-eight, but in a short period of time, as a session drummer, had a career that defined the sound of that decade. He was, literally, a part of every big pop and rock record that charted in the 1980s. Along with many of his bandmates, Jeff played on megahuge records like Michael Jackson's *Thriller* and so many other albums and singles of that era.

That was years ahead, but I'd been aware of Jeff even before he showed up in Boz's band. People talk about talent like his the moment it emerges on the touring circuit, and after watching him play just once I was quite intimidated that he was in our supporting band. His style was so technically perfect and consistent that it gave me a huge dose of the Blackboard Syndrome.

It didn't help that once the tour got under way I noticed Jeff sitting at the side of the stage watching me each and every night. He and I had met but we hadn't spent much time together, and that didn't change as the tour drew into its second, then its third week. Still, there he was, every night, watching me play, for the entire set. It rattled me, but I played through it, with the aid of a few additional servings of brandy and red wine. Eventually I'd forget he was there and go about my business. Then sometime during the third week of the tour he came to my dressing room.

'I give up,' he said. 'I can't figure it out so you've gotta tell me. Tell me how you do it.'

'How I do what?' I asked, completely befuddled. I really had no idea what he was talking about.

'I've watched you, I've tried to understand it. Nothing you do up there makes sense, but it sounds beautiful. What's your method? What are you doing during that last fill in "Go Your Own Way"? I can't figure it out! I've been watching every night. What do you do in the last measure on that last beat? Is the snare ahead or behind? Is the hi-hat off beat by two quarters or is it a little more than that?'

'Oh,' I said, taking a huge breath. At least I had an answer, just not the one he wanted. 'Oh, *fuck*. Really . . . I have no idea. I'm telling you, truly, Jeff, I have no idea at all.'

Jeff Porcaro didn't believe me at first; in fact it was clear that he thought I was being coy and pretentious. I don't blame him because the idea that a drummer with my experience had no idea of musical nomenclature was ridiculous. It was only after we continued to talk that Jeff realised I wasn't kidding around. We eventually had a tremendous laugh about it, and when I later told him that I was dyslexic, it finally made sense. He analysed my playing from the perspective of a trained drummer and explained to me that my fills weren't precisely the opposite of what a traditionally trained drummer would choose to play, but they were something close to it. Yet all of it worked, which is what Jeff couldn't get his head around. I had nothing to offer, because I don't ever make a conscious decision to place a hi-hat accent a half beat behind the beat while my snare is just ahead, what I do just comes. I do what feels right and I always have. It's something that Lindsey Buckingham has come to rely on me for and I'm very proud of that. I have what he calls *the feel*.

I might as well say it now: I have no idea what I'm playing, each and every time I play our songs. I've never played the same thing the same way twice – which has driven many a producer and recording engineer to near madness. I really don't know what the hell I'm doing up there. Lindsey Buckingham can vouch for me when I say that there have been more times than either of us would care to count that he's had to tell me what to play by sounding it out. He and I share a language all of our own comprised of noises that fall within the 'boom-crash-buh-bump' category. At this point we are fluent in it.

In 1985, during the writing and recording of *Tango in the Night*, which Lindsey also produced, he was keen to have my drum tracks replicated on a portable drum machine so that he could take them home with him and do further work on the songs there. That is when I think he truly understood just how deeply embedded this dyslexic drum style of mine is, and just how little I know about what I do in a conscious, calculated manner. Machines are logical and methodical and just like Lindsey's brilliant approach to music, machines make sense. Try as he would, there was no way he could programme what

I was playing in the studio into a drum machine, because none of it adhered to a set repeating rhythm that could be tracked on grid. It's not that I was ever out of time, it's just that I never played the basic rhythm of the songs the same way twice from verse to verse. Lindsey isn't one to give up so he did his best, but eventually he realised that how I play doesn't adhere to anything the drum machines of the day could be programmed to do.

It's always been this way, since my second professional gig as a drummer. I've always needed a translator. Back in 1967, I played briefly for a great guitarist named Billy Thorpe (whom I would reunite with years later in my band the Zoo) who had to come over to me before every song to dictate the beat, and usually did so by singing horribly sexual lyrics in the tempo and rhythm that he wanted me to play. It would go something like this: '1,2,3,4, They're going to bang it in your ass, they're going to take it in the ass,' which, to me, would spell out where the bass drum, snare and cymbals needed to fall within the beat.

My father was a military man, but in the true sense of what that means, he was a man who knew the value of service to others and he strove to pass that on to my sisters and me. He wasn't ironclad in his beliefs when it came to how this should be done, however. He allowed all three of us to follow life paths that were far from the straight and narrow because he believed in us, and – along with our mother – he always helped us along the way. His faith in us was a source of strength to me and I feel lucky, because other fathers from a background like his would have been very different. Many men of his generation might have looked upon my dreams and goals as something to be plucked out like a weed, rather than be nurtured like a flower. My dad imparted something to me as a very young man that has stayed with me and set the tone for how I've lived my life. He told me that no matter what I chose to do with my life, if I had a chance to be a part of something I believed in, I must never let my ego get in the way.

He said that it was better to let someone else take the credit for your work if that's the way it had to be, so long as the work got done, got out there and was of service to people. The act of doing good, of making something that served the good of everyone in and of itself, was more important than getting the credit for it, according to Dad. I do believe he was right. When I look at how my life has played out, I know I took his advice to heart because I've spent all of my energy keeping something going that has been for the whole more than it has ever been for my own personal ego satisfaction. There is something to Dad's choices and efforts in that way that I know is within me as well. I don't think it's entirely philanthropic either. It has something to do with deep-seated issues regarding self-esteem and I mean that for both of us. It was hard for Dad to take a compliment and to truly acknowledge how many wonderful things he'd achieved in his life. I am the same way, though these days I'm doing my best to give myself a break.

One of the values my father had, which wasn't typical for a lifelong military man of his generation, was that he valued the arts tremendously. My father always wanted to be a writer, and I believe that is why he supported my sisters and me when we gravitated toward pursuits that were hardly practical. My sister Susan became an actress, attending drama school and eventually enjoying a respected career in theatre and film. My sister Sally went to study at the London Polytechnic when she was sixteen, became a sculptor and eventually a clothing designer. When I showed an interest in playing the drums, my father, who on paper should have been against it, was completely in favour. Rather than browbeat me for having little interest in school (though in truth it was really an inability to properly participate), he and Mum supported the one interest they clearly saw that I had: playing drums.

I love them so much for that, because in my early teens I wasn't easy. I failed miserably in every school they sent me to, and I ran away from several of the boarding schools they enrolled me in, hoping that the well-documented brand of stiff-upper-lip education practised in those institutions would break me from my school daze. That didn't happen, so as the old adage goes, I had two choices, fight or flight, and I always chose flight.

My first exposure to the power of live music came when I was ten or eleven. During a family summer holiday in Italy, we'd all gone down to the beach one day, when I was still young enough to know nothing of sexuality, but my sister Susan had begun to mature. She was looking absolutely gorgeous and this young chap came up to her in a pair of Speedos with a big hard-on. I remember seeing it, just right there, nearly sticking out of his swimsuit, so I ran to tell my dad because Sue was young, probably fourteen, and I didn't know what it all meant.

That night Mum and Dad let the chap take Sue into town to go to a dance and charged me with going along as the chaperone. I'm not sure if it was more cruel for them to send me along, or for Sue to have to bring her little brother on a date, but I forgot about all that when we got to the dance. There was a local band doing nothing exciting, just covering songs by surf-rock pioneers the Ventures, but they had the entire town audience in the palm of their hand. That was fandom: the entire town knew those guys, and they were all dancing, young, old and every age in between. All I could focus on was the drummer; I was fascinated with what he was doing. It was a great feeling.

My parents saw me tapping along on cardboard boxes or furniture to whatever song was on the radio and by the time I was eleven, they rewarded my initiative with a drum set. I'd play along to hits by the Shadows or Acker Bilk and his Paramount Jazz Band, and Mum used to play old 78 rpm records by Charlie Kunz, a great American piano player who came to England in World War II and never left. We listened to a lot of Charlie Kunz and still do. Mum would be humming to the radio and she also liked to make up songs off the top of her head and I learned to play listening to her. When we got our first tape recorder, she used to hum into that and I'd tap out rhythms to her little songs. I never studied music at school, it was entirely a home-grown exercise.

My parents supported my musical interest entirely, even letting me turn a shed out behind our house into my personal rehearsal space, which my mother fondly dubbed 'Club Keller'. By then I was attending a progressive day school, a very enlightened institution. I enjoyed my time there more than any other school I attended, and perhaps if I'd started my education there from the beginning I would have been able to complete school, but that wasn't the case.

The school was based on the Rudolf Steiner philosophy of teaching, and was one of a thousand Waldorf Schools that Rudolf Steiner's followers had started founding as early as 1922. Steiner's schools preached a very individualistic philosophy that was suited to me because it meant I could literally do what I liked all day, so long as I was learning. I do think that Rudolf Steiner had the right idea, but looking back it may have become watered down by the time it got to my generation. I was able to more or less do what I wanted, to learn about maths by juggling, for example, but I still found a way to not quite 'get it' as far as proper learning went. I can't say that I flunked out, because that idea didn't exist in the Steiner universe, but I came as close as possible to doing so. Somehow, I stuck out from the crowd at a place where anything went. I wasn't a misanthrope at all, I was quite social. I just really wasn't myself in any type of regimented school environment.

That is why I chose to spend every minute I could in Club Keller, playing drums, making any kids from the neighbourhood who chose to come by as happy as I could. I took some of my father's old fishing nets and hung them on the walls, I borrowed the family's wind-up Victrola gramophone to play my mum's 78s out there, got some Coca-Cola and invited all the kids I knew to come by after school. I'd charge them admission and give them soda and they'd listen to me play drums along to the records. It was the first time I realised that I might be good at something, which was bringing people together and showing them a good time.

I was inspired to do so because I had caught a fleeting glimpse of what I wanted to do with my life. When I would go to and from boarding school, as a young boy, I'd usually pass through London and spend a night with my sister Sally at her place in Notting Hill. She was in the art scene and she'd take me to an art school party or to Café des Artistes, a famous club in the Chelsea area, where I'd see things that blew my mind.

As a young schoolboy I saw beatnik culture, people reciting poetry, girls in men's black turtleneck sweaters and sunglasses smoking French cigarettes. There was jazz playing, people beating on bongos, wild paintings on the walls and performances of all kinds going on. It was a wonder to me and I cherished those odd nights I got to spend with my sister. Sally was my guide, my protector and in every way my catalyst, because without her I'd never have experienced any of that. I would not have grown into the man I am today. I doubt I'd even have pursued the drums with the same degree of fervour that I did because if she had not taken me around with her, I'd never have known that such a wonderland existed. I saw there was a place for me. I just had to figure out how to get there, because it was close by, just barely out of reach.

CHAPTER 2

HIGH TIMES ON CARNABY STREET

I arrived at a state of determination while I was at the Rudolph Steiner School. Playing drums as a way of life was still a vague, fanciful wish, and I saw no realistic path to that goal aside from collecting instrument catalogues and dreaming. I had a pile of them, from which I'd build fantasy drum kits in my mind's eye, and I carried them around for months, until they'd all become so weathered that I needed to bind them together with tape. I was distraught about school and the dim prospects in my future, so one day I hiked up a hill on campus far away from where anyone might find me, to seek solace under a shady tree. I sat there for hours, feeling desperate, until I could take it no longer and cried out for help. With my catalogues in my hands as if they were holy texts I offered up a forlorn prayer. Confused, sad and earnest to the depths of my soul, I pleaded to God and the universe to hear me. I begged for help to get me what I wanted. I knew I could do it and I knew where I had to go, I just needed someone, or something to *please get me to London.*

I experienced what I consider to be a divine episode under that tree, much like Buddha, though at the time I hadn't yet learned that fable. I saw myself in London, playing drums in clubs, in those smoky rooms I'd seen with my sister. In my vision I was *there* and I was doing it. It was so real I could feel it. I was uplifted and I had the sense that what I saw was there just waiting for me. It was all possible, but when I opened my eyes and looked to the sky I was acutely reminded that it was still out of reach. It was as if I were looking into the window of a store for which I couldn't find the door; I could see it, but I didn't know how to walk into that dream.

So I sat there, under that tree and began to plead aloud. I stayed all afternoon, four hours or more, crying most of the time, talking to the greater powers the rest of the time. When I'd exhausted myself, I got up to leave, none the wiser, but I'd found my determination. I wasn't going to wait for it to happen, and I wasn't going to suffer any more. I wasn't going to stay the course. I was going to strike out on my own, and wherever it might lead me, I intended to get inside of that vision of mine. I walked back down to school knowing that I had to leave for good, come what may.

Telling my parents I was through with education was difficult, but they couldn't have been surprised given my struggles. When I told them my mind was made up, they let me go without a fight, even though I was just fifteen. I'll never forget telling my dad of my decision because it was one of the few occasions I ever saw him with tears in his eyes that weren't from laughing. We were at a little café near our home, having a heart-to-heart and I just came out with it.

'I can't do it, Dad,' I said. 'I don't want to go back to school, and I won't make it through college. I don't know how to do all that. I need to leave school and get on with my life. I want to play drums and move to London.'

He held my hand, making me feel safe, and we both started

to cry. I knew at that moment that he really loved me and that I would be okay because I had his support.

'Well, we will have to sort you out. We have to get you a proper drum kit if you're going to do this professionally. You'll move to London and live with Sally, but you'll have to get a job.'

My father had a way of tempering his criticism and reprimands with the honest insight of a man, not a father, and I found that very enlightening. It allowed me to understand why he might not agree with me, or wished I'd reconsider, but ultimately that he understood my point of view. He did that when I ran away from school, telling me that he knew school wasn't for me and he didn't expect me to think about college, but that I needed to get back in the saddle and finish high school. When I was in a shooting phase with my air rifle as a ten-year-old and I shot an endangered local seagull off the back of the house barge, he told me every reason why what I'd done was wrong and said I needed to shoot tin cans. At which point I frowned and started to feel pissed off.

'However,' he said. '*Damn* good shot.'

I know it wasn't easy for my parents when I left for London, nor was it easy for me; but my parents handled their decision with the same grace, love and wisdom as they did everything else when it came to raising their children. They must have known that they'd instilled within me the tools to find my own way. As a father myself, I appreciate now that it takes great strength to let your teenager move to the big city with nothing but a drum set by way of a future. God bless them both for their faith in me.

I'm sixty-five now and I have my own Club Keller; it's called Fleetwood's on Front Street in Maui, and it's been a journey getting that off the ground, but it's been worth it, every bit.

When I signed the lease on it and set about designing the kind of restaurant where live music, great food and great wine would be the main event, my mother Biddy, who as of this writing is ninety-four, reminded me of something.

'You always did want your own club didn't you? Always inviting your friends round, selling tickets, that was grand. Quite precocious for a teenager. Well now at least you can serve more than Coca-Cola can't you!'

I was gone and away, on my own, leaving behind the last elements of a traditional British teenage upbringing. I had not the slightest idea of what it meant to be a young man of the world and was naive about what lay ahead. I'd never even played in a proper band, but thanks to my father, I was sent off to London with a brand-new full-sized drum kit. It was very flashy, slick black with a glittery finish that seemed as if only a professional should dare play it. A professional show-off at least.

I moved into the attic space at the top of my sister Sally's house and she continued her role as my saviour and cultural guiding light. Sally lived in the Notting Hill area with her husband John Jesse, who was an art dealer, and after I settled in I did the only thing that made sense and went to find a job. I landed one at the department store Liberty, where to my utter bewilderment, they hired me to work in the accounting department. I would have understood if they'd put me on the floor to sell goods, because I could compose myself and was friendly and determined enough to move product, but placing me in an office with paperwork involving numbers? That was madness. In terms of my Blackboard Syndrome, mathematics has always caused my heart to palpitate dangerously. I really have no idea how I got that job. I don't recall the interview, or whatever I wrote on the application that convinced them I was their man. Clearly they didn't ask me to do calculations because if they had the next words I'd have heard would've been 'We'll be in touch' instead of 'You start on Monday.'

I can't be trusted to keep track of how much is coming in or going out when it comes to my own finances, though I've always been good at it when it comes to others. When I was Fleetwood Mac's acting manager, I knew our budgets and stuck to them. But my own? Well, that has been an ongoing saga involving a number of business managers who often produced no better results than I could have. As a result I've seen my share of ups and downs.

But all of that was in a very distant future when I was still a lad of fifteen, living in my sister's attic, a space I accessed via a rickety iron ladder. As a member of Liberty accounting department, I was tasked with reviewing applicants for the store's charge accounts. I had a small office, where I'd sit and pretend to work. I'd have a notepad to doodle on alongside my actual work so that if someone passed by my doorway it looked like I was busily writing away. I'd open the folder that held the application and the documents the applicants were required to provide and I'd arrange all of that on the desk, before starting to draw on my doodle pad. When I grew bored of the current doodle, I'd stamp the application 'Approved', move on to the next and begin a new drawing. Most days I also enjoyed a satisfying nap after lunch.

The guy who'd hired me thought I was well-spoken and well-dressed (clearly the only reason I got the job) and he told me that if I applied myself and stuck with it, I might have myself an office like his one day. His was much larger and better appointed with a window and all the trimmings, but it looked like a fucking cage to me.

I needed the job but I didn't want it. I also couldn't quit

because the family would have been disappointed, so instead I decided to get fired. I did everything I could not to fit in. Liberty was very posh and proper, and I'd dressed the part for my interview, but once I'd decided they must make me go, I wore more casual clothing, typically a roll-neck polo sweater in place of the expected starched shirt and tie. I also grew my hair long and didn't comb it so that it might be more unruly, and I chewed gum as visibly and often as possible when in the company of my superiors, because that was a clear violation of the etiquette guide given to all Liberty employees. I made sure to stride just over the line of acceptable behaviour and my plan worked famously.

Within a few months, my co-workers began logging complaints about me and soon my boss could ignore it no more. He called me in one day and told me that Liberty wasn't the proper fit for me and so it was, with a heavy heart, that he had to let me go. I was probably smiling like a fool the entire time. I remember agreeing with him heartily, as politely as I could. As I walked out of the store that day, I'd never felt more relieved in my life. That was the first and last time I held any manner of straight job. My parents weren't angry, but they didn't offer to support me, though when I did run into problems they gave me a few pounds here and there to sort me out in the short term.

The only problem, of course, was that soon I had no money. That troubled my family more than it bothered me. I was willing to trade money for my freedom. Without a job, I could spend every single day playing my drums in my sister's garage, which is why I'd come to London – to play, though not exclusively in a garage. Sally's garage was a great place to start though, it was a spacious double-doored affair, originally built to house horses. There was plenty of room for my kit, and it sounded nice too. With no gainful employment to take me away from practising, that's all I did, all day, every day, all by myself.

I had no idea what I was going to do next but I found a great comfort in that; the kind of strength a person can only derive from committing themselves to a course of action, come what may. It's not to be done lightly, it should be the result of a very brave, or conversely a tremendously foolish perspective. It can also be inspired by having no other choice, which in my opinion is when it means the most. That's how it was for me; after failing at school and having no prospects ahead, my back was against the wall. Playing drums was the only thing I wanted to do. I had no idea if that would see me through life, I had no idea if I was even very good at it. I didn't care. That was how I felt and it was liberating. If I'd been mature enough to consider the ramifications of such a pledge, it would have been a bit scary, too.

As a shy young man, it wasn't easy being tall (I'm six feet six) and all the more noticeable because of the way I chose to dress. I wore bright-coloured blousy shirts, tight trousers, big belt buckles, boots, and I wore my hair long. Perhaps shy isn't exactly the word, because I've always been social and jovial just like my dad, but when I think about my first days in London, what strikes me is how shy I was in the presence of girls. I'd always liked the girls at school, but I was suddenly out of my league. The girls in London were absolutely gorgeous and enchanting and they were *everywhere*. I was awestruck in their presence and would fall apart just walking down the street. I could be chatting with a bloke about the blues, confident and knowledgeable, but the moment a beautiful girl walked by I became a complete idiot. This may be odd to hear from a guy who adores meeting fans and chooses to hold court to thirty or forty of them every night on tour before the show. Nowadays I have no problem greeting people, whatever the situation. But when I was young, girls were my kryptonite. I wanted to talk to them but I couldn't. I was completely dumbstruck.

I didn't lose my virginity until I was almost eighteen and by then I'd been a gigging musician for a few years. That's kind of pathetic, considering my advantages and the mores of the time. My introduction to sex was very late and basically I had to be railroaded by my first girlfriend, Sue Boffy. Sue was a society girl who always got what she wanted, and when she saw me on stage one night, she decided that I was it. She had me all right. She took me back to her flat in Chelsea and taught me what it means to be a man and a woman.

I was a sheltered country boy in so many ways. I didn't even know what homosexuality was until I moved to London. I had to ask my sister about it because I kept hearing people saying that so-and-so was 'queer', to which I would just smile like I knew what they meant. It reminded me of being at boarding school, when I realised that I didn't know what being a virgin meant. I was even less happy when I found out that I still was one. If I hadn't learned to play in bands, I can't imagine how much longer it might have taken me to lose my virginity.

The world I'd landed in fascinated me and I became a sponge, soaking up everything I could. Though I was not an astute student, I am a keen observer and I took in all of the new customs and concepts that presented themselves to my young mind. It was 'swinging' London, when the mod fashions in Carnaby Street were all the rage, and the sensory overload was incredible. I went anywhere that I heard something interesting might be going on and attended all manner of happenings, where people gathered and talked about ideas. My sister's house was in a cul-de-sac called Horbury Mews in Notting Hill, which, along with neighbouring Ladbroke Grove, was the epicentre of the underground movement in art and music that was soon to define the sixties counter-culture as we now know it. Those neighbourhoods were the real shit, the low-life, hip, starving-artist reality. Jamaicans and art students lived side by side and the working class of all races had to find ways to get along. Out of these burgeoning cauldrons of people and energy, the music, the art and everything that played a part in changing England's cultural identity, and then the world's, started to happen.

Notting Hill is a very different place now; it's extremely expensive to live there and the former diversity and bohemian elements are long gone, but back then it was glorious and larger than life to me. Even at my age, with my inexperience, I knew it was significant. I could feel that this moment in time was *something*. I was aware that I was living in an historic period. If you lived there you were instantly a part of it too because these vibrations were all around you. There was a tangible shift occurring on an international level too, which made for a uniting and vivid moment in time that I don't think can be appreciated properly now.

Today the world is united through technology, so ideas spread and knowledge is shared in a much less organic, human way. It is all done so quickly – only to be replaced with new information. The transaction of sharing ideas is fundamentally different. But there was a time when a band like the Beatles or the Rolling Stones or later on, Fleetwood Mac, united likeminded people around the world the way the Internet or Facebook does today. Bands were a reason for people to gather in groups and exchange ideas – and they used to have to do that in person, not from the comfort of their computers.

31

Bands were a way for people to *connect* with each other and if the bands were good, then their fans were able to plug into something greater than all of them. People are still fans of bands in the same way, and music still accomplishes that goal, but back then was the moment that type of relationship was born. The founding fathers of rock and roll started it, but the bands of the 1960s made it a language that teenagers (and the rest of us) still speak today. It was a revolution that brought a shift in values and a change in times.

In the United States, because of the Vietnam War, that revolution was much more dramatic and visceral than it was in the UK. It had a purpose and a common goal, to end the violence, whereas in the UK it was more about fashion, music, art and a loosening of that traditional British reserve. Everyone was united by music, because music was our vessel to a deeper, mutual understanding. The fact that they loved the Beatles and 'I Want to Hold Your Hand' was something teenagers from both Dusseldorf and Des Moines could agree upon, no matter how different they were. Love, rhythm and teenage lust are universal, and so is shouting 'Yeah! Yeah! Yeah!' at the top of your lungs. If more people did that together more often, the world might be a better place.

I didn't give up on my dream and kept playing in my sister's garage day in and day out, with no audience until the day a guy from the neighbourhood, just a few years older than me, poked his head in to listen. I wasn't playing along to anything, I was just making up beats and fills and enjoying myself so much that I didn't notice him there at first.

'Hey! Hello,' he said. 'I'm Peter Bardens.'

And with that, I awoke into my living dream. If it weren't for Peter Bardens, I could have been alone in that garage for five years. Peter was well-educated, intelligent, extremely witty and always stroking his hair out of his eyes when he spoke. He was eloquent and a great musician, and I suspect he would have been a great writer because his father Dennis Bardens was a well-known author and journalist. Peter was also a great draughtsman and was always drawing satirical comics that were hilarious. He was a complete dreamer, more so even than me, and we shared an ineptitude for handling finances. Peter never deserted his dream, and struggled as a musician, achieving recognition and a modicum of success, but until his death he was still envisioning the next band, the next album, and next project.

Peter was my entrée into the scene; he was already playing in bands and living just a few doors down in the cul-de-sac, Horbury Mews. He wanted to put a new group together and was interested in recruiting me, though he had yet to find the remaining players.

'That other band isn't quite together yet,' he said. 'But in the meantime, how would you like a paying gig?'

'Well yes, of course!'

Suddenly I was thrust into the world I'd been searching for – and with a job. All my doubt was gone; I could tell my family that I'd done it, I'd actually got myself a job as a drummer! I nearly jumped over the drums and bear-hugged Peter that day. It was only one gig, but I didn't care.

I joined a band called the Senders and played exactly one gig with them, in a youth club. We mostly did covers by the Shadows, a band whose records I'd listened to while learning to drum. They were Cliff Richard's backing band, (to all of you in America, Cliff was our Elvis) and they were huge during my childhood. I absolutely adored them and knew all the songs by heart. I did the gig, playing with a real band to a real audience, and the exhilaration was dizzying. There is no feeling quite like it and once I got a taste, I wasn't letting go.

By the summer of 1963, Peter Bardens had got his pop-rock act together and I became the drummer, alongside Eddie Lynch on guitar and vocals, Peter Hollis on bass, Roger Peacock on vocals, Phil Sawyer on guitar and Bardens on keyboards. We were called the Cheynes, named after a fashionable street in Chelsea called Cheyne Walk, where everyone from Mick Jagger and Keith Richards to Marianne Faithfull, Lawrence Olivier and Henry James have lived. The Cheynes' repertoire consisted of Bo Diddley, Buddy Holly and Little Richard covers, plus a handful of originals and we did put on a good show. We toured Britain extensively, playing regular gigs in London as well as short trips on the university circuit with bands like the Yardbirds, the Animals and the Spencer Davis Group.

I must say that, considering our relative youth and great inexperience, we were a pretty hot act for the time. As a band, like a thousand others, we all went to a shoe shop called Anello and Davide and got ourselves Beatle boots, which were basically Spanish dancing boots (they're also known as Chelsea boots). They were a cool thing before the Beatles, but afterwards they were mandatory. We had a crooked booking agent, who I believe was the one who came up with a uniform for us all to wear: leather jerkins, pink Dr Kildare shirts, and brown mohair trousers to go with our boots. We amassed a following locally, and my favourite regular venue was a dive in Soho called the Mandrake. The place was open all night, every night, and when I wasn't playing I usually stopped in there to see who was on. I was still only sixteen at the time, but thanks to my height, no one ever questioned whether I was old enough to drink or be in the club – which I wasn't. I learned so much with the Cheynes, not only about playing, but also about what rock and roll was becoming and what the music had begun to mean.

I saw all of this close up by having the chance to tour and open for the Yardbirds, which we did quite often, and usually at the original Marquee Club on Oxford Street. The Yardbirds were not then the influential band that history has proven them to be, but they already had fans – dedicated, knowledgeable, die-hard fans – something I'd never seen before. It was the first time I realised exactly what that meant. Before then I'd always seen my fellow audience members as people like me, there to absorb the music. This was different, these were people who were there just for the Yardbirds, to see them play songs that they already knew by heart because they'd seen them many times before. These people shouted out to their favourite band members as if they were old friends. This was very early in their career, too, at a time when the Yardbirds had a blonde lead singer with one lung named Keith Relf and a young guy on lead guitar named Eric Clapton, who was good, but at that stage, honestly, he was still just a guy in a band and didn't stand out whatsoever.

Later I would see the same thing when I saw the Rolling Stones play gigs at Eel Pie Island, a tiny piece of land in the middle of the River Thames. Those audiences hadn't just come to hear blues and rock and roll, they had come to hear *those guys* play blues and rock and roll. That might seem silly to say about legendary acts like the Stones, the Yardbirds and Clapton, but at the time they were nothing more than cover bands with a few original tunes in their repertoire. They hadn't even begun to find themselves, so to see that degree of dedication from an audience was eye-opening. The energy of that idol worship was tangible and when we opened for the Yardbirds I could feel it, even though the fans weren't there for us.

That moment in time was the start of 'bandmania', an unfolding phenomenon that soon went completely viral as we'd say today. This happened to the Cheynes as well; we had people following us from pub to pub around London. With the Cheynes I also lived through every cliché that young inexperienced bands endure. We were ripped off by promoters and kicked out by venue owners without being paid after playing a great show. Our booking agents gave us a van and a PA system to tour with but had included words in the small print of our contract that required us to repay them at a loss. We'd play gigs all week long, driving for hours in a freezing cold van, only to end up with pocket change. But I wouldn't have traded it for the world, and eventually, by being as thrifty as I could, I moved from my sister's attic into a small flat that I shared with one of my bandmates. It was about then I also got my first car, an old taxi. I've always been a nut for motor cars.

The Cheynes recorded a few singles, gained momentum around London, and in 1964 did a tour with the Rolling Stones just as their star began to rise. The Stones had been booked on a tour of old cinemas, and we'd been hired to play as the back-up band for the pop legend and opening act Ronnie Spector and the Ronettes. Ronnie, aside from taking the house down every night with her unparalleled vocal gifts, answered patiently our never-ending questions about her then-husband Phil Spector. Like almost everyone in the world of music, we were fixated on his famous 'Wall of Sound', on every technique he used to capture such massively beautiful soundscapes. 'How many guitarists did he have doubling those parts on "Sleigh Ride?" How many musicians were required to lay down the basic tracks? What was the room like?' We didn't leave her alone for a minute!

When she told me how Phil had built a platform that hung

five feet from the floor by thick chains to hold the drummer's kit, I nearly died. He'd built it because he believed that drums should be recorded from every side, including below. I was grinning from ear to ear; this made so much sense to me because no one knows more than a drummer how much reverberation is created and how much is dissipated into the ground as we play. That echo is a powerful feeling that both grounds us and drives us. The fact that Phil Spector had tried to capture the sensation that a drummer felt when his bass and snare vibrated his stool was genius as far as I was concerned. I could barely contain my envy, vowing to myself that one day I'd record with a producer like him, if not Phil himself.

That tour was magical to me. The Stones really took care of us, looking after us like little brothers, and that is when and how I got to know Brian Jones quite well. I feel lucky about it because Brian was a special soul, in many ways far too sensitive and perceptive for this world. A brilliant, fluent multi-instrumentalist, he was the one who founded the Rolling Stones and he had the creative vision that helped them to evolve organically from a mop-top blues-pop group into the mystical rock gods they became – something that many people today might not realise. Brian had a huge heart and we became friends very quickly. We'd sit and talk about the blues for hours, trading stories we'd heard about the recording of the songs we both loved.

Later, Brian and I became even better friends when I was dating the young beauty who became my first wife, Jenny Boyd. Our social circles became intertwined and we saw each other all the time. Jenny and I used to go round to Brian's flat to hang out and even to participate in the séances he'd hold at his mews cottage in Fulham. At the time Brian had a girlfriend called ZuZu and the two of them would pull out the Ouija board and we'd attempt to communicate with the dead. Peter Bardens' father had written a book about ghosts that we had all read, so we were scared and fascinated at the same time.

I'm far from the first to have said so, but I'd like to confirm that Brian Jones was, without question, one of the sweetest human beings and the most visionary musician I've ever met. He's yet another who died too young, at twenty-seven, the same age as far too many of his peers – Janis Joplin, Jimi Hendrix and Jim Morrison, as well as Kurt Cobain and Amy Winehouse in the years to come.

Bill Wyman was a great mentor to us as well. The Stones bass player took an interest in us and brought us a song he'd co-written with a former bandmate named Brian Cade (they were in a group called the Cliftons together) called 'Stop Runnin' Around.' Bill played bass on it and co-produced it with Glyn Johns, whose work with everyone from the Beatles to the Eagles to the Clash is iconic. The song came out as a B-side to our song 'Down and Out' in 1965 though it didn't chart (none of our singles did), it was just so cool that Bill did that for us.

There is a reason why Mick Jagger was with Marianne Faithfull at that time and their relationship encapsulates all that was changing in the counter-cultural scene and in English society as a whole. Marianne came from a very sophisticated family and dating Mick Jagger, who was well-educated but very much associated with a working-class band and movement, was symbolic. It was the epitome of the cultural shift and their relationship was a catalyst for it. Marianne was one of many well-bred members of the scene, such as Tara Browne, an heir to the Guinness fortune, and many like him were of the younger generation and wanted to be a part of this new movement. They included members of the aristocracy, some in their twenties and thirties and others who were even older, lords and ladies and members of parliament, who aligned themselves philosophically with the more radical ideas of sixties culture. All of these people could be found hanging out at the same clubs where we played and at parties in posh properties where the Stones would be the main course.

The Rolling Stones were the crown jewels that the wildest of the rich, young and privileged felt they had to possess. They were the best party favour anyone could hope to have at their gathering. I'm not sure if any of their party hosts realised it, but as funny, fuzzy and odd as they saw the Stones, these eccentric entertainers were the ones who truly held the cards. They became the linchpin to those aristocrats' social lives more than they would have thought possible when they started inviting them round.

After the Cheynes toured with the Stones, we were accepted and we found ourselves invited everywhere that they went. At the end of that brief tour, I wondered if I'd be seeing Brian again soon and I remember him turning to me and saying, 'Well, you'll be coming along with us now, won't you?' It was that simple and we did.

It was a moving scene that would start at a number of pubs or clubs and usually move to some elegant townhouse that lads like us would never have imagined being inside. Rolls-Royces and Bentleys would be parked out front, antiques were every-where, and the men wore gorgeous velvet jackets. I wanted clothes like that too. So I saved my pennies until I could afford to have one shirt made and I scoured the second-hand shops for the right funky old scarf to wear with it. Everyone looked so cool and it was all so exciting.

In the way that people talk about Paris in the 1920s, everyone who was a part of London in the 1960s knows what I mean when I say there will probably be nothing like it in this lifetime.

The working classes and the children of the rich were sharing the same space for the first time, all of us finding ourselves. Everyone was like-minded and anything was possible, and why not? Musicians were the pied pipers who rallied the socialites, the fashion folks, all of the mods, the models – just about everyone.

Music was our shared playground, but I must say that without those younger aristocrats unwilling to follow the path set out for them, a lot of it wouldn't have been as swinging. They were the patrons, just like the families throughout history who commissioned great works, from Wagner to da Vinci. Their patronage wasn't as directly influential or recognised, but they furthered everything. The easiest way to think about it is that something exploded and it was heard. Then it grew bigger until it was no longer exclusive to the lucky ones sitting in town-houses in Chelsea and it became everybody's property.

The Stones and the Beatles became the spokesmen for a generation, the vehicles that allowed a large number of people to come out of their shells and that had a lot of repercussions. For one thing it caused a much deeper, eventually dangerous degree of fandom. You only have to look at how obsessed people became with John Lennon, or any of the Beatles, and how personally they took it when John hooked up with Yoko Ono. It made no sense that people should feel failed by an artist for the decisions he made in his personal life, but it happened. This was the start of that kind of devotion when it came to our cultural public figures. The Stones and the Beatles were living billboards for a movement that changed from day to day, just as they did as people, because everything was new and in flux then. They were the flag-bearers and they ended up bearing the brunt of a storm that wasn't necessarily of their making.

When the government and the more conservative lawmakers

tired of the younger generation's taste for drugs and flamboyant living, they went after the figureheads. The Stones were busted for drugs, constantly harassed and eventually forced into exile in France. It was all reported in the newspapers, served up as a morality tale by the powers that be, but they didn't win in the end. They tried their best but they couldn't hold back the tide of change. By the end of the 1960s, the counter-culture was accepted, but only after it was deemed fashionable.

Now, looking back on what happened then in London, I am reminded of a story my dad told me about a journey he took by canoe, as a young man. He rowed his way down the Rhine, through Germany and France, and though it was well before the Second World War, he saw things he could not ignore. He observed the start of the Nazi movement and he wrote about it in his journals. There was something afoot that he didn't understand. He knew only that something tremendous was about to happen there and it was but a matter of time before the pieces came together to form a larger, and in this case ominous, whole.

Forgive me for drawing such a negative parallel with the sixties scene in London. I do so only because I remember how my father spoke of that trip and I felt the same way about that particular moment for me. Things were happening, there was something coming together, but I didn't know what it was. I knew it was bigger than me. It was bigger than all of us, even those at the centre of it all. And it was coming our way.

CHAPTER 3

JENNY

By 1965, the Cheynes had wound down to a logical demise. None of our singles ever really hit it big and we were going in circles creatively. Since we had the same agent that booked most of the top British blues bands, among them John Mayall and the Bluesbreakers, I came to know a man who has never left my side since – my best friend, the other side of my brain, and the fellow without whom musically I'm only a fraction of what I can be. That would be Mr John McVie. When I met him, John was one of the untouchables because he was in the Bluesbreakers, whom everyone had huge respect for. He and I had been on so many of the same bills that we became what I call 'nodding partners'; one of those people you see often but don't know, so you never talk but you nod at them, 'Hey, how you doin'?' and keep walking.

John was known to be a great guy but also had a reputation for being a lot of fun. If you were going to be hanging out with John McVie, you'd better saddle up if you planned on keeping pace with him. I noticed John because he was always turned out in a classic blues band style. He'd have on perfectly faded jeans, a pair of gym shoes, white T-shirt and his Fu

Manchu moustache. He had a very cool, 'don't fuck with me' air to him. He wouldn't leap around, he'd just stand there and play beautifully. He's never changed.

John was born in Ealing, West London, and like me, he learned to play his instrument by listening to the Shadows. His first bands played Shadows covers exclusively and John learned to play bass to be contrary to all of his peers, who only wanted to play lead guitar. John left school at seventeen, and after a stint as a tax collector and gigging in a few bands, he ended up playing in John Mayall's Bluesbreakers for about two years before we met. Mayall's band, unlike the Stones and the Yardbirds who went off to conquer America, had remained in Britain and focused on becoming purists of their form.

So when American electric blues became an internationally acknowledged art form for the first time, John Mayall and his outfit became the backing band of choice for every great American blues master who journeyed across the pond. The demand was there and those that came to the UK were received with open arms because they completely blew our minds. From John Lee Hooker to Sonny Boy Williamson to B.B. King, when those great bluesmen toured England they toured with John Mayall, thanks in part to the Stones for going to America and flying the flag there for the blues.

This is where John McVie cut his teeth playing bass and that is why he does so as divinely as he does. John possesses a tone and rhythm and a progressive sense unlike anyone I've ever heard. Back then he was a cut above, and he's done nothing but improve with age. He is the greatest dance partner; the type who knows what you're going to do before you do it, because they've been leading you all along.

John and I became instant friends and we began to spend time together in the clubs and at my flat, sharing pints and our love of the blues. To this day, we've never been at a loss for things to talk about. John was one of my first close friends. I didn't have mates from school because I changed schools so often, so Peter Bardens, then Peter Green, and then John McVie were the first real male friends I had ever made. It would be some time before John and I would be able to translate our friendship to the stage, however.

After the Cheynes, I answered an ad in the weekly music newspaper *Melody Maker* and landed a gig in a band called the Bo Street Runners, who had been put together via a contest on the pioneering music TV show *Ready, Steady Go!*. That was fun and more importantly it paid the bills. The lovely thing about being in the Bo Street Runners was that I formed a friendship with our singer John Dominic that has lasted a lifetime. He is one of my closest friends in the world and he always will be.

At this time I also began a relationship with Jenny Boyd, who became my first wife years later. I'd been obsessed with and was utterly in love with Jenny from the first moment I laid eyes on her. I'd see her coming home from school each afternoon as I sat having my breakfast in the window of one of my two favourite cafes in Notting Hill. She was an absolutely gorgeous young girl, the same age as me, but I couldn't muster the courage to speak to her, let alone ask her out. I was besotted. All I knew was that I wanted one of those.

Jenny and I have been through so much together, including raising our two beautiful daughters, Amelia and Lucy, and I'm blessed to say that we are still the very best of friends. She's a part of me, and so much a part of my early life that it feels right to include some of her own memories of those early days here in this book. Jenny has a PhD in psychology and has written two books of her own, so her recollections of those days and her analysis of our relationship are as valuable as mine.

Jenny recalls the first time she saw me: I was a sculpture. Literally, I was a piece of thin copper wire bent into the shape of a boy sitting on the edge of her friend Dale's desk in the stifling summer heat of their classroom in 1964. Her teacher was reading to them from *Macbeth*, which was far less interesting to her than the sculpture with the long legs that Dale had fashioned.

'What is that?' she whispered.

'It's a boy called Mick Fleetwood, who is fab,' Dale replied, her eyes opening wide. 'He plays drums in a group called the Cheynes. He's got long, straight hair and these long, long legs.'

Jenny stared at the copper version of me as Dale sat it in her inkwell. Jenny was intrigued.

'Come with me to meet him,' Dale said. 'He's always at the Coffee Mill cafe. He's so cool.'

The Coffee Mill was one of my two aforementioned hangouts, where I ate before heading off to gigs, and it was situated on a bend in the road, not far from Portobello Market. That is where I was when Dale and Jenny came and met me one Saturday afternoon.

As Jenny recalls, I was wearing black mohair trousers held up by a dark belt with a large metal buckle. Above that I had on a pink shirt with a white collar. I was tall and skinny, with thick, brown shoulder-length hair covering most of my face. When I did sweep my mane aside she's told me that the most enormous cow-eyes she'd ever seen would look directly at her, then flicker like a butterfly about the room before landing on her face again. She found me very gentle and softly spoken.

When it was time for me to get ready for my gig later that afternoon, I invited the two of them.

'We're playing in Brentwood at the Town Hall. Why don't you catch the train? It's not that far.'

They agreed to come and off I went, as my ride was waiting outside, a transit van full of my bandmates.

The girls came up to Brentwood early enough to be there while we set up. Jenny sat on the edge of the stage watching as I loaded in and assembled my drum kit and once I was done I went and sat with them. Jenny recalls that when I did, my foot came to rest on hers and when she tried to move it away, the pressure increased until I'd pinned her foot to the floor. I have no recollection of doing this consciously but the body wants what it wants, so I'm quite sure my subconscious was at play. Whatever the motivation, Jenny's sixteen-year-old self took this as a sign that I liked her. And did I!

She liked me too, but she wanted to be a loyal friend to Dale, so she tried to hide it. She has said that if it weren't for Dale, she and I would have got together a full year before we did and that she'd never have dated our singer Roger Peacock. Good Lord. How cruel retrospect can be. Dale and I never even went out, for God's sake! Receiving knowledge like this at my stage of life is a double-edged sword, because you can't change the past, so it makes you wonder just how much wasted time you might have spent otherwise.

The Cheynes were the first live band Jenny had ever seen and she says the experience transformed her. She'd never seen a crowd go mad for rhythm and blues and she'd never heard the power of songs by Bo Diddley, Chuck Berry and Howlin' Wolf played live. She spent the night in the front row, where our guitar player Phil winked and smiled at her and, as she told me later, she decided she was in love with rock and roll. Oh to be sixteen again. At the end of the night we gave her and Dale a lift back to London in the group van and she drifted off to sleep at home with the sound of a cheering crowd in her head.

After that I began to see Jenny more frequently at the Coffee Mill or the other cafe I frequented, the Mercury. Typically I'd be sitting around eating an omelette and chips with my flatmate Roger Peacock and Peter Bardens, waiting for the other guys to show up with the van, when she'd pop in after school. I adored her, but did nothing about it. It didn't help that Jenny was just as shy as I was, and when we spoke about this period for the book, it brought tears to my eyes. We were just so innocent; reliving it warmed my heart. We were two kids, completely in love, in awe of how love felt and utterly incapable of expressing it to each other.

The first of many downsides to this was that I stood by paralysed as my friend and bandmate Roger made a beeline for the girl who'd stolen my heart and to make matters worse, he managed to make her his girlfriend. That was Jenny's first relationship, and as his flatmate, I bore witness to the entire thing, which was torture to say the very least. I began to avoid them at the flat and everywhere else, because I couldn't bear it. I felt like a coward for not making a move first, but I'd lacked the confidence, and that left me feeling utterly inadequate as a young man. All of this while my friend enjoyed the girl I couldn't stop thinking about – it was a hopeless situation for me. What I didn't know was that while I tried not to be at home when she was there, Jenny used to hang around the flat hoping to see me. She's told me that whenever we crossed paths, all she kept thinking was that she'd rather be with me than with Roger.

When she turned seventeen, after she and Roger had been together for a year, Jenny left school and began working as a house model for fashion designers Foale and Tuffin on Carnaby

Street. She began to travel to New York as well and had a promising career ahead of her. The candle I held for Jenny never went out and I stayed in touch, always making sure I knew where she was and what she was doing. For me it was simple: I loved her and I wanted to be with her. I believed it would happen because my feelings were unwavering.

One day I decided to pop by the shop in Carnaby Street to surprise her. Roger and I no longer lived together so I hadn't seen her in some time and I missed her. She was sitting there between fittings, looking gorgeous, when she noticed me standing in the window. As she's reminded me, I was wearing a long white cardigan, which was more or less my uniform by then, and black flared trousers. I'd cut my hair short into the Vidal Sassoon bowl cut that was all the rage at the time. I was hanging about with a couple of friends, obviously there to see her, but trying to look casual about it. She's told me that the new hairdo did wonders when it came to exposing my 'smooth baby face' and that she was very pleased to see me. I came in and sat down and then my buddies, great wingmen that they were, drifted off and left us alone.

I pulled out a cigarette, a habit I picked up for a very brief time, and for appearances mostly. I felt like smoking made it easier to strike up conversations with strangers.

'Would you like one?' I asked her. I was incredibly nervous.

'No thanks,' she said.

Jenny says that cigarettes didn't suit my baby face and she suppressed a smile when she noticed how I didn't even inhale.

'I've joined a new band,' I said.

'Did you?'

'Yes. It's called the Bo Street Runners. Those guys that were just here are in the band, too.'

'That's great!' she said.

'They won a talent competition on *Ready Steady Go!* that was held to find the band that would replace the Beatles.'

She smiled at me. 'Are you playing around here any time soon?'

'Yes we are, we're playing at the Marquee Club in Soho next week. You ought to come.' An uneasy pause. 'Would you like to?'

Jenny tells me that after I said that, I stared at her long and hard and didn't look away. She felt herself blush.

'Jenny,' I said. 'I heard from my sister that you aren't going with Roger anymore.'

'That's right,' she said. 'Going off to New York to model made me grow up. It was good for me. When I came back I realised how arrogant he was.'

'Well, I could see that, right from the start,' I said. 'He never treated you properly.'

This opened something up between us; we'd both had our fill of Roger, and he gave us something to commiserate about. It wasn't an act, I really had hated the way Roger treated Jenny. She was a plaything to him.

'Living there while you were together wasn't easy, Jenny,' I said. 'I could barely stand seeing him at gigs, because he'd be there laughing, bragging, talking about how many times he'd stood you up at the Coffee Mill. How he'd leave you waiting there for three hours just for fun.'

'Sometimes he wouldn't arrive at all,' she said, lowering her head.

I stayed as long as I could, until it was time for me to meet my bandmates and hop in the van. We had a gig out of town to get to, but before I bid her farewell, I bent down and kissed Jenny on the cheek. I wasn't going to let her slip through my fingers again.

'I will see you soon. Let's go to the cinema one evening.'

'I'd like that,' she said.

A few days later I paid her another visit at the shop. I arrived in the afternoon with newspaper in hand and stayed until they closed, dutifully researching films that Jenny and I could see in the West End that evening, when I wasn't staring at her. The cinema was the perfect setting for us; we could be together, consumed by our feelings, and free of the onus to say what neither of us was capable of saying to each other.

By then I'd moved into a large flat in Finchley with Peter Bardens, who was playing with a band called Them from Belfast, in Northern Ireland, led by a fiery, soulful vocalist named Van Morrison. The place was one enormous room, a proper loft as large as a banquet hall, with a small bedroom at one end and a kitchen and bathroom at the other. We had so much space that our friends were always coming and going, sleeping on the floor or just laying about smoking dope. It was the perfect crash pad and practice space in one, where music was always happening.

This was also a good setting for Jenny and me, at least in terms of our awkwardness with each other. We could just *be* in that flat; we could sit there holding hands, listening to Mose Allison or Bobby Bland while sharing a joint. Although, according to Jenny, and I do agree, the more stoned we got, the more deafening the silences between us grew.

Fortunately when that happened there were always distractions to snap us out of it. No one ever went to sleep before 3 or 4 a.m. in that flat, so it was typically littered with bodies until late the next afternoon. Poor Jenny would have to pick her way through the human minefield on her way to work in the morning, trying her best to look put together after a mere two or three hours rest. She was the only one who saw the morning light on the other side of 6 a.m.

I wasn't much help to her either. That was my home and that was my world and I was in it. I'd do things such as call her at work to play her a drum fill I'd come up with while practising, after I'd arisen at 1 p.m. One day I called and asked her very seriously to listen, and then embarked on a solo that never ended. Later she told me that she listened as long as she could, so as not to hurt my feelings. Eventually she put the phone down, helped several customers, and then returned to discover that I was still playing. I was off in the ether.

I can understand why, because Jenny and I were now officially together. I was over the moon and wanted nothing more than to be with her every moment of every day. By the way, Roger Peacock never got over this. He held a grudge, to the point that one day we were in a pub together and someone told me that Roger had a knife on him. When Roger asked me to come outside and have a chat with him, I was convinced I was going to get my face cut up.

Jenny and I also started hanging out with her sister Pattie and her boyfriend George Harrison. He was friendly, kind, thoughtful, natural in his own skin, and loved to laugh. He was a whole load of fun and we formed a friendship, but he formed a bond with Jenny that lasted their whole lives. George taught me the value of spirituality, because even as a young man he was very in touch with his soul. I learned a lot just being around him and, in retrospect, even more. George was talented musically but in my opinion his real contribution was the lifestyle and cultural change he brought to the Beatles and therefore the world. They went to India because of him and look at the effect that had. George was responsible for all of that and it was because of his spirit.

Jenny and I would go out to nightclubs such as the Scotch of St James, the Establishment, and the Crazy Elephant, which were the places to go at the time. We'd sit with the rest of the Beatles and their wives and girlfriends, and it couldn't have been better.

Jenny's favourite club was the Scotch of St James, which was dimly lit and packed with tables surrounding a small wooden dance floor. That was where we met Keith Moon of the Who one night and he introduced us to a little pill called methadrin. It was a stimulant and after we took it, we had no problem talking. We literally didn't shut up for hours. Those clubs were places where guys as famous as Keith or the Beatles could just enjoy themselves. They were special because there was a camaraderie and a mutual respect between the musicians and those like-minded people who just wanted to hang out. It was all about how you looked and dressed, and the music you liked spoke volumes. I say this because I'm not sure anyone can appreciate how back then, in places like that, being famous or a celebrity didn't mean anything. There was no elevation, no idol worship, no one ever asked anyone else for autographs. Everyone was a part of the same family ideal-istically, famous or not. It was unspoken but obvious to everyone. We were all one and we were in it together, because we all understood.

We drifted along into the summer of 1966 and before we knew it Jenny and I had been together a year, which was when I felt the pang of heartbreak for the first time. I'd never known a deeper loss and it was devastating. In the twelve months since we'd been an item, Jenny's modelling career had taken off and she'd begun to spend more and more time abroad. I was happy for her, though I missed her when she left. I wanted no one else and I thought she knew this, but apparently that wasn't the case. I don't blame her; I think it's clear that I had a hard time being demonstrative, but none of that made it hurt any less.

One day after we had spent the night at my sister Sally's house in Notting Hill, Jenny got up early to catch a plane to Rome for a week-long modelling gig. From what she's told me, I bid her farewell, but didn't kiss her goodbye and was far too casual about it, which she took as an indication that my feelings for her had cooled. That couldn't have been further from the truth and what she didn't know was that I watched her from the upstairs window as she walked out of the mews, watched her until she was out of sight, and longed for her return the moment she was gone.

Jenny left thinking I didn't care and did her best to avoid thinking of me while she was away. Unintentionally, she felt insecure and rejected by me, which isn't how a guy wants his girlfriend to feel on a journey alone, to a place as romantic as Rome. She stayed in a beautiful palazzo, took part in a fashion show held in a railway station with a live band playing. From the sound of it, her trip was magnificent and somewhere in there she took a shine to an American guy who was playing in the band. They had a brief flirtation, but when she came back to England she told me that she'd met someone, and that it was over between us. Since then she's told me that her time in Rome had given her a taste of independence, which she didn't necessarily want but pursued because she thought my feelings for her were only fleeting. I was too shocked by the news to react.

Jenny was dead wrong about my feelings, but it's my fault for masking my love for her with nonchalance and detachment. This pattern plagued us for years, and we were never capable of overcoming it, though we tried to make things work over and over again. Whenever I'd seem uninterested and too far away, it triggered her insecurity, which then caused her to act out and hurt me. The tragedy was that I cared a lot, always, I was just paralysed by shyness and an inability to put my feelings into words. I assumed she knew how I felt and she didn't.

After Rome we split up and stayed apart for two years. During that time I spent countless nights in my car, parked outside the house Jenny moved into with the incredibly gifted R&B singer Beryl Marsden. I'd sit there, watching her bedroom, waiting for her light to go out. I was back where I'd been at sixteen, once again unable to approach her.

I dealt with the heartache by immersing myself in music. I'd already left the Bo Street Runners and joined Peter Bardens' new band, Peter B's Looners, later shortened to just the Peter B's. That was a good outfit. We were entirely instrumental, playing R&B and soul in the style of Stax bands like Booker T & the MG's. After a month the original guitarist left and as his replacement Peter Bardens found an eighteen-year-old who'd never held down a regular professional gig as a musician before. The guy's name was Peter Greenbaum but he went by Peter Green.

Peter Green was unlike anyone I'd ever met before and unlike anyone else on the scene – which really was saying something. He hailed from a working-class Jewish family, born in the East End of London and raised in Putney. His childhood hadn't been easy and he'd worked as a butcher and furniture polisher, while playing bass on the side for a number of local bands. As a child his musical pursuits were shunned by his family as indulgent and impractical. But he had a gift and after he first saw Eric Clapton, he picked up the guitar. He chose to play a Gibson Les Paul because Eric did and when Eric joined John Mayall's Bluesbreakers after leaving the Yardbirds (where he was replaced by Jeff Beck), Peter began to follow them just to watch Eric play. Peter was determined to join that band and when Eric ran off to Greece on a whim, leaving Mayall without a guitar player, Peter filled in until Eric returned. That was the extent of his experience.

None of that mattered, of course, because Peter Green was meant to play the guitar. In the Peter B's, Greenie came into his own. The first time he played with us, I was impressed but not awestruck. Honestly, I wasn't sure that he'd be of much use to our sound. He was capable of playing the expected blues but I didn't see him creating much beyond that. I told Bardens what I thought but he told me to be patient, to wait and see. He believed that this guy had a talent that he was too inexperienced to understand. There was a player in there and I'd see him too, if I stood by and supported him properly.

'I'm not so sure Peter,' I said. 'How long do you want to wait?'

'Won't be long. You'll see.'

Well, Bardens was right. In no time Peter Green found his tone – and what a tone it was. Once he'd settled in and trusted us backing him, Peter Green's playing became the voice no one could ignore. He could be running through a blues progression we all knew, one that we'd heard a million times, but after he'd emerged from his shell, when Peter played it, those same old notes sounded brand new. Peter's guitar tone was wailing, high and lingering. It gave me shivers every single night. It still does today.

I can say without hesitation that Peter Green was the most brilliant musician I have ever played with. When he was well, he was on a par with a genius like Miles Davis. Like Miles, Peter said things about music that as a young man I didn't understand but never forgot and now, after a lifetime of playing, make complete sense. He was my mentor, he was my teacher, my captain and for a time, my best friend.

Peter is a hero to so many guitarists, from heavy-metal bands like Metallica to blues connoisseurs like Aerosmith. He wrote 'Black Magic Woman' in 1968, the song that made the band Santana famous two years later, which is why Carlos Santana asked Peter and me to play that song with him at the Rock and Roll Hall of Fame induction ceremony in 1998, as Fleetwood Mac were being inducted the same year. Since the last time he'd even played that song, probably ten to fifteen years earlier, the complicated mental illness that seized Peter in 1970 had transformed him from the friend and co-pilot I'd loved so dearly, to a mystery I still can't fathom.

His desire to perform publicly had been erratic; his career full of short tours here and the odd contribution to my records and others' there, often not credited by demand. All of it had been random, dictated by whatever his mood at the time happened to be. Since the onset of his condition, Peter had struggled morally with the fact that his gift – his beautiful, singular guitar playing – was something that could be commodified. At times, no matter how it was put to him, he refused to acknowledge that his playing should be celebrated, let alone rewarded. Rather than let that happen, he would refuse to play.

I explained this to Carlos Santana, promising him that I'd talk to Peter but I couldn't guarantee anything. When I put it to Peter, I gave it my all, because no one wanted to see him play that song more than I did.

Somehow I got Peter to agree to play with Carlos at the ceremony. I was shocked, because getting Peter to join us at the induction at all had been a feat in itself. Picking up an award at a formal ceremony seemed to me to be exactly the type of thing I expected Peter to reject without question. He was generally in good spirits about the whole thing but I knew that could turn at any second, so I just went with it, and when it seemed like the right moment I asked him if he'd like to play with Carlos and Pete said yes. He even agreed to do a rehearsal with Santana.

I don't think Carlos realised just how much of a miracle this was and frankly how could he? At the rehearsal, Carlos played us a beautiful recording of Peter soloing on 'Black Magic Woman' sometime in the late 1960s, a perfect specimen, one that captured all the highs and lows and profound beauty in Peter's playing. Carlos then told us how much that song and Peter's playing had influenced him and that he'd not be the player he is today if he'd never heard Peter Green play guitar.

You could have heard a pin drop. Peter stared at Carlos blankly for a very long and awkward minute or two. Then we did a run through of the song and when it came time for Pete to solo, he laid down one, maybe two sustained notes and nothing more.

Carlos was understandably concerned about the performance to come and asked me to talk to Peter.

'Carlos,' I said. 'I promise you. I'll do all that I can. But it may make no difference.'

I asked Peter if he liked what he'd played.

'Not really,' he said.

'Maybe if you played something like you used to when you played that song, you might like it again. Things might be better if you do it the way you used to,' I said. 'Do you want to hear that? I have tapes of us doing it live back when the record came out.'

'Play me what he wants me to play,' he said.

I cued up the tape and watched Peter Green regard the

speakers as if they were sputtering gibberish in a foreign language.

'What is that?' he asked.

'That's you, Peter. That's your playing and that's what they want you to do. Or something like it.'

'But why?' He was truly perplexed. 'Why do they want that? Why would I want to do *that*?'

'Well, that's you. You're the one that wrote the song and did it that way and it was great. That's what made Carlos become the player he is. He wants to celebrate that.'

'Yeah, but why would I want to do that? Why, when I've already done it?'

I had no answer for him there. He silenced me. He was right and he'd cut through all the shit, straight to the heart of the matter.

Until that moment, I'd never quite understood Miles Davis and his deliberate dissection of form; his insistence on playing one long note or turning his back to the audience. In the same way I'd had a hard time appreciating contemporary artists like Mondrian, who painted one perfect black line across a canvas and called it a day. But, sitting there with my old friend Peter Green, all of it made sense to me, and it has ever since. It was almost too much to bear. Peter had been so far ahead, he'd done all of what the rest of us considered the only thing to do. He'd done all that could be done within the confines of structure so expertly that the only thing that made sense to him anymore was one bold black line on a blank page.

Still, he agreed to perform with Carlos, but when he did, Peter kept turning his guitar down. Every time he did that, Carlos turned it up. It was a civil, respectful tug-of-war.

Peter Green didn't give Carlos Santana what he wanted, but the Green God was present. No one heard him live on stage that night, but he was in the house, he just didn't want anyone to know it. Believe me. I went to the control room after the show, because I wasn't going to leave before I heard what Peter had actually played. The engineer turned the feed way up, and when he did, there it was. Peter had laid down a stark, melodic solo that was as beautiful as it was a huge 'Fuck you'. It was a broadcast from the fringe of purely individual thought, something precious for no one else to enjoy but the man who played it. It was the hardest line to paint. It was a lone, bold, black mark down the middle of a canvas.

༄༅

CHAPTER 4

THE BLUESBREAKERS

The Peter B's really were something there for a moment and I've got no reason to err on the side of hyperbole. We were one of the two or three acts chosen to support the best of the best, because Bardens was a visionary musician. Under his guidance, the Peter B's later became the Shotgun Express, which featured me and amongst others, a very talented, impossible to ignore, raspy vocalist named Rod Stewart. After Bardens was done playing that manner of blues and rock with all of us, in the 1970s he broke new ground as a solo artist, experimenting in the type of synth-based music that laid the groundwork for the electronic music of today. Peter was great and he was taken from us far too soon in 2002, at the age of fifty-six, by lung cancer.

But back then, once he'd put together the Peter B's, we were booked solid. We filled support slots at every prestigious gig there was, which is how we got invited to play at Tara Browne's birthday party. I've mentioned Tara already in passing, but I've not taken the chance to say that he was, truly, a wonderfully warm Irish lad. He was one of the heirs to the Guinness brewing fortune but you'd never know it unless someone told you. His wealth and influence had nothing to do with his charm; Tara was who he was and it came through.

He was a sprite, a dashing patron of all manner of culture to be sure. He was always there, always in the moment. He made the rounds with the Beatles and the Stones and he always did it right, he was never a nagging tag-a-long. So when Tara was set to turn twenty-one, every single person in our little bubble world was up for it, because we knew he would do it right. He chose one of the most gorgeous properties I'd ever seen, one that had been in his family for nearly a century. It was a castle in County Wicklow, Ireland, set in a wide green valley, complete with a staff, chauffeurs, stables, everything but a legion of hunters on horseback awaiting the release of the red fox. Tara flew up the two hundred or so guests in two private jets, including John Paul Getty, Paul McCartney, Mick Jagger and his girlfriend at the time, Anita Pallenberg. This party was special and those invited knew it too; all of us arrived in decadent, splendid costumes, whether they'd been kitted out at thrift stores or bought from a posh boutique. There was a glamour to it all that befit the setting.

I spent hours that seemed endless with Brian Jones at that party, because as soon as I walked into a hall as grand as a cathedral, he was the first person I saw. He beckoned to me to follow him upstairs before I had time to register the scope of the place.

'Come on, Mick, let me show you something.'

I followed Brian upstairs. He led me down a hall, looking back to make sure I was with him, smirking in that knowing way of his. He opened a door and there, in the middle of the room, was the biggest block of opiated Moroccan hashish I'd ever seen in my entire life. There was nothing else in the room but that hash, a beautiful glass hookah and a bed.

'Is this yours Brian?' I asked, ogling that massive block of drugs.

'Sure it is, Mick. It's mine. It's all of ours. It's here for everyone. So let's have some.'

This was the birthday party to end all birthday parties. For one thing the music was stellar, full of various bands playing everything from blues to all manner of Eastern excursions; in short, every musical genre the English rock-and-roll scene was currently into. The environment was indulgently magical, with jugglers and people dressed up as goblins and other mytho-logical figures.

Tara being Tara, he even had a surprise for those who thought they knew everything. He'd arranged to have the Lovin' Spoonful flown over from America to play during the height of the weekend. He'd told no one. At the time the Spoonful had a huge Top 10 hit in the States with 'Do You Believe in Magic', which we all knew, whether we liked it or not. What mattered was that Tara had flown in the hottest new group in the American charts that week – because he wanted them to play their hit song at his birthday.

That moment was beyond words. Just to be able to do that, so nonchalantly, as a surprise to your guests, was amazing. The Spoonful impressed me, for what it's worth. I had thought they were bubblegum crap, but seeing them live, right there on the stairs of Tara's house, I changed my mind. They could play; they weren't just a piece of candy, they were the real deal. They blew everyone's mind, because all of us who'd doubted them saw first-hand that John Sebastian had the goods.

Tara was quite the host, as he always was. Sadly, he left us about seven months after that party. He was killed in a car crash in December 1966, while speeding in his Lotus Elan through South Kensington. He failed to see a traffic light and smashed into a parked lorry. His passing touched us all.

There was some debate about it – on record even Paul McCartney and John Lennon couldn't agree – but I've come to accept as truth that the Beatles' song 'A Day in the Life' was inspired by the newspaper headline that Tara Browne had died and I couldn't imagine a more beautifully appropriate song to be his eulogy.

In the spring of 1966, months before Tara passed and all that happened, the Peter B's cut a single called 'Do You Wanna Be Happy?' and we added two additional singers to our roster, one male, one female. It made a huge difference, so much so that our name no longer made sense, so we changed it to the Shotgun Express. Our two new singers were the best anyone could hope to have. They were Beryl Marsden, one of the most powerfully beautiful R&B singers I've ever known and as I mentioned earlier, Rod Stewart, a North London chap who needs no introduction.

Can you imagine how great that band was? Those two singing, the bassist Dave Ambrose and me holding it down, laying back in the groove and letting them loose with Peter Green beside them – it was fucking gorgeous. In those days, Rod was the embodiment of the recently-deceased Sam Cooke and with Beryl up there with him, they could melt iron. Peter Green was coming into his own and it was powerful every night. Greenie was becoming known as 'the Green God', up there with Eric Clapton, who some people had begun to equate with God in graffiti all over London.

The Shotgun Express was a shooting star, too full of talent not to break apart. We were a powerhouse live, each of us doing our bit, but not always together. Although Rod Stewart was an equal band member, he was already a star because he behaved like one. It was my first experience of working with a prima donna, yet it made complete sense. Rod the Mod and his fantastic full head of hair, which if I remember correctly stood up on the strength of a mixture of sugar and lemon, could not be counted on to unload the van if it was raining.

'Lads, I don't think I'll be doing that,' he'd say.

'Well, why the fuck not?'

'Because the hair will get fucked up. And someone's got to look good out there.'

It was hard to argue with him because it made sense, and he did look so damn good out there and sang so well that no one wanted to mess with that. After a while we never asked for his help again and let Rod the Mod sit there. No one minded because he did his magic on stage. Rod also taught me about clothes and was the first person to make me realise that being my size, shopping in stores was a waste of time. What I needed was a tailor, something I knew nothing about. Rod and I nearly worked together again, when Jeff Beck called me up to tell me he was forming a band with Ron Wood and wanted me to be their drummer. Peter Green and I had already formed Fleetwood Mac, so I turned Jeff down, but if I hadn't, I might have become one of the Faces.

Shotgun Express was a group of talented individuals playing our hearts out, but missing the glue that turns a collective of musicians into a living, breathing band. Peter Green was the first to leave Shotgun Express, after which the rest of it fell apart. Rod went on to join the Jeff Beck Group, while Peter went back to playing for John Mayall, because after a year in the band Eric Clapton had set out on his own. I was the only one left jobless.

Back in the Bluesbreakers, Peter really took flight. He became *the* Peter Green, the stuff of legend. But fans of the Bluesbreakers were not receptive to him at first, because he was now the guy stepping into Eric's shoes, and Eric had become the high priest of the blues. Doubt be damned, Peter showed them a thing or two. He became living proof that John Mayall was a true patron of British blues. He was a forward thinker too, a master of spotting young talent, as he still is today. He was like a father-figure, very businesslike. When you worked for him, you showed up on time and when he said he was going to pay you, you'd be paid. You knew where you stood with John Mayall, so playing in his band was a very secure place to be. John also gave his players all the credit and took care of his flock.

I was unemployed for the first time in four years when the Shotgun went bust. Lord knows I'd saved nothing, I'd been living week to week which was fine, but once that was gone I had to sort something out. The best idea I came up with was starting a business with a friend of mine named Dave DaSilva to clean windows and also to decorate them for the various shops and boutiques around London. My father came to our rescue by loaning us the money to buy what we'd need – ladders, buckets and brushes. We got ourselves properly kitted out and spent the next few months advertising our services, but we were all dressed up with nowhere to go. We tried, we really did, but Dave and I landed precisely zero jobs.

I tried to keep this from the family; I'd make up stories of how Dave and I had just cleaned some windows and how we'd been hired to install a few mannequins. My sister Sally didn't buy it for a second, so she came round and saw how Dave and I were living. We were starving, eating the least expensive canned goods we could afford. Sally, my angel, out of the goodness of her heart, hired us to paint her new home off Kensington Church Street, across from a gallery space that her husband had bought.

That put more cans in the cupboard for a while, until Peter Green came calling, thank God, and asked me to join him in

John Mayall's Bluesbreakers. I was overjoyed but also shocked actually, because that band had one hell of a drummer. His name was Aynsley Dunbar and he was a fucking powerhouse, far superior to me. I don't know exactly what happened there, but from what I heard it sounded like Aynsley was a bit too good for his designated role in Mayall's outfit. He was such a massively-skilled drummer that he wasn't content playing straightforward blues and couldn't contain himself. He felt held back and had started to express himself through solos that became somewhat of a problem within the context of the band.

Peter Green had played with me in the Peter B's, and he suggested me to John Mayall when things came to a head with Aynsley. They'd get no masterful insubordination from me, because even if I'd wanted to, I couldn't hold a candle to Aynsley's playing.

I didn't solo then, but in the years to come I learned how. In Fleetwood Mac my solo became a part of our repertoire, though it was never conventional. Usually it was a glorious mess. I'm not sure when in the late 1960s drum solos became expected in rock and roll, but it happened, and that lasted well on into the 1980s in all styles of rock. If history has deemed it a crime then I am most certainly a culprit.

When it all started, I was up for it, exhilarated by the pressure to captivate the crowd, and for that I felt I'd need props. Lacking much else, one night I absconded with a pair of wooden balls attached by a chain that made up the flushing lever of the toilet in the pub where we were playing. These were quite common, they were what you pulled to flush toilets in pubs all across Britain. Yet until then, I'd never seen them as rhythm instruments until the night I pulled them down, tucked them through my belt and started beating them with my sticks once I got back on stage. They sounded pretty good, and there they were right on my belt – my pair of wooden bollocks.

Those balls came to inspire all of my solos; I'd tap on them like a mad man, start dialogues with the crowd, I'd shout out whatever was on my mind. It might be nonsense such as 'Please don't leave me sitting on the toilet!' or something inadvertently personal like 'Have you phoned your mother lately?'

Solos eventually got me out from behind the kit, which was new and a great opportunity to follow whatever muse came to me. Peter Green loved it, he encouraged it, and even gave me an African talking drum, which allowed me further indulgence. A talking drum is a sublime instrument with an hour-glass shape, a drum head at either end, and stretched leather cords along the sides that allow the player to modulate the sound with his or her body. When you play a talking drum you lean into those cords to morph the sound the way a guitarist does by bending strings, and in both cases the result can resemble human speech. There's nothing else quite like a talking drum.

My solos began as a way to keep the ship afloat when the shit hit the fan. If someone broke a string or the power went out, I'd start playing a Bo Diddley rhythm and hum and make noise until we'd got things sorted. But they grew from there, especially once I got the talking drum. I began to have my 'Mick moments' in the show and slowly became a bit of a showman, and I found that I liked playing the part. I'd get out there with my snare drum first, then fetch the talking drum, and I'd dance about like a mad jester. I'd clap my wooden balls together, I'd chant, I'd do whatever came through my mind. However shy I still was in my private life, during my solos I became someone completely different from myself, and I relished the transformation. I developed a confidence via that character that I may not have done otherwise. Those moments in the spotlight and the evolution of that role I played were what allowed me to eventually become the bandleader – and the ringleader – of Fleetwood Mac.

What I would call my first proper solo used to come at the end of 'Green Manalishi' when Peter would do long six-string bass improvisations. They would sometimes last twenty minutes and begin with just me on hi-hat, and eventually some drums. That same hi-hat style is there in what I do today, because I play one all the way through 'World Turning' which is a part of my solo section today. When we did it on 'Manalishi', it served as an intermission of sorts, and that moment has remained in the band's live show in one way or another ever since, though my solos grew more ornate and outlandish with time. In the 1980s I even had a vest constructed, wired with digital pads that played samples of drum sounds when I hit them. It was a marvel and it allowed me to play with myself in front of thousands of people without fear of arrest.

Peter Green was the reason I joined John Mayall's Bluesbreakers and though I didn't play with them for long, I consider it an honour to have been a member at all, because that band is a legendary institution. I'd watched every bluesman worth his salt become known to the world by playing with the Bluesbreakers. Mayall was a true professional and a consummate gentleman who made me feel welcome. There was nothing he could do to make the fans accept me, however.

You see, the people who came to see John's band knew every member by name, so when they saw a new face, like mine, they'd shout about it.

'Where's Aynsley?' they yelled.

'Who the hell is that?'

Then they started booing. Very, very loudly. It took me back a bit, because I honestly wasn't expecting such a visceral rejection. That's when John McVie, who in all the years I've known him has preferred to stay in the background and do his job, took it upon himself to set the crowd straight. We'd started the first number, with the audience continuing to shout that I was no good and that Aynsley Dunbar was better, when suddenly John McVie stopped and started waving his arms until the rest of the band halted as well. Then he walked up to Mayall's microphone.

'Hey!' he shouted. 'Why don't you fuck off? Just *listen*. Listen to him play. Then boo if you want.'

Most of them stopped – not all, but I no longer heard them. John had silenced them for me; his confidence in my ability dissipated my jitters and allowed me to play on with renewed vigour. I already liked John tremendously, but with that one gesture he cemented my loyalty and love for him forever. John has never let me down, not once, to this day. He was my brother from that point forward.

I found my place in the Bluesbreakers and as we did more gigs I really loved it, mostly because McVie and I became tighter as a rhythm section with each passing show. I have, as a true dyslexic, always played slightly behind the beat in a very idio-syncratic manner. John plays just slightly ahead of the beat which isn't exactly perfect either, but when you put us together, it is. These aren't things you can teach someone to do. When you find that kind of musical marriage, typically it's a beautiful coincidence. That's how it is between John and me; we've never had more than one or two conversations about how to play together or how we should play together in forty odd years. We just do what we do with no premeditation required.

John was the ideal partner for me, the only bassist I'd encoun-tered whose playing effortlessly intertwined with mine. We were soon inseparable off-stage too, because we shared the same affinity for drinking and carousing. John was better at all that than I was, actually. And he had to be. John Mayall didn't look down on enjoying a drink, but when it came to the shows, he ran a tight ship and inebriation wasn't tolerated.

It's not like McVie and I were the only ones who weren't angels. There was a night when Peter Green didn't even show up and I was far too gassed to go on. We figured without Pete, we'd cancel the show, but Mayall wouldn't do it and made a point of going on regardless. He planned to play Peter's parts, his own, and everything he was capable of. God bless him for it, I only wish I'd been in better shape to back him up. I was three sheets to the wind, and that was a very big mark against me. The last straw came a few weeks later after a gig in Ireland. Keep in mind that we were all good friends, so my dismissal wasn't cruel or even awkward. We all laughed about it. It was clear that the rhythm section had too much fun together, so one of us had to go – and we all knew that McVie was not the kind of bassist you fired lightly because no one held a candle to him. So I was out and I knew it. I decided to make it easy on Mayall by bringing it up myself as we drove to our next gig. Mayall was going over the tour schedule and laying out the coming few weeks and months. After he mentioned a gig a week or so away, I interrupted.

'So John, that gig you just mentioned, I'll be gone by then, right?'

He couldn't help but laugh with all of us and just nodded his head. 'Yes, old boy, I'm afraid you will.'

It was without a doubt the easiest 'you're out' conversation I've ever been a part of. You have no idea how horrible those are, whichever end of the equation you're on.

In the history of my band, John Mayall must be celebrated, because if it weren't for him, Fleetwood Mac would never have existed. I did only one studio session with his band during which I played on two recordings that were released as a single and to tell you the truth I can't even remember the names of those songs. I mention that session though, because afterwards I stayed on to play with Peter Green and John McVie. Mayall had bought Greenie a few hours of studio time as a birthday gift so that he could record some songs he'd written. This was at Decca studios up in West Hampstead where we were recorded by Gus Dudgeon, the Decca house engineer there who went on to become extremely famous for his work with Elton John, which includes *Honky Chateau, Goodbye Yellow Brick Road* and other Elton classics. John McVie and I were Peter Green's rhythm section that afternoon and it was magical, and I don't say that lightly. We did two covers and three instrumentals, the last of which was a twelve-bar up-tempo R&B number that Peter over-dubbed with a harmonica solo. It was a dirty bit of Chicago-style electric blues and it was fucking *hot*. It was by far the best track of the lot.

'I've got a name for that one,' Peter said with a knowing grin, as we listened back to it in the control room.

'What's that, Pete?'

'I'm calling that tune "Fleetwood Mac".'

He took a pen and wrote it on the white tape on the lid of the tin holding the finished two-inch tape.

'You mean as in him and me?' I asked, pointing to John and me. 'Why would you call it that?'

'Why? That's easy. Fleetwood Mac is the name of my favourite rhythm section.'

The English obsession with American blues during this period is an interesting cultural phenomenon. At the core of American blues, and jazz and gospel, are slave songs sung by African-Americans brought involuntarily to the new world as cargo, to build a fledgling nation from the ground up. Those slave songs were a secret language among them, through which they could express the pain they dared not vocalise, under fear of torture or death, in any other fashion. This tradition evolved into the blues, which eloquently and harrowingly expressed the suffering that African-Americans continued to endure after their liberation. They were free but they weren't accepted; they were poor, they were still treated as lesser beings. That pain and the alleviation of it through song is at the core of the blues, and later, jazz.

None of that had any direct historical connection to English history or society whatsoever. There was no logical reason for musicians in the early 1960s to become taken with American blues, nor for younger guys like me and other kids of my age to flock to it in the way we did. It may not be logical, but the reason is the Second World War.

The pioneers of the English blues scene were members of the generation just older than mine – guys about ten to fifteen years my senior. I'm talking about musicians like Alexis Korner and Cyril Davies. Many of them weren't necessarily super-talented, but all of them deserve credit for being the troubadours of an American art form that was all but dead in the country that gave it birth. Blues was too much for America in the 1950s and early 1960s; it was an uncomfortable reminder of a past that the country had yet to come to terms with or acknowledge properly. Rock and roll was different; although it was considered morally corrosive to the youth, it was safe compared to the raw honesty and societal verity intrinsic in the blues. It took a decade of unrest, from the Civil Rights Movement to Vietnam, to realign America with its own legacy, both the good and the bad. It also took two generations of English musicians celebrating and honouring the blues to reintroduce it to the country from whence it came.

The early English bluesmen were old enough to have been children in the Second World War and to have come of age in the ruinous aftermath. Our country was devastated by the war and they had seen it first-hand. They grew up playing in rubble, waiting in queues for food, many of them without homes for most of their formative years. Most had lost their fathers and uncles in battles on foreign soil or lost other family members in deadly German air raids. That didn't happen in America, because, aside from the tragic attack on Pearl Harbor, the country wasn't ravaged by war in the same way as the UK and Europe.

Post-war America turned its industrial machine to building highways, putting up supermarkets, and giving the boys back from war the life they deserved, whereas in England we were left licking our wounds, bound together by the necessity of rebuilding our ruined homeland. The UK, like so many other European countries, emerged from the war with a demolished infrastructure, a nearly bankrupt financial system and a population going hungry. This wasn't the same suffering that inspired the American blues, but it was very real suffering nonetheless. I believe the blues appealed to those musicians because it echoed their pain. The source of the anguish was different, but the sentiment was the same.

There was also a yearning for something new, something to put the past behind us, and the blues provided us with that in England. It was music that our parents' generation had no knowledge of, so it became a generation-defining movement. It was obscure and it made those of us who knew it and loved it feel a part of something powerful that was also very much our own. It had the same unifying power that the punk movement would have a decade and a half later.

It didn't hurt that the music was so infectious and irresistible, either; the blues is impossible to ignore. It came over to the UK via American GIs, black Southerners mostly, who were stationed on our shores and it fanned out from there. The first wave of English bluesmen spread the word and the second wave, of which I was one, really took up the call. It was an interesting time, even more so when we English bluesmen carried the blues back across the Atlantic. For quite some time it felt like we were educating our audiences, and the fans we met, on their own history. We'd be playing gigs while legends like Muddy Waters were playing smaller venues just down the road. We made no bones about telling people that they were at the wrong gig. They had no business seeing us when the real deal was in their backyard and had been all along. In England we were running as fast as we could towards this American musical tradition, while America was running away from it just as fast. Aside from a few regional radio stations, there was nowhere to even hear the blues in the States.

Meanwhile in the UK, a generation of extraordinary guitarists was emerging through blues-rock groups, and the fans could not get enough of them. There was Eric Clapton's Cream, of course, and the Jeff Beck Group, as well as a virtuoso from Seattle named Jimi Hendrix, who'd recently taken up residence in London and was in the midst of putting together a band. It was 1967 and as the saying goes, it was all happening. The Beatles had just released *Sgt Pepper's Lonely Hearts Club Band* and a guy named Mick Taylor, who would later join the Stones, was taken on as Peter Green's replacement in John Mayall's band.

Mick Taylor is yet another reason why the English government should erect a monument to John Mayall, because Mayall maintained a high-functioning finishing school and breeding ground that gave the world some of the best guitar players in the history of rock and roll. The point is that the blues is somewhat simple musically but that doesn't mean it's simple to do. There's nothing worse than a lousy blues player, believe me, and I think anyone who has suffered through a set by a sub-par blues band would agree.

John Mayall set the bar very high and kept it there. His guitar players in the 1960s, one after the other, became legends, and Mayall was the first to give them a proper stage upon which to shine. Eric Clapton, Peter Green and Mick Taylor, all of them passing the torch to each other in Mayall's ranks. He knew how to spot and develop talent, so his band became an invaluable institution, like the Count Basie Orchestra, which not only gave us Quincy Jones but also introduced us to so many incredible vocalists from Frank Sinatra to Ella Fitzgerald and Sarah Vaughan. John is still out there making music today and still flying the flag of the blues, backed by great young players. I think his example of never letting change hold you back, and always looking for an infusion of new blood to keep his musical endeavours fresh, influenced John McVie and me immensely. It's certainly how we went about it in our band.

As it happens, Peter Green did not have a plan to leave the Bluesbreakers, because he was very happy there. He didn't have to front the band, he didn't have to sing if he didn't want to; he could just play lead guitar and follow his muse. Nothing was ever done in secret behind Mayall's back, the way some written history has implied. But something happened that day in the studio when Peter played with McVie and me. I think our chemistry, without the boundaries of being in the Bluesbreakers, got Peter thinking how it might be to have his own band, although bearing that burden as a frontman didn't appeal to him.

Peter talked about going on a soul-searching trip to Morocco, as Eric Clapton had done, until he knew exactly what he wanted to do with his music and his life. That never happened, because Mike Vernon, a producer and the founder of Blue Horizon Records, where Fleetwood Mac would release their first few records, influenced Peter to stay in England and start his own project. Peter respected Mike greatly and thought it over for a few months. Once he decided to do it, he asked John McVie and me to be in his band. Mike wanted us too and he had a vision for Peter, which included enlisting the guitarist Jeremy Spencer. Mike Vernon is another behind-the-scenes player who deserves tremendous kudos for his guidance, not only in our career, but for many others in the English blues scene too. He did more than anyone knows to further the music and nurture the artists.

CHAPTER 5

AND AWAY WE GO

After Peter Green had decided to start a band with John McVie and me as his rhythm section, the new band was dubbed Peter Green's Fleetwood Mac by the agent who started to book us gigs. Peter never wanted his name up front and centre like that, so he dropped it as soon as we'd developed a following and fans knew that Peter was in the group. Peter had never thought he would sing or be a frontman either, but he changed his mind about that as well after seeing how Eric Clapton did it in Cream. Still, Peter wasn't crazy about being out there leading things, which is why he had named the band after the guys in the back line.

There was just one problem – John McVie had yet to sign on as a member. I signed up in a split second, but John was still playing bass with the Bluesbreakers and had been earning a good living that way for nearly five years. McVie is a pragmatic fellow; he wasn't going to leave a comfortable paid situation to follow Peter on a reverie, no matter how much he loved playing with us. John turned the two of us down so squarely that we were forced to hold auditions, even though Peter had no intention of changing the name of the band; we figured that would show John how serious we were about wanting him. We hired a great guy named Bob Brunning to play bass and told him from the start that once the band got off the ground, John McVie would be replacing him.

The original line-up of Peter Green's Fleetwood Mac was Bob Brunning, Peter Green, Jeremy Spencer and myself. Jeremy, a diminutive eighteen-year-old was a devotee of Elmore James, the great American bluesman who was known as 'King of the Slide Guitar' and who had died a few years earlier in 1963. Peter had seen Jeremy play with his old group, the Levi Set Blues Band, when they opened up for the Bluesbreakers once or twice, and it was Mike Vernon who had the idea of putting Jeremy and Peter in the same band. Jeremy was something to see, a tiny chap, pretty quiet off-stage, who became a whirlwind of raw power once he plugged in. He was a white, British incarnation of Elmore James – it was uncanny. He had the same stirring voice and the same lightning-bolt tone coming from his overpowered guitar. Jeremy was a dynamo on stage, impossible to ignore, and Peter just loved him. Elmore was his go-to style, but Jeremy was an incredible mimic and could serve up pitch-perfect renditions of Elvis, Cliff Richard, Little Richard, Buddy Holly, and every other 1950s rock-and-roll great.

Our fledgling band developed a handful of instrumentals anchored by Jeremy's slide playing and highlighted by Peter soloing in the Chicago electric-blues style he loved and tossed off effortlessly. Our first vocal numbers were sung by Jeremy. We made our first live appearance at the three-day Windsor Jazz and Blues Festival on 13 August 1967, among an amazing line-up for the day: Cream, John Mayall and the Bluesbreakers, Ten Years After, the Crazy World of Arthur Brown, Jeff Beck and Donovan. Pink Floyd were supposed to headline as well but they were forced to cancel due to Syd Barrett being unable to perform. There were about fifteen thousand people there and we played for an hour, turning in a great set, as far as I remember.

John McVie was also there on that day, because the Bluesbreakers were on the bill, and he spent our entire set watching us from the side of the stage. We knew he was there, in fact to me it felt like we were auditioning for him. Some written accounts have claimed he found us 'boring', but that's not true at all. McVie wished he were out there playing, because what we were doing was exciting and he knew it.

The Windsor Festival was a landmark moment in the history of Fleetwood Mac. It was the band's live debut, and the moment that John more or less decided to join us, but that wasn't all. In a tent playing on another stage was a band called Chicken Shack, featuring a singer and pianist named Christine Perfect. Christine would go on to join our band in 1970 after she married John McVie. In the meantime, she and her bandmate Andy Sylvester, the bass player, became huge fans of Fleetwood Mac; they came to see us play all over the UK and even did a few tours with us. Andy and I shared a flat for years and he is still one of my very best friends, despite the fact that he later had a brief affair with my wife, Jenny Boyd.

By December 1967 John McVie had left the Bluesbreakers and officially joined Fleetwood Mac, at which point we evolved from a skilful, purist blues band into something else altogether. Many times I've thought about how best to convey what John and I are when we play together but the words still escape me. He makes my form of expression effortless and I do the same for him. If you can imagine doing whatever you feel comes most naturally to you and then finding a partner that accompanies you so perfectly that neither of you need to even talk about it, then you're close. Imagine doing that together year after year; the only constant in a life that has shown you all manner of ups and downs. If you can get a sense of that, you've caught my drift.

Once we had John McVie we were a tight musical juggernaut, off and running. We'd record late-night sessions in studios after playing for hours in seedy blues clubs and in doing so we quickly became a well-oiled machine. I can't say it enough – John taught me everything, his playing freed me up, and he made me a better drummer. With such a strong backbone, Peter and Jeremy were able to get out there and lay it down like they never had before.

We released our first album, *Fleetwood Mac*, early in 1968 on Blue Horizon Records and recorded it at CBS Studios in London. It is a collection of blues covers and originals, written by Jeremy and Peter, who split the vocal duties, and it was recorded in just three days. That album includes a song of Peter's called 'The World Keeps on Turning', which we later truncated to 'World Turning', that is still played by today's Fleetwood Mac. To me that song is important; it's the intersection of both eras of the band. It became a Christine McVie number, although today Lindsey and Stevie handle it, and it's the bluesiest song we do. It allows Lindsey Buckingham to cut loose with some blues picking and he just kills it. That moment in our set is a link from past to present and I love it.

Much as it did in 1975 when a very different band released an album called *Fleetwood Mac*, the 1968 version gave the band unexpected and immediate success. The album spent nearly forty weeks in the UK charts and hit number 4, though in the US it didn't make a dent. We were overrun with positive reviews from the British music press and I suppose I had always wanted that, but I never thought it would happen to any of my bands. I also didn't care, as long as whatever band I was in fulfilled me and allowed me to play music for a living. So a bit of 'Macmania' occurred for us straight away. Our smaller gigs, which were always well attended, became complete mob scenes overnight. Suddenly, for a time, we were given the same degree of coverage in the music press as the Beatles and the Stones.

Peter's response was to record and release a single that was the furthest thing from a chart hit, 'Black Magic Woman', the alluring bit of blues that Santana made famous a couple of years later. It was Peter's first 'fuck you', I suppose; a four-minute collage of solos that no edit could fit into the radio format of the day. The record reached only number 37 in the UK singles chart, though it was added to regular rotation on rock-and-roll radio stations around the world.

Our first album was almost entirely Jeremy Spencer doing his thing and it was amazing to see it played live. Peter loved having a new undiscovered talent with him and Jeremy did not disappoint. He was beholden to the blues and rock and roll and owned it so well that if you closed your eyes, you heard Elmore James. Jeremy was the focal point on stage, which was great for Peter because it allowed him to do his own thing, playing evocative, soulful leads and rhythm lines there in his corner of the stage.

Jeremy had a long-time girlfriend and by the time he joined the band they'd had their first child, even though they were still teenagers. He was quite religious and used to carry a Bible at all times and pray, but on stage he was a complete wild man. I loved it because the juxtaposition of the real Jeremy and the stage Jeremy was astounding. Humble Bible reader by day, possessed bluesman by night – it doesn't get any better than that. At our shows, Jeremy would really carry on, cursing and making bawdy comments, all of which made the proceedings so extreme that it was a bit tongue-in-cheek. It came from the heart, but it had the effect of keeping us from being too earnest and precious as a blues act. We played plenty of cover versions but we weren't a tribute group, we were something else and we had a sense of humour about it.

Jeremy and I were the unelected court jesters of the band and the fact that we roomed together on tour made it that much more fun for us, though quite often a nuisance for the others. As room-mates we had plenty of time to think of new pranks and other ways of stirring up mischief. Jeremy is massively funny and as I've mentioned, an incredible mimic, which made him even more adept at comedy. He could imitate each of us in the band so well, down to our facial expressions and turns of phrase, that it felt as if you were sitting in front of a mirror. There were times when this lost its charm, of course; after hours and weeks together in a van, Jeremy's antics were more annoying than a fly you can't shoo away. No one hated him for it, but sometimes we'd beg him to stop. Usually he wouldn't.

Like Jeremy's on-stage persona, our live act was also lewd and rowdy by design. Jeremy would fill condoms with beer or milk and hang them from his guitar, with a reserve pile at the side of the stage. At the end of the night, we'd throw however many were left at the audience, by way of thanks. Jeremy also liked to change the lyrics to a song, making them as bawdy as could be, and we'd all join him in the choruses putting extra emphasis on the dirty bits. We were lads goading each other on, which is how Harold came to join the band.

I don't know whose idea it was, but Harold became our new member and we introduced him as such, complete with a properly grand entrance. Harold, you see, was a pink, sixteen-inch dildo that our road manager, dressed as a butler, would bring onto the stage on a silver tray, surrounded by glasses of cognac for the rest of us. We would toast Harold as our road manager affixed him to the top of my bass drum, where he would spend the rest of the show undulating to the vibrations. His real moment in the sun came when Jeremy poked Harold through the fly of his gold lamé trousers, while he sang a few Elvis songs.

We were so entrenched in what we were doing that we never gave much thought to context, until we realised the hard way that there were places in the world where our little stage routine would not go over well. One such location was the Marquee, the venerated jazz and blues club in Soho, where we were pulled off stage mere moments after Harold made his appearance. It was just too nice a venue for that and we were banned from playing there for a while afterwards. We got into even more trouble in America, the land of the free. The audiences we encountered on the coasts loved our raucous rock-and-roll revue, Harold and all, but the rest of the country was hit or miss – mostly miss. The worst reception came at a Christian college in Texas, where we didn't censor ourselves at all and found ourselves surrounded by local law enforcement officers before we could even get off the stage. They intended to haul us in for disorderly conduct and public indecency; the same rap that befell Jim Morrison with the Doors quite often in those days. I have no idea how our manager got us out of it, but he did, probably by promising we'd leave and never return.

We were definitely different. We had a dancing phallus, plus the wooden balls hanging from my belt – what more could you want in a rock-and-roll band? As silly as it all sounds, we were serious about it. I still have that same pair of wooden balls and I still strap them to my belt every night before I play with Fleetwood Mac. They are a part of my performance persona. Have a look at the cover of *Rumours,* you'll see them.

God bless Jeremy Spencer for inspiring that irreverence, because it allowed us the liberty to be ourselves. Looking back, I think what Jeremy was trying to do was subvert things from the inside. As a performer he paid tribute to the past in a very pure way, honouring his idols and the music by channelling it with a perfectionist's attention to detail. Yet by taking the piss out of things the way he did, he made it all new and very much his own. He challenged accepted norms and pushed the envelope, which brought it full circle because, of course, that is what rock and roll is all about. It was punk rock behaviour, well before punk existed, and we wouldn't have been able to cut loose that way if it hadn't been for Jeremy leading the charge.

Fleetwood Mac did their first American tour in 1968. We played one gig at the Wollman Rink in New York, before heading west to California. We were on a bill at the Shrine Auditorium in Los Angeles with the Who, Arthur Brown, and Pacific Gas and Electric and that was one hell of a gig. I remember Arthur Brown being *way* out there, doing his Screamin' Jay Hawkins thing, while Pacific Gas and Electric delivered true acid-rock American music and the Who – well, at that time they were simply unstoppable. They had their amps turned up to the point of combustion and *really* meant it; they were just a powerhouse. Then there we were. We got up and turned out beautifully rendered blues followed by very straight-ahead rock and roll.

Since the other bands were quite bombastic, I worried that we'd be lost in the shuffle, but that wasn't the case. It's a testament to Peter's talent, because you could have heard a pin drop when he stepped up to sing a slow and pretty blues tune. I had even suggested that we change our set and do only the loudest material we knew.

'No, Mick,' Peter said. 'We're gonna do what we do.'

He was right. We did a lot of slow, poignant blues and the crowd was right there with us. They weren't bored, they weren't distracted, they were in the palm of Peter's hand. His control of his instrument was sublime.

That short venture was the first of our many forays into the drug-heavy West Coast rock scene. There were drugs back in England but the degree of acid, pot and other hallucinogens going around in the US were on another level altogether. It was ingrained in the music, in the experience, in the fashion, and everything else. We caught a glimpse of the centre of it all when we went to San Francisco to play a few gigs with Grateful Dead. Phil Lesh and Jerry Garcia, who became great friends of ours, met us at the airport and had us stay at their house. We also met their friend and then-manager Owsley Stanley.

The London sixties scene was nothing like the American hippie scene and there's a clear reason for this: Britain was not at war. The US was entrenched in a losing battle in Vietnam, as thousands of young men continued to return home in body bags. The Civil Rights Movement had turned society upside down as well and more than a few student protests had turned violent. America was a tumultuous place.

Walking into that other world on the West Coast at the height of the 'Summer of Love' was an education. We saw it all first-hand – the Hells Angels, the acid-tests, the free love, the communal crash pads. The Grateful Dead were our tour guides and I really adored Jerry Garcia from the start. He was such a warm, amazing guy. They played all the time, so even though our first visit was short, we played a handful of gigs. We loved it because the Dead had a proper PA system that was leagues beyond the crap we were used to playing through in the pubs and clubs back home. The band and their fans already knew and loved Peter Green, so we were accepted everywhere, and I think the Dead's noodling, inventive approach to improvisation really inspired Peter to new musical heights.

On that first trip, despite Owsley's best efforts, none of us indulged in the LSD he was constantly pushing on us. Owsley was still their sound man – the one responsible for that grand PA – and he'd alchemised his own mix of acid, called LSD-25. Frankly, there was enough to take in without hallucinogens. We were used to hash and fashion and music, so we declined at first.

When we got back home, we recorded *Mr Wonderful,* an album influenced by our trip out west and the first one to feature Christine Perfect. We knew she was a great pianist, but even so she blew us away. She had Otis Span's style down pat, along with all the greats. She was the blues babe and she was immediately part of the rhythm section, which was an amazing addition to our sound in my opinion. Chris never got up there with something to prove, she just instantly became the glue. That is what makes Chris so great; she's a band player, not a solo act. She loved playing with us because she'd been such a fan of ours while she and Andy were in Chicken Shack, and since we knew her so well, she was one of the boys. All of the guys in Fleetwood Mac took a shine to Chris immediately because she is irresistible, but Peter and John really liked her. At first Chris fancied Peter, but as we all know, she and John ended up falling in love and getting married.

Peter had a vision for the band and our time among the more improvisational acid-rock bands in America inspired him to move things forward. To do so he needed a new musical collaborator, someone other than Jeremy Spencer. Jeremy was devoted to pure blues, he didn't have any interest in experimenting with

First steps, Hayling Island 1948.

Mike and Biddy on their wedding day.

At five taking in the sights.

My family, Hayling Island, 1949: Susan, Sally and Me on Mum's lap.

At thirteen in Gloucestershire
wondering what's coming next.

The Bo Street Runners, Baby
Never Goodbye Promo Shoot,
back when I was called "Mike".

The lads of Fleetwood Mac: Jeremy, John, Me, Danny and Peter in 1968.

An early Fleetwood Mac TV appearance, Denmark, 1968.

Steering the course with John,
Peter, Danny and Jeremy.

Rave on! An ad for our
headlining show at the Lyceum,
midnight 'till 7am.

Rehearsal at the Royal Albert Hall in 1969.

Spring is in swing: an ad for
a 1970 gig in Reading with
Chicken Shack.

Fleetwood Mac with Cliff Richard, 1969.

Ready for kickoff, 1960s.

At Kiln House, 1970.

Danny Kirwan, Bo[
Welch, Me, John an[
Christine McVie, on [
rock at Kiln House[

Danny and John
sitting in the garden
at Kiln House.

Peter Green during his
time with John Mayall's
Bluesbreakers.

John Mayall in the studio.

With my trusty portable tape recorder, on the road, 1970.

My first marriage to Jenny, 1970.

Ready for the beach, somewhere in America.

Jenny and I on holiday in Corfu, Greece.

Our first winter. Taken at Benifolds with the band and friends, 1970. Jenny heavily pregnant with Amelia is on the left with Bailey the dog.

Jeremy and I - and my balls. Backstage at the Boston Tea Party, 1970.

Walking with my balls sometime in 1971.

something that he already found perfectly satisfying. There was never any question about Jeremy leaving the band, because Peter and the rest of us loved what he brought to us musically. In a similar way to John Mayall, Jeremy knew who he was as a musician and was happy to stay that way.

Peter Green was an entirely different animal; he was the type of creative person that needed to evolve. His nature was to mutate, once he became comfortable doing a chosen form. The truly talented players in our scene did that and did it well. Led Zeppelin were the greatest at it; they evolved from covering Willie Dixon's 'I Can't Quit You' to 'Ramble On' in a short period of time. Peter had the same drive to push his own boundaries, which is how Danny Kirwan came into our lives. Danny was a nineteen-year-old guitar player in a very average band who was a huge fan of Peter's. Danny would see us every chance he got, usually watching Peter in awe, from the front row. He was such a sweet guy and such a true fan that we became friendly, chatting after gigs. Peter and John and I went to see Danny's band a few times and it was clear to us that he needed to be with better players. They were holding him back and we told him as much, and did our best to think of who we could hook him up with, until in the end we just invited him to join us. It was one of those *ah-ha* moments when you realise that the answer is right there in front of you; Danny's style of playing complemented Peter's perfectly because he was already a disciple of the Green God. We added him to the line-up and so became two bands in one.

Danny and Peter were a natural fit, with Danny's sense of melody on rhythm guitar really drawing Peter out, allowing him to write songs in a different style than he'd been able to previously. Rock songs poured out of him, much of them with a ferocity unlike his earlier work. The new material steered the band further into rock and roll than we'd ever been before and so began Peter's most powerfully creative period.

The fans, the press and the music scene went wild over our new direction. Peter was so thoroughly respected that he was even given his own column in the weekly music paper *Record Mirror* where he would espouse vegetarianism, whatever our band was doing, and whatever other bands he liked at the time. Peter didn't want to be a star, but he did need to express himself. He was entirely self-made and had a real presence off-stage and on that made people take notice of him. His playing, of course, spoke for itself. He knew what he wanted to do by this point and he had a lot of drive. He was also very giving and encouraging to the rest of the band. He didn't take shit from anyone; he didn't want to be the king of the castle, although by shining so brightly, he couldn't avoid it. He was also a lot of fun and had a great sense of humour, which he needed in order to put up with the shenanigans that were going on in the band. To his credit, Peter loved that irreverence when many others wouldn't have done, particularly as the leader of a band known for flying the flag of the blues.

We spent the next few months touring Europe, where we had a number of top charting hits in several countries. Some of those, in my opinion, I considered to be our least exciting new material. After those live dates we went right back into the studio where Danny and Peter split the writing duties on a whole new album.

No song better signified our new sound than 'Albatross', an echoey, over-dubbed extended exploration that I just adored. The song hit number 1 in England, which we heard about while on tour in America. Soon afterwards 'Albatross' was played on the weekly TV show *Top of the Pops,* which signalled the beginning of Fleetwood Mac's career as a pop group. Our thirty-date tour of America was almost entirely sold out, including a few huge festivals.

We began that tour on the West Coast opening for Grateful Dead at the Fillmore Auditorium in San Francisco. We ran into Owsley Stanley, of course, and decided that we were ready to try his acid. We didn't do it then, we waited until we had checked into the Gorham in New York City, which was a well-worn party hotel where all manner of bands stayed, and we gathered together in a room to make a ceremony of it. What ensued was a mind-melting experience that wasn't at all what I expected. As it kicked in, we ended up sitting in a circle on the floor holding hands, consumed with anxiety. Each of us panicked in our own way that we were having a bad trip and had done immeasurable permanent damage to our minds. I glanced at Peter, saw him as a skeleton and thought he was dead.

It was horrible, we were all a wreck, and then the phone rang. The clang of the bell sent us through the roof, I remember us staring at it as if it were a piece of alien technology. Eventually someone answered it, not me, and miraculously, Owsley was on the other end. He must have felt our vibrations; like an LSD super-hero he sensed that we were in peril. The phone was passed around, all of us weeping and blubbering to him. One by one he expertly talked us down, the way he had with so many others. It worked and soon we weren't scared anymore and were just enjoying the trip. LSD was a bonding experience for us that we did together on other occasions, each trip unique in and of itself. It was a tool that brought our collective consciousness together, as it did for so many of our generation. It never became a regular thing for all of us in the way that hash and pot and alcohol were, though Peter and Jeremy indulged more than most, but LSD played its role and it cannot be underestimated.

This tour marked a change in our live show. We'd taken off in terms of our renown, so Harold and the most ribald aspects of our act didn't get as much stage time. Aside from a wild show at the Whisky A Go-Go club in Los Angeles and a few others, our antics would have got us into too much trouble because this was no pub tour of England. We did get up to our old tricks, though, when we shared the bill with Big Brother and the Holding Company, and Janis Joplin got a real big kick out of Harold. She thought it was the greatest thing she'd ever seen.

Just because we learned to control ourselves on stage doesn't mean we'd mellowed in any way. As a concession to toning things down while performing, we turned things up off-stage by uttering deliberately filthy things very quickly, in proper English accents, to all manner of unwitting Americans who crossed our path. No one knew what we were saying except us, which was endlessly amusing. We did this a lot at restaurants and Jeremy was the absolute master of it. When the waitress came to take our order he'd say, 'Can I have the vagina burger with the hot sloppy mess on top? Do you have that?'

'The what? No, I don't think we have that.'

'All right. Well, do you have a shitburger thing on rye then?'

'No, sir. Is it a hamburger that you want? I'm sorry I didn't understand what you said.'

'Yes, that's fine, I'll have that. Hot slop on the side.'

We'd be sitting there, biting our tongues, waiting for the day when someone would catch on and beat him up. Jeremy loved upsetting the norm like some mischievous pixie. He'd shout obscene things at kids on street corners in nice neighbourhoods. He'd say things that were often quite profound, or intended to make them think, though as usual, Jeremy often took it a few steps too far in the same way he did with his imitations of his bandmates.

That tour of America was amazing: we opened for Muddy Waters in Chicago and booked some recording time at the famous Chess Studio before it closed down. We were able to cut a few tracks with a handful of our heroes from the Chicago blues scene, who were all sceptical of us at first. We had Otis Span on piano, Willie Dixon on bass, Walter 'Shakey' Horton on harmonica and Elmore James' famous sideman J.T. Brown on saxophone. None of them had ever seen or heard of us before and when they got a look at us, I could tell that they thought we were another loud, over-distorted, acid-rock blues band from England, the type who turned it up to mask their fairly basic skills. But we showed them otherwise; they saw that we were a tight little act who could put them through their paces. Peter, of course, won the day with his taut soloing, his guitar tone and the deep soul in every bit of his playing. The resulting album, *Blues Jam in Chicago*, captures a truly great recording session.

When we got back home to England, 'Albatross' was on its way to selling a million copies. We'd set off with a decent roster of gig offers, but we returned with TV spots to do and *much* larger venues at our disposal. It was very exciting but all a bit dizzying. I took it in stride, as best I could, but it took some getting used to. Once I got my head around it, I did like the attention. It gave me a sense of confidence and that gave me the courage to endeavour to rekindle my romance with Jenny Boyd.

After we had broken up, Jenny went on a journey to find herself, after experiencing what she calls a spiritual awakening. She moved to San Francisco for six months, right at the start of the Flower Power movement. Then she went to India with her sister Pattie, George Harrison and the Beatles, to meditate with Maharishi Mahesh Yogi. She became so involved with it, as did the Beatles, that she intended to take part in setting up a Maharishi centre in London, to help raise consciousness locally, and then globally, in an effort to bring peace to the world. That didn't happen. The Maharishi turned out to be not quite who he had seemed to be and she grew disillusioned. Jenny returned to London in the summer of 1968 and began to sell Art Nouveau and 1930s china in a small shop called Juniper, which she ran with her sister Pattie.

I'd never stopped pining for Jenny and I wasn't the only one. Donovan, who was a huge pop star at the time, was so taken with Jenny that he wrote the song 'Jennifer Juniper' for her just before she left England. Then he followed her when she went to India and declared his love. Luckily for me, she never fancied him.

During our tour of America I wrote Jenny a letter, addressed it to the shop I'd heard she had opened and hoped she still had feelings for me. Things were going great for me with the success of 'Albatross' and our American tour, because we'd finally got some recognition and a larger global following than we ever thought we'd have. I wrote about how wonderful it was to play with Peter – I believe I said he 'oozed with feeling' – and I told her how I'd come to realise that I'd never be a great drummer, but had learned to really understand and appreciate music more than I'd thought possible.

I also asked her to marry me.

We hadn't seen each other in over six months, and when we did it was in passing, so my proposal was a bit of a surprise. It made complete sense to me, of course, because in my head I knew how I'd felt all along – I just never managed to let her know it. My timing couldn't have been worse, because Jenny had just made plans to move to Wales with a fairly new boyfriend.

I wasn't going to let that happen, so when I returned home,

I drove my car up to Wales to visit her. She was living in a communal house on a very rural piece of land, with no modern conveniences and no other buildings in sight, surrounded by sloping fields that were covered in snow, dotted with woolly sheep huddled together for warmth. There were about five or six of them living in an old stone shepherd's cottage, with an outhouse and no heat aside from one large fire. It was a very hippie scene; they'd cook rice in a pot balanced on the logs and spend their time reading, wood carving or going on walks. They listened to Bob Dylan's *Nashville Skyline* album quite a lot on the record player.

As Jenny has reminded me, I showed up looking like a Cossack in a floor-length Afghan coat, which made me appear even taller. I looked sharp and smart and in those parts, I was clearly a 'townie' beside everyone else in their country, hippie clothes. Truthfully, I wasn't one of them. I came from a different tribe, as Jenny has told me. I was one of the nomads, one of the musicians, and that tribe wasn't always on the same wavelength as the hippies. My type of people drank heavily, swore often and did things, well, like we did in Fleetwood Mac. Given the chance, hippies wouldn't have thrown condoms filled with milk or beer into the audience.

I had to find something to do for the night with these people up there in Wales, so I settled on wood carving. One of the girls had shaped her piece of timber into an angelic statue and one of the boys was busy whittling a flute to play. I joined in, carving an homage to Harold – just a blunt, crude, wooden dildo. Jenny flushed with embarrassment when she saw it, because it was so base and contrary to the Flower Power rules. I could tell that she really wanted to giggle. I didn't do it just for shock, by the way, I put that dildo to good use; it became the gear-shift knob in my car as soon as I got back to London.

It was so flagrantly a wooden dick that I had to buy a leather pouch to put over it so that anyone looking in would think it was a regular shifter. My sister Sally thought this was so hilarious that she bought me a set of small sterling silver balls to use as a keychain for my car with the dildo gear-shift. I still have those balls and still use them to this day.

Jenny had told her new boyfriend, Martin, that I was an old friend coming to visit for a night, so they put me in a little bedroom downstairs where I slept in my clothes, including my coat, because it was so terribly cold. The next morning I drove Jenny to the nearest town for breakfast at the local tea shop. I told her all about the tour we'd just finished and how the band was growing day by day. Jenny told me that when she saw me in Wales she knew I was different. I had more confidence and she saw how excited I was about the future and the band.

'But Jenny, what about you?' I asked her. 'Did you give up your store to live here?'

She nodded.

'It's very quaint,' I said, looking around. 'The countryside is beautiful, I get it. But you're going to be bored out of your mind eventually, don't you think?'

She just smiled at me. We both knew I was right. I also knew her.

'I mean, there's nothing going on here,' I said. 'Jenny, what are you doing?'

'I don't know,' she said, as we stared at each other, then started to laugh. 'I'm not sure what I'm doing really. A whole bunch of us had been hanging out together, smoking pot, cups of tea, getting a bit hippie, and I guess I fell into being with Martin.'

'I can see what they're doing, the back to nature shit, I saw a lot of that in San Francisco,' I said. 'But it's tough living that kind of life. It's great if you're on the West Coast of America. But here? In Wales? It's fucking freezing, Jenny!'

We were both laughing near hysterically by now. Jenny had tears running down her cheeks.

'I mean, having to pump the well to get water?' I continued. 'Having to go outside in the snow to take a shit? What does that prove? They're mad!'

When our giggles died down, I asked her what I'd come that far to ask.

'So you got the letter I sent?'

'Yes,' she said, staring into my eyes.

'I meant what I said. I would like to marry you, Jenny.'

'I want to be with you, Mick.'

I held her hand and felt my eyes water. 'Let's get your stuff and get back to London. I leave for a tour of Europe tomorrow.'

CHAPTER 6

FLIGHT OF THE GREEN GOD

After our time apart, getting back together with Jenny felt like coming home, and I know she felt the same. We settled into a flat at 74 Kensington Church Street in west London, with a little attic room upstairs that I set about soundproofing, so that I could play up there when I was learning new material. I nailed blankets and cushions to the window frames and stuffed my bass drum full of them too. As the band's direction changed I spent more and more time up there working it out, sometimes – as in the case of 'Oh Well' – terrified that I'd never get it because I wasn't good enough. I'd think myself into a corner, then let go, and eventually find my way.

That flat might as well have been a rehearsal space and poor Jenny had to put up with very barebones living. In our sitting room we had a great stereo system and a lot of records, but other than that just a deckchair, a mirror above the fireplace and grey carpeted floors. Later we got a long wooden table, but for most of the time we lived there, we had nothing else. I used to spend nights in that room listening to music with friends like Andy Sylvester who lived downstairs. We'd put on headphones, sit on the floor and listen to James Brown albums, nodding at one another as yet another drum break or bass line blew our minds. The next morning, the entire floor would be littered with vinyl.

Jenny came with us when we returned to America that winter, and I couldn't have been happier because I wanted her to see all that we'd achieved. We had a new album to support, our second release in the States, and greater popularity over there than we'd ever had before. Our record company, Epic, had released *English Rose*, which was a selection of the best cuts from *Mr Wonderful* (that Epic had declined to release the year before) as well as 'Black Magic Woman', 'Albatross' and four new Danny Kirwan tracks.

Our show had evolved into two long sets, which by the end became an inspired free-for-all. The first set was comprised of traditional blues-based compositions led by Jeremy on slide guitar as well as Danny's material. Then Jeremy would take a break, leaving Peter and Danny free to launch into long impro-vised excursions like 'Rattlesnake Shake' that drove our fans completely insane. Then we'd all take a half hour break, have a few drinks, then return to the stage for Jeremy's set, where he'd don his gold lamé suit and introduce us as 'Earl Vincent and the Valiants'. He had his proto-Elvis character perfected by then; he'd grease his hair back, snarl appropriately, and do perfect covers of 'Great Balls of Fire', 'Tutti Frutti', 'Keep A-Knockin'' and more.

We went on like this for three months or so, some gigs good, some bad, and though I was happy to have Jenny there, she didn't feel the same. She was excited to witness what our band had become, but touring life was not for her. We stayed in seedy Holiday Inns or at the Gorham Hotel in New York. Everyone in the band was a night owl, but Jenny was not by nature, so playing music, drinking all night and sleeping late was not how she'd organically choose to spend her time. She had to find ways of entertaining herself and of spending time with me, which I did as best I could during the afternoons. I remember us being in Chicago on that tour and going on a quest for Levi's jeans, which you couldn't get anywhere in England at that time. The only pair that would fit me because of my height were the very largest pair, which looked like clown pants on me.

When we got home, Jenny altered them on her sewing machine and since that was such a chore, one of her hobbies became sewing patches onto my Levi's when they wore out at the knee or the bottom, which they did constantly. Over time they became embroidered works of art. Jenny also knitted me a scarf while we were on tour. She was just learning, so it ended up being much longer than it needed to be. I would wrap it round my neck several times and it would still fall to the ground on both sides of me. It wasn't how she intended it, but I absolutely loved it because it had an element of costume, which I embraced in my style of dress.

Jenny was with us one unforgettable night when we played with Grateful Dead in New Orleans. They were headlining a new venue called the Warehouse, which was a huge old barn where cotton had once been stored after picking. It had been converted into the first concert hall of its type in New Orleans and we couldn't wait to play there. As diverse as New Orleans has always been, it is still the deep South, a place where the police were hostile toward scruffy long-haired types like us.

The backstage area at the Warehouse was up a set of rickety wooden stairs, right above the stage. There was a table laid out with the usual cold cuts, carrot sticks and celery, with bottles of Coke and beer stuck in a cooler tub filled with ice. I remember going up there and having some, then doing our sound check. Peter's voice sounded beautiful in that big open space.

I don't remember where I was when I realised that Owsley had spiked the drinks. Jenny told me that she was upstairs in that dressing room and had started to feel cooped up. She wanted to get downstairs and watch the crowd walking into the venue. At the bottom of the stairs she bumped into Danny Kirwan.

'Jenny, Owsley spiked all the drinks,' he told her, grinning impishly. 'I don't think I can go on. I can't play my guitar!'

'You can do it,' she told him, even though she could see how jittery he was. Truth be told, Danny always seemed a bit nervous, but this was beyond that.

That's when Jenny's trip kicked in. She remembers looking out at the crowd and seeing their eyes glistening. She saw bits of straw in their mouths when anyone smiled. Later as she watched me play, my whole body turned into a skeleton, just as I'd seen Peter's do when we'd first tried Owsley's acid. It was too much for Jenny as it had been too much for me, and she looked away in horror.

Meanwhile I was out of my mind, sitting at my drum kit, trying to make sense of what we were trying to do. At least we were all in the same boat; when Peter got on stage, he grabbed two sticks and banged them together for a while before reaching for his guitar. Once he did, things fell into line and somehow he led us through it. Still, it was a roller coaster from start to finish.

Time becomes a laughable concept when you're on LSD; it can crawl to a halt or fly past you at the speed of light. During that set there were moments of both and then suddenly it was over. All of us were flying all the way through the Grateful Dead's performance and on into the night. The entire place emptied out and still John McVie, Danny Kirwan, Jenny and I were there, wandering around the empty room. We had no idea where or when the others had left. I managed to find someone to drive us back into town. We intended to go to the Grateful Dead's hotel, where the party was going to continue. We were staying in a different motel.

Jenny and I sat in the back of the guy's car, with me right behind the driver, and John and Danny in the front. As we started moving, I noticed that the driver's head was bowed, so I looked over the seat and saw he was looking into his lap, rolling a joint with no hands on the wheel. I did the only sensible thing and reached my arms over the seat to steer the car for him. When he was done, we just kept driving like that because it seemed perfectly normal.

I have no idea how long we cruised the streets looking for the Grateful Dead's hotel, but we never found it. I think we spent several hours going in circles, passing old warehouses and driving over decrepit rail road tracks, not venturing far from where we'd started. Somehow, some way, we eventually found our motel.

It's a good thing we did, because if we'd been at that party, it would have spelled the end of Fleetwood Mac. That night the authorities raided the Dead's hotel because they were after Owsley, who they knew was an LSD chemist, and they arrested everyone else present. The incident became the inspiration for the line 'Busted down on Bourbon Street/Set up like a bowling pin', in the Grateful Dead song 'Truckin''. If we had been arrested with them, we would have lost our visas and the ability to tour the States for many years.

Instead when we got to the motel we found our bandmates and hung out in Jeremy Spencer's room. The acid was still far from over, so we spent the rest of the night and on into the morning talking about our beliefs. It was a rare moment of sharing amongst us, because we usually spent our time guarding ourselves from ridicule when we weren't making fun of each other, in the way young men in bands, or groups of any kind, often do.

Jenny remembers that night well, she's told me that it changed her life. She saw musicians as modern day disciples, spreading the word of something greater through their music. Music was the only way to do so because it brought people together and everyone understood. I think that was the closest all of us got to ever discussing religion, despite the fact that religion was a large part of Jeremy's life and would soon become a part of Peter's.

With all that was happening for the band, we failed to see that our leader, Peter Green, was changing. He'd grown moody and brooding, which came through in his new material. There was a sadness to his lyrics that hadn't been there before, which you can clearly hear in 'Man of the World', the follow-up single to 'Albatross'. Considering lines such as 'There's no one I'd rather be, but I just wish that I had never been born' and 'I could tell you about my life . . . about all the times I've cried, and how I don't want to be sad anymore', it's all right there. But it's not as if Peter was suddenly morose; like the narrator of that song telling the listener how amused they'd be to hear about his life flying around the world, seeing all the pretty girls, outwardly that's still who he was. But not so internally. Regardless, 'Man of the World' reached number 2 in England and kept us on a roll.

Our next album, *Then Play On*, was even more of a departure, because for the first time we didn't record live in the studio and then choose the best take. We employed editing and over-dubbing extensively, because for the first time we could and also because it suited where were going creatively.

Peter was squarely at the helm of the ship on this; we'd jam for hours in the studio and then leave him there with the engineer and producer to edit things down to a shining jewel. For the first time, Jeremy was entirely absent from the proceedings; in fact I don't think he played a note on that album. Stylistically we were two bands in one, but the division became distinct and the new album didn't have room for Jeremy. It wasn't a rejection and Jeremy didn't take it that way, because we planned to release an EP of his tunes shortly thereafter, possibly as Earl Vincent. It was just that Peter didn't want the album to be a mix of styles. He had a vision to communicate via the songs and the studio as well, using it as an instrument the way the Beatles and Stones had with their most recent albums.

Then Play On was entirely Danny and Peter, with Peter letting Danny write most of the songs, trying ever-harder to hide from what was expected of him as Peter Green, The Green God. Try as he may, Peter's songs were the ones that made the album special. His playing was sublime and his lyrics, even at their most depressed, were expressive and poetic. Peter had become disillusioned with our success, and whatever the cause, this period of time is where the onset of his mental health issues emerged. I have no doubt that they were brought on by his use of LSD, but when it comes to the human mind, nothing can be that black and white. Peter's illness would have happened regardless, or maybe it was just part of his quest, but in my opinion LSD fractured his mental stability sooner rather than later.

Then Play On became Fleetwood Mac's biggest hit, selling over 100,000 copies in the States and reaching the Top Ten in England. It included 'Rattlesnake Shake', perhaps the most enduringly famous song from the album and that era of the band, which is an ode to masturbation as a cure for the blues. I'm named in it, as a guy who does the rattlesnake shake to jerk away my sadness whenever I don't have a chick. That was an appropriate immortalisation of my younger self, to be sure.

McVie and I were convinced that Peter's choice of single, 'Oh Well', was too sad and we even bet him that it wouldn't chart. Well, were we ever wrong; it went to number 2 in England and Peter took our money. The album was the right piece of music at the right time and it made us a bona fide mega-act in Europe that year. It felt like we'd finally found ourselves and were onto something, and all of us were ecstatic about it – all except Peter. Our popularity, our tour schedule and our record sales had the opposite effect on him; they put him into a dark, depressed cocoon of his own making. He'd started talking matter-of-factly about leaving the band even before 'Oh Well' exploded.

This happened fast, and as someone who knew Pete well and felt that I understood him, I tried every which way to get him to open up about it. I wanted to know why our success made him sad. We'd come up together, we'd walked the same road, put our shoulders to the same burden and I thought we'd shared the same goal. I expected us to be toasting the fact that we had no lack of gigs and could enjoy the creative freedom that comes with success. We had earned it.

'Mick, why did you start playing?' Peter asked me during one of these chats.

'Because I love the music and because I don't think there's anything else at all that I'm very much good at. I don't even think I'm very good at what I do, Pete, but I know I should be doing it, because I love it.'

'I started playing because I wanted to, Mick,' he said, staring at me for a long moment. 'I still play because I want to. I never did it for the business. I never did it to make a living. And the more I'm in it, the more I know that I'm not cut out for this business. I can take it or leave it at any time. I see it for what it is. It's just playing.'

That threw me. It was like talking to someone I didn't know. 'But Pete, aren't we playing, together, every night? Isn't that what you're doing? Isn't that what *we* do? Don't you like being on stage with us? Do you not want that in your life?'

He stared off for a moment and then looked back at me. 'I really don't know. I don't think I want to be on a stage at all anymore.'

'But Peter,' I said. 'I'm trying to understand, but I'm not sure I do. You and John and I have worked so hard, we've all worked so hard, to be able to do what we want, to play what we want. We've worked hard and now we're finally there! We have the freedom to do what we like. We can write whatever kind of album we decide we want to write, and we can play it for people all around the world, people who are there just to see us. You understand how much of a privilege that is, don't you? I can understand that you may be tired. Touring is hard, and the routine wears us all down. But we've just got to the point where we can call our own shots. We've finally made it. All of that tedious stuff is over for us. Now we can really start to enjoy what we set out to do.'

'That's where you're wrong, Mick. What looks like success to you is horrible to me. There's nothing in this to hold me here. We play every night but we play the same fucking thing. Night after night after night we play the same thing and it's making me sick. I don't want to play the same thing; I want to *jam*. I don't want to ever do the same thing twice. I don't want to know where it's going when it starts. And I can't do that here. I'm going to have to move on to something new.'

Peter had taken more than a dozen LSD trips that I knew of by then, and continued to do so. We will never know how that played into it. What matters is that Peter changed, fast and drastically. He'd never done so before, but he began to talk about religion incessantly. He was Jewish but that wasn't what he talked about. He'd decided he wanted to convert to Christianity. For a month or more, he turned every conversation to Christ and his conversion and then, just as quickly, he never spoke of it again.

Since the day I'd met him Peter adored the attention of girls and sought out love. Among all of us, with McVie coming in second, Peter was the guy pulling girls after gigs, before gigs, pretty much all the time. Overnight that behaviour stopped because he found it disgraceful. He was consumed with an all-encompassing ideal of 'doing good', a pursuit Pete now believed all human beings should be devoted to. Playing music professionally did not fit into his new program.

'Peter,' I said to him one time, 'we are doing good. We do a job that makes people happy. That is doing good. People who do jobs that bring other people happiness or do good deserve to be paid just like everyone else.'

My words were met with a Peter Green X-ray vision stare. However much he'd ever trusted me, I could tell that he no longer did. He looked angry and suspicious.

Very softly he said, 'Mick, I don't want to waste my life. That's what I'm doing. I'm wasting my life. I don't want to die thinking I never did a fucking thing for anyone.'

I had nothing to say, because there's no answering that.

'You know Mick, sometimes I think music is everything, sometimes I don't think it's anything. I don't know what it is and that's all right. All I know is that I don't give a shit about the money.'

I'd had nothing to say before; and even less after hearing that.

*

Fleetwood Mac marched toward 1970 with more accolades than ever before, mostly thanks to a dedicated fan base. In the 1969 year-end polls in *Melody Maker*, we were voted the number one progressive group – the Beatles were number one pop group that year – and Peter was the number three composer behind Lennon–McCartney and Jagger–Richards. We'd also outsold the Beatles and Stones in Europe in record sales and concert tickets. We were one of the biggest bands in the world, but with a leader who was fading fast.

Peter grew more disillusioned, more sensitive, and increasingly hurt by the suffering he saw all around him. On tour I'd find him in his hotel room crying at the evening news and at one point he gave £12,000 to various charities. Then he approached the band and asked that we give all of our earnings to charities of our choosing. He wanted us to refuse any gigs or deals through which we could make money; all of it should be given away. We weren't averse to charity, but this was too much. We'd discuss it with him for hours, but there was no changing his mind. Peter wanted us to live and tour monastically and to donate one hundred per cent of our profits to charity.

'We won't stop working,' he'd say. 'We will dedicate it to purpose. It is the only way to make a difference.'

'But Pete,' I said, 'you like your money. You like to have cash and you like having people look after you. All of that costs money.'

'You're wrong, Mick,' he said. 'You're dead wrong. I can walk away from it. I don't *need* it. There's so much poverty. I would feel better if I earned money and gave it all to the poor. That is how you make a difference.'

These debates were endless loops that arrived inevitably at the same impasse. Peter didn't want to make money from music and the rest of us felt there was nothing wrong with that. To be clear, we were willing to do free concerts to raise money and to donate to organisations that helped the poor and under-privileged. But Peter wouldn't accept anything short of complete and utter selflessness when it came to what we earned as a band. So we'd always end up staring at each other in silence. And it got worse from there.

Once he understood that the rest of us weren't going to change our minds, Peter began acting crazier with each passing day. He took to wearing robes, caftans, and a huge wooden crucifix. He grew his hair and beard very long and when he spoke to the press he would only discuss his search for God. Later, when he'd see his words in print, he'd feel violated and ashamed and that would send him to a dark place that was hard to watch. To be fair, his words were often taken out of context and exaggerated outrageously, but he had made extreme statements to begin with. Peter took it all so personally that he suffered tremendously. In the span of a few months he degen-erated from a vibrant, confident man into a sad and fragile soul. I felt helpless and devastated watching him slip away.

I recalled a conversation I'd had with Peter years before, when John had finally joined the band.

'You know there's something else to the name, Mick,' he said. 'If I ever do leave, you'll be okay.'

'What do you mean, Peter?'

'You'll be okay without me if I leave, because you'll have a band. I don't want something that's all about me. That's why I chose a name that is the two of you, not me.'

'Yeah, but it's your band, Pete,' I said. 'We wouldn't be here without you. And this band is all of us, isn't it?'

'It is, but Mick, you have to understand something – I don't really want any of this. But you do. And now you have it. No matter what happens, you've got a band. You and John have a band named after the two of you. I don't matter and I like that. I can leave if I ever want to.'

He did matter, of course, but he was right about how he'd set things up. His choice of name left us a band and a legacy, and a built-in emergency exit for him.

In the end, Peter left because the rest of us didn't want to give it all away. We agreed with the beauty of his idealism, but we were practical. We didn't see ourselves as materialistic for wanting to earn a living from music – we couldn't have been because our living was quite meagre. No one in the band was rich by any means; for example, Jenny and I lived in a third floor walk-up rented flat. Our dream was to have enough saved to buy a place of our own where we could raise a family. We had yet to enjoy the fruits of sustained success but it seemed that we were about to. Peter found that idea repulsive. He was the only one amongst us that wanted to live like a pauper.

Pete left the band for good during a sold-out European tour in February 1970, but was very responsible about it, agreeing to fulfil all of his obligations. We were in Munich when a bunch of well-to-do German hippies got a hold of him and took him to their commune. They all lived in a big old house where Peter joined them in getting fried on LSD for a few days. He met us at the gig and played with us, but it was the last we saw of him for quite a while. John McVie and I have had years to discuss it all and we've decided that Munich was the moment when Peter was truly gone for good. We weren't sure what to do and after a few days our road manager and I went to fetch him. We found him tripping but lucid enough to tell us he was through.

'I'm not coming with you,' Peter said. 'I'm going to live here now. I have everything I need.'

These Germans were taking advantage of him and whether he stayed in the band or not, we weren't going to leave our brother in their care.

'That's fine, Pete, you can come back and live here for the rest of your life, but you need to come with us now,' we said. 'You have some things to settle before you come back here for good.'

'I do?'

'Yes, Peter. Come with us, it won't take long.'

With much coaxing, we succeeded in getting him out of there and back to our hotel. We tried to convince him to finish the tour, but were unsuccessful because Peter was in a panic like we'd never seen before. He'd start talking about the money we were making, then just mumble, repeating himself endlessly. He'd get worked up, upset and inconsolable, and then go into a paranoid, feeble panic. He kept saying that he was simple, he was working-class, and that the money we made was too extravagant.

'The money, I don't want it,' he'd say. 'The money. It's an anchor around my heart. It drags me into darkness.'

Once he'd come down somewhat, Peter didn't change his mind about leaving the band, but he did decide that he wanted to play the rest of the shows on our tour. He felt that he owed us that and wanted to do right by the band. We had gigs booked through May, so it was a real commitment on his part.

A few of the German hippies who'd got a hold of him followed Peter back to London and moved in with him, where they continued to trip on acid together. Peter grew more erratic and started talking about his 'unclean money', with the same zeal with which he once spoke about Christ. He was coming undone and every bit of it can be heard in Peter's last single with Fleetwood Mac. His swan song was a pulsating slab of blues rhythm chords topped with howling solos that he called 'The Green Manalishi'. The tune is about the devil, the darkness within, and the alluring temptation of descending into madness. He wrote it one night after waking from a nightmare. Gripped with terror and paralysed by dread, Peter was unable to breathe. When he was finally capable, he grabbed his guitar and a pen and paper and wrote out the chords and lyrics. The song came out of him in a feverish sweat and we recorded it just as it was written, changing nothing.

Peter's final gig was at the Lyceum Theatre in London with Grateful Dead and he was once again sky-high on acid. Some claim that he tried to set his amps on fire backstage. I didn't see that, but he was so high that I don't doubt it. 'The Green Manalishi' went on to become our fourth straight hit single; it rose to the Top 10 on the British charts after Peter had left the band. That was a bittersweet victory and one we'd not enjoy again for a long while; it took Fleetwood Mac six more years to crack the Top 30 in the UK.

Losing Peter was like taking the rudder out of a sailing boat. As a band we were still afloat, but we were drifting, with no map and no land in sight. We had some growing pains ahead of us. They weren't the first and they wouldn't be the last. Just like the ones I suffered as a boy, they would be abysmal, yet they were the only path to greater heights.

CHAPTER 7

A HOUSE BECOMES A HOME

Our leader Peter Green was gone; the reason we'd all come together. That would have spelled the end for most bands and everyone in the scene expected the same fate to befall us. But that wasn't an option as far as John McVie and I were concerned. The band had been named after us and we didn't want to look like quitters. I still believe, and time has convinced me that I'm absolutely right, this was Peter Green's plan all along. John and I weren't going to let it all dissolve, particularly when we'd finally got a taste of success. Then again, we didn't have to front the band, write lyrics or sing. Jeremy Spencer and Danny Kirwan were charged with those duties and understandably they had their doubts about doing it all without Peter. They were such different players, united only by Peter, who could glide effortlessly between their two styles. He'd play sideman to Jeremy, laying down incredible rhythm guitar and harmonica, and with Danny he'd come to the fore and sing, or support his numbers by playing lead. Peter could do all of those things without a thought. He also had the charm and vision to lead us.

But he was gone and we needed a new leader, so out of

necessity, I stepped into those shoes. I didn't see any other way for it to happen and I thought it would be a temporary role until Danny, Jeremy, or perhaps a new frontman picked up the reins. Forty years later, I'm still at it, but hopefully with more wisdom and grace than I had back then. I had no experience in making decisions for a group, nor did I have a distinct musical direction in mind. I did have all the passion in the world and that is what won the day, as it has continued to do over the years. I wanted nothing more than to keep the band together, by whatever means necessary.

John has always been my confidant and co-pilot, so he and I decided that we had to get our guitar players some assistance in fronting the proceedings. Luckily we knew the finest blues-woman and piano player in all of England, Christine Perfect.

Chris was born in Birmingham into a musical and intellectual family. Her father, a professor, played organ and her mother sang and played several instruments as well. The house was full of music, which inspired Chris at a very young age to pursue it professionally. She went to art college in Birmingham and during that time met a young man who would become known as 'The Professor' and also played music, named Spencer Davis. The pair dated for a short time, fronted the university jazz band for a bit, and used to busk together around town. While doing so, they met a fifteen-year-old schoolboy named Steve Winwood who would spend his lunch hour playing blues piano at a local pub before going back for his afternoon classes. Spencer immediately snapped Winwood up and formed the Spencer Davis Group, at which point they were off and running. Steve Winwood, even at that age, already possessed the clear, wispy voice that has blown people's minds ever since.

Chris went on to join a local band called Sounds of Blue, playing keyboards and singing, with Andy Sylvester on bass and Stan Webb on guitar. They gigged together for about a year, playing songs by Mose Allison, Ray Charles and Amos Milburn. By then Chris had graduated from college with a degree in sculpture and went off to London, where she got a job as a window dresser and looked around for a new band. When Andy asked her to join his new project with Stan Webb she jumped at the chance, because she hated working in fashion.

That band was Chicken Shack and Chris had to learn a great deal more about playing blues piano very quickly. She did it the right way, by picking up a stack of Freddie King records and studying the moves of Freddie's legendary piano player Sonny Thompson. Chris's style became an offshoot of Sonny's, which in turn informed her singing. Her style evolved and although Chicken Shack was celebrated for their guitarist's heavy presence, Christine Perfect's plaintive blues interpretations set the band apart from their contemporaries. It didn't hurt that women performers were very few in the English blues scene and Chris was hands-down the best of them.

Mike Vernon discovered Chicken Shack and immediately signed them to his Blue Horizon label, which is how we caught wind of them. He told us that Stan Webb and the rest were great, but that we should pay close attention to Chris.

'Don't miss them at Windsor Fest,' he said. 'Chris Perfect is going to take your breath away.'

Mike was right, she certainly did.

Chicken Shack, like every band starting out, put in months of touring in pubs and concert halls around the country, so we shared the bill with them often, especially as we were both on Blue Horizon. We all became great friends, which is how Chris came down in 1968 and played piano on our second album, *Mr Wonderful*. As I've said already, Peter and John both fancied Chris, but John made the move. He asked Chris out for a drink when she came round to one of our gigs. He might have been dating a girl at the time, but that was long gone the moment John and Chris got together. They had both met their match and it was lovely to watch.

They were a serious item, but much like the moment Jenny and I got together, Fleetwood Mac took off on a tour immediately afterwards. We went to America, while Chicken Shack departed for a tour of Germany. Chris was, and still is, such an irresistible, special woman that while she was away, I believe a German disc jockey asked her to marry him. Honestly, it was constant; there was always some man asking Chris to marry him. From what I understand, after she refused her German suitor, she wrote John a long letter telling him how she felt for him and when we returned, John proposed and Chris said yes. They were married ten days later, in August 1968, and we had quite the party.

Afterwards though, it was back to being apart from each other, because if we weren't on the road, Chicken Shack was. They couldn't go on like that, so Chris left her band to be with John full time, joining us on tour at the beginning of 1969. Mike Vernon understood her decision but he wouldn't let Christine sit on her laurels. He got her into the studio to record a few sessions, which became the album *Christine Perfect*, a debut that went on to win her all manner of awards. She was voted best female vocalist for the second year running in *Melody Maker* as well as being celebrated in every other piece of the English music press. Though Chris was glad for the compliments, she wanted none of the attention that came with it. She announced publicly that she was retiring from the music business, which was met with tremendous disappointment.

That lasted all of two months.

*

This period of transition taught me what it means to be a band. A true band is a family and, like any family in crisis, a band must gather together privately, devoid of outside influence when under duress. It is the only way to re-establish the bonds that exist, for that family to remember who they are, and to decide their next steps together. To do that well, a refuge is required, which is why I insisted we go to Kiln House.

The fragmentation caused by losing Peter was amplified by the fact that none of us lived close to each other. Getting everyone together to rehearse and discuss what would come next was a project and a drag. London was full of so many other distractions that I knew we wouldn't survive that. The only thing that made sense to me was a move to the country. Fresh air, a change of scene, and a bit of communal living was what we needed. Once again, my sister Sally came to the rescue and via a friend of hers, I arranged for us to rent a quirky old oast house near the old market town of Alton in Hampshire, that had been converted for domestic living. Oast houses are common in regions where hops and barley are grown for brewing beer; they are two- to three-storey structures where those grains are spread out to be dried by hot air rising from a large wood- or charcoal-fired kiln situated below. The house we lived in had once been two oast houses; it had a long narrow room upstairs, a simple kitchen at one end, and a long thin table in the middle of the room where we'd gather together at meal times. There were bedrooms leading off both ends of the great common room and at the very top, on the third floor, there was an attic that became our rehearsal room.

The band, our wives, children, and roadies all moved into Kiln House. They included me and Jenny (she was pregnant with our first daughter Amelia by then), John and Chris, Jeremy and Fiona and their son Dicken, Danny and his girlfriend, and the others, and we lived there for six wonderful months. I still look back on that time as some of the most creative and overall positive times of my life. It was summer in the country and we eventually turned one of the wide kiln rooms into our recording studio. We brought lots of hash – great big blocks of it – that we had lying about for all to share if they chose to.

Jenny and I got married there on 20 June 1970; I'd allowed the band's schedule to come first for far too long. It was time. We set off at noon in my old Austin, which Jenny had nick-named Lettuce Leaf, even though it was blue. I still have that car, by the way, it's on my farm in Maui and when I had it restored, I had it painted green in honour of the name she gave it. That very hot day we drove down the country lanes to the public registry office where we met the rest of the band, our parents, our friends and families. Everybody filed in, but I took a moment and remained outside, soaking in the enormity of it. It was happening. I was going to marry my first love, my Jenny!

Lost in a reverie, I had no idea that everyone else had been waiting inside for over five minutes. Jenny told me recently that the registrar threatened to kick everybody out because he had more marriages to do that afternoon. She went to the window, bouquet in hand, and saw me there in my beige corduroy trousers, pink shirt, and fitted brown-checked waistcoat wandering in the garden, with my hands behind my back looking at the flowers, the trees, and up at the sky like I had not a care in the world. She was wearing a long custom-made dress in Liberty Print floral cotton with a rust-coloured background. It took a rap on the window and a stern glare from the registrar to snap me back to reality.

I'd asked Peter Green to be my best man and he'd agreed to,

but in the end he showed up too late and when he did arrive he made a point of telling Jenny and me that he didn't believe in marriage. I would have asked John McVie but he's rather shy; doing something like that all on his own wouldn't be fun for him. Instead, our long-time road manager and friend Dennis Keane stood in and did a wonderful job. Peter was there but he was distant; he was still hanging out with the German hippies and taking acid regularly and was on his own plane, further away with each passing day. It wasn't easy to see him, but I'm glad he was there. Our wedding reception was bucolic and gorgeous; the sun was out and we all sat on the grass at the foot of a wooden stepladder that led up to Kiln House. We ate sandwiches, drank wine and passed joints all afternoon, into the evening and then into the night (except for Jenny, who was pregnant), sitting there around the table in our country home. Jenny's pregnancy made her feel nauseous and combined with her necessary chemical abstinence, it made her feel out of place.

That was a beautiful day, but it wasn't always like that; there were many nights when the pressure got to everyone. We had to follow up *Then Play On*, we had to prove we were something without Peter Green, and all of us knew it. At one point or another every single member aside from me, McVie included, wanted to quit. John used to have a go at us all the time, saying he'd like to be a roadie for a while instead of a member. I was the one to step in and convince them, some nights one after the other, not to leave. I became the torchbearer, the zealot, the one urging everyone to play on, by hook or by crook. Somehow it worked. Little did I know how often I'd find myself in that position in the years to come.

It took a full six months for us to find the answer and reconfigure ourselves. We didn't plan to bring Christine in as a songwriter and member, but we leaned on her a lot because we didn't know what else to do. Jeremy was terrified of being the frontman on his own and the pressure on Danny's sensitive temperament was tremendous. We'd jam for hours and days and work out some great musical ideas, with Danny humming 'la-la-la' into the mike. It seemed he was scared to write, to sing or to fill Peter's shoes. We knew what we could do, but there was a terrible vacuum there without Peter. We needed it all to sound better and Chris was safe, familiar, and more than capable of elevating us. Her piano playing fitted in perfectly with our blues numbers and she filled the harmonic space that Peter had vacated. She found herself, sang a few songs that she knew well, and eventually began to write new ones. The lyrics to one of them, 'Jewel Eyed Judy', emerged from words she wrote with my wife Jenny while the pair sat together at the communal table, when Jenny was about four months pregnant.

The band's new formula remained true to our roots, showcasing Jeremy's skills, while allowing Danny to do more melodic rock. In the end Christine became the glue; she not only drew the cover art for the resulting album, *Kiln House,* but filled out our sound beautifully. When we set out on a three-month tour of America in August 1970, Chris did so as an official member of our band and was from then on known professionally as Christine McVie.

The lease for Kiln House ended when we left for the tour but I didn't want to let the vibe of the place go, so I suggested pooling our money together to buy a country house of our own. I didn't want us to lose our momentum and I worried that if we separated again we might splinter for good. Everyone agreed, so we bought a place jointly for £23,000, most of which came from the advance on our next record. It was a secluded Victorian mansion up on a hill and it was called Benifold. This place was also in Hampshire, just a few miles from Kiln House, but it wasn't rustic at all; it had been built in 1899, had twenty rooms and was truly gorgeous. At the time it was owned by an ecumenical society that took in devotees of any religious denomination seeking a spiritual retreat. It sat on seven beautiful acres of forest and had a dilapidated tennis court surrounded by lush trees. To us it was paradise. We had a billiard room and set up a music room so we could rehearse any time of day or night. There were bedrooms for everyone and plenty of extra space for guests and relatives to visit when we weren't on tour.

I'd found the house while Jenny and I were searching for a place of our own, and as was the way in much of our relationship, I substituted our needs for the band's when I saw Benifold. It didn't register with me at the time, in fact I've only just learned this through talking to Jenny, but that decision truly hurt her. She had a dream of starting a family with me in a country cottage and she craved a haven of normality in our lives. That dream and her needs went out the window the instant I laid eyes on Benifold and it made her very sad. She had wanted to start our marriage in a home, not in a commune. If I had been more in tune, more considerate, I would have seen it. But there was no time; shortly after we bought the house, the band was off to America. Since we'd done nothing to make the interior of Benifold hospitable, Jenny went to live with her mother for the next three months.

That three-month tour was very tough on our families. I'd wanted Jenny to come on the road with me, but she was pregnant and I understood how hard that would be on her. On that tour we focused primarily on our new material in the first set, followed by a second set where Jeremy played blues and oldies the way we'd always done. It was well-received by our fans, although in England it didn't touch the commercial success of our work with Peter Green.

Around that time Peter released *The End of the Game*, an album of acid-rock guitar excursions on wah-wah pedal that left me bewildered and hurt. He'd talked so much about wanting to go in a new direction, and it was, but it wasn't so far off from what we'd been doing. The way he spoke about his intentions I expected his next music to sound completely different and it didn't. He could have done those songs with us and I didn't understand why he hadn't even tried to. We would have followed him into whatever uncharted musical terrain he chose to explore, without question.

We continued to tour and after about five months, we really found our identity as a collective. Christine was a smash, and her playing and voice became a focal point, filling the gap between the two guitarists.

Our first year of living at Benifold was heaven. Jenny and I lived in what used to be the servants' quarters, which were large, because a mansion of that size would have demanded a sizeable staff. John and Chris had their own wing with its own kitchen and living room, and Danny and his girlfriend Clare, who was pregnant with their son and whom he later married, lived upstairs in the attic. Jeremy and his wife also lived there for a short time.

John and Chris's quarters were the nicest because Chris knew how to make a cosy home. Jenny used to get upset with me because when I was there, I'd spend most of my time over in the McVies' wing, sitting at their table, talking about the band. This didn't lessen her alienation in an already large and rambling manor, when she'd wanted time alone with her husband after waiting patiently for his return. She had no friends living close by, but that wasn't it, she wanted me to be more of a part of her life when I was around, particularly during the last term of her pregnancy.

We were on tour in Scotland in January 1971 when our first daughter Amelia was born and it was one of the scariest days of my life. When I got the call, I was told that the delivery was going wrong and both the baby and mother might not survive. I fell to pieces; there were no mobile phones then, no way to stay in touch moment to moment, so I boarded the plane to return to Jenny, with no idea what news would greet me when I landed. The doctors performed an emergency Caesarean section and though it was hard on both of them, Amelia and Jenny pulled through. I was there at her bedside when Jenny woke up and I'd never been happier to see her face. Our mutual joy was short-lived however, because I had to catch a train the next day to rejoin the band.

Talking to Jenny for the book all these years later, her perspective has taught me so much about me, about us and about our marriage. The hardest pill to swallow was just how poorly we communicated, both of us, and just how much of our marriage she spent oblivious of how deeply I loved her. We're soulmates, always have been, and we've remained close through the years, connected not only by the bond of the two beautiful daughters we brought into the world but also by a bond of true friendship. Yet I have to laugh to keep from crying when I grasp the fact that we're both in our late sixties and only now are we able to speak to each other honestly and openly. I'm so thankful to have had the chance, because life is about understanding who we are and why we are here, and that process continues – if your mind remains open – until the moment you draw your last breath.

After Amelia was born, life at Benifold was even tougher for

Jenny, because she was torn between two different lives; the one she lived when the house was full and we were home, and the one she lived on her own during the long weeks we were away. She's told me how scary it was for her at first, living there with a newborn baby, all alone in a big old mansion in the woods. Gradually she adjusted, fell into a routine and came to enjoy her privacy and the stunning natural setting. When the band and crew returned, however, the house filled up and was transformed and what Jenny had come to see as her personal space was overrun with a rowdy group of miscreants who had been gone so long, they were virtually strangers to her, myself included.

A band on the road, even without the type of trauma our circle had come to regard as routine, is a tightly-knit unit. The shared experience of the effort of getting from here to there, of performing, of living in the moment of whatever collection of songs you're out there delivering to the audience, is an adventure that only those who are a part of the endeavour understand. The inside jokes you make to pass the time, to alleviate the strain and exhaustion, the shared memories both good and bad – to an outsider all of that time spent together becomes a language they can't decipher or hope to learn. In the same way, those who lived it first-hand can't explain it to those who weren't there, because it won't make sense. I never wanted Jenny to feel like an outsider but it was unavoidable. She didn't possess the constitution or desire to spend her life on the road. She didn't want to deny me that life, she just wanted a private life with me that existed apart from all of that. She never got to have that, so our love, deep and true as it was and still is for each other, simply couldn't survive.

Jenny has told me that when we did return, she saw how tight we'd all become, how bound together. It was as if we'd re-emerged from a secluded alternate reality, where we'd relied on each other and no one else to get through it. She saw that bond amongst us and longed for that with me, but knew she could never be a part of it. She saw how we all looked out for each other, how if one of the team had strayed from their partner on the road, the others, ever their ally, never uttered a word. She said that she saw us protect each other and how that fortified her alienation. She felt that it was all of us against the world, which included her. I was never unfaithful to Jenny, because she would always find out if I were. There was one rare occasion when all the boys in the crew convinced me to bring some girl, who was up for it, back to my room and I was eventually drunk enough to agree to the idea. We got up there and I had to go to the bathroom, so I told the girl whatever she did not to answer the phone. As I was going to the bathroom, the phone rang and of course the girl answered it, and of course it was Jenny. I told the girl to get lost and I talked to Jenny, who I don't think believed me when I said there was a party in the hallway. We never spoke of it, so I don't know if she believed me, but the truth is I was always faithful. In fact, I was the guy on tour reminding the other guys that they had girlfriends whenever temptation crossed our path.

I saw very little of my newborn daughter in the next few months because our manager Clifford Davis kept us touring non-stop, and though we weren't fighting him, we were being stretched to our limits. We returned to America in February, this time for three months, and that US tour nearly destroyed us. An English or European tour might have been easier; less travel and less time away from loved ones, but the truth was, our audience and our album sales had shifted to the States. At the time we were on the charts alongside Jenny's brother-in-law George Harrison's 'My Sweet Lord', which was at number 1, and Santana's meringue-flavoured tribute to Peter Green, their cover of 'Black Magic Woman'. We were nowhere close to that anywhere else in the world.

I should have known that things were not well with us the moment the plane set down in California on our first tour stop. When we arrived in San Francisco, Danny and Jeremy took some mescaline and it really did a number on them, Jeremy in particular. The effects of the drug seemed to last far longer than they should have, and I saw it first-hand because I still roomed with Jeremy, the way I had for years. Something was off and I was concerned. He was consumed with reading his Bible and completely detached from the group. I had to coax him into doing his set that night, which was bizarre because we'd never had to wait for Jeremy to take the stage; usually he was like a racehorse chomping at the bit. For the first time since the day I met him, he was uninterested in playing. He dragged his feet and he wasn't himself, though when we finally got him out there, he was positively on *fire*. I found that even stranger. Nonetheless I was transported by him; his performance was stunning. He was possessed, playing at a level I'd never seen from him, just absolutely out of this world. That also turned out to be Jeremy's last show with Fleetwood Mac.

Our next stop was Los Angeles, which had been rocked by an earthquake severe enough that our arrival was delayed. News of the earthquake sent Jeremy into a state of foreboding; he didn't want to go to LA and insisted that something dreadful was going to happen there. It took all of us to talk him down and assure him that we would be safe. He kept repeating that Los Angeles was full of evil (he had a point there), so we told him that we had each other and we'd be all right. We'd just go down there, do our job, and leave immediately. He eventually came round, though he still wasn't the Jeremy we knew and loved. I was terrified that the psychedelics he'd taken had done permanent damage to him and that he was going the way of Peter Green. I tried to put that fear aside and focused on keeping him close by. He was all right on the trip to LA but once we got there, he was nervous and jumpy. He grew calm again once we reached the hotel room and I felt like Jeremy was back. We chatted, made a few jokes, and for the first time in days I felt as if he was himself once more.

'Mick, I'm going to go out for a bit,' he said. 'I want to go down and browse this book store on Hollywood Boulevard that I like. Be back in a bit.'

I didn't think anything of it, but clearly I should have, because he never came back. We waited until six o'clock, when we had to cancel the gig, then we set out together to track him down. We went to the bookstore, which was actually a head shop, and learned that the owners hadn't seen him. We tried to remain calm and did some deductive reasoning. We knew Jeremy – there was no way he'd gone off with some girl, and he wasn't the type to meet a stranger and hide out doing drugs with them. The remaining possibilities were more sinister. Either he'd been kidnapped or killed or, more logically, he'd run off with one of the hippie Christian sects that fished for converts on Hollywood Boulevard. We'd passed a few of them earlier in the day. I felt so foolish for letting him go out on that walk alone.

Jeremy didn't return that night, so the next morning we went to the police. We asked around about those cults, who were known for taking in runaways and others ripe for the picking. They'd sequester them away and brainwash them until they'd renounced their former lives, donated their worldly possessions, and pledged allegiance to the cult. We didn't wait for the police, we went out and searched on our own for four fevered days among the destroyed buildings and roads of a city recovering from an earthquake. We got Jeremy's picture on the news and on flyers and with the help of several local Christian churches, we learned where the city's more radical cults were housed. One of them was out in the San Fernando Valley, close to the epicentre of the earthquake, and driving out there was bleak. Surrounded by fractured highway overpasses and felled buildings, all of us felt desperate that we'd never find Jeremy. When we got to the door of the house, they wouldn't even open it, nor answer our questions. The expressions of the pale, thin faces peering out through the windows were chilling.

After four days, we received an anonymous tip at the hotel. We'd find Jeremy if we went to the Children of God's warehouse in downtown LA. He was staying there under an assumed name. I was so spooked by then that I didn't go, but our manager Clifford Davis did. He conned his way inside by claiming that Jeremy's wife was seriously ill and he found a very different Jeremy. His long hair had been shorn to his skull, he was wearing dirty clothes and he would only answer to the name Jonathan.

As we guessed, he'd been approached by the brethren on the street and been taken with them. He'd seen the earthquake as a portent of the end of the world and had decided then and there that he had to pursue salvation. He didn't care about the band, the tour, not even his family back home.

'Jeremy, don't you—' our manager said.

'My name is Jonathan.'

'Jonathan, don't you want to see your wife and child? What will become of them if you don't go home?'

'Jesus will take care of them,' Jeremy said.

He'd been completely brainwashed; he was like a child, star-struck. Jeremy Spencer was gone.

We had six weeks of the tour left; the revenue we'd lose cancelling those dates would cost us our house, Benifold, and probably the band. We were at a loss as to what to do, we really were. Out of desperation we reached out to Peter Green and asked him to fill in. We had little faith that he'd do it; his album had flopped and we'd heard from mutual friends that he'd given away all of his guitars. When our manager got in touch with him he learned that Peter had taken a job doing manual labour on a farm. I'm not sure what Clifford said to him, but he convinced Peter to play with us for the six weeks, though he insisted repeatedly that he had no interest in playing music anymore. He said he'd do the tour in honour of the friendship he'd shared with us for all those years.

Whatever the reason, Clifford got Peter a flight to California, while Jeremy flew to Texas, where he was joined by his wife Fiona and their son to live with the Children of God, while their youngest child remained behind to be raised by Fiona's mother. Jeremy became a major recruiter for the sect and the two of them spent the rest of the year visiting branches all over the country.

Peter showed up looking the worse for wear, but his playing was great, though he had a few demands that we had to honour. He agreed to play 'Black Magic Woman', at whatever point in the set he felt inspired to do so, after which we would do ninety minutes of free-form jamming. This made for an interesting six weeks because not once did we take the stage knowing what the set was going to be.

Stranger still, that six-week tour ended up being the most lucrative American run we'd ever had. Peter never once engaged with the audience, he'd come to the mike occasionally to murmur something or just laugh. He took none of it seriously, yet at times his playing was so beautiful that it raised gooseflesh on my arms. Those moments made it all the sadder; this was the long goodbye.

At the end of the tour, Peter went back to his life on the farm and we retreated to Benifold. We were exhausted and at our wits' end, which made Jenny all the more self-conscious about the presence of a crying baby, knowing the state of everyone's nerves. We'd been through a lot, but to be fair, she'd been on her own raising a baby. Once Jeremy's wife and child had departed, she was quite literally all by herself. She began to resent the band for taking me away from her and I began to feel it, although I dismissed it, blaming it on the stress of caring for the baby. Neither of us ever talked about how we felt, so things between us would work themselves out slowly, non-verbally. After a tour it would take a few weeks for us to feel connected again and to resume our normal life together. But as soon as we'd re-connected, it was usually time for the band to set out on another tour.

Now that I look back on it, the best times we shared in those days were spent away from Benifold. We used to get away, at Jenny's urging, and go to Salisbury to visit my parents, Mike and Biddy. They lived in a long white house with a river running past the bottom of their garden called Bridge House. My mother would make delicious meals and we'd sit at their dining table for hours telling stories and laughing. The atmosphere was warm and inviting, the evenings filled with as much serious discussion as with crude jokes and silliness. Jenny loved my family as they did her; our family dynamic was quite a departure for her, as she had come from a broken home. She treasured my parents, regarding my mother as her role model when it came to raising our children, and my father as the wise, gentle influence he was to everyone who knew him. She saw the value of family from my own family and wanted to emulate that environment with me.

CHAPTER 8

A SERIES OF BEGINNINGS

After Jeremy's departure, once again we were a band in need of a guitarist and yet another fresh start. Through Judy Wong, a long-time friend of ours, we ended up hiring Bob Welch, an LA native. Bob had grown up on the Beach Boys and rock and rollers like Little Richard, before moving to Paris where he cut his chops as a sideman backing expatriate American jazz greats such as Bud Powell and Eric Dolphy. After a few years he returned to LA and played in an R&B group called the Seven Souls for a number of years. They never quite made it and neither did his next outfit, Head West. Bob had just about sold his last guitar and given up his dream of playing music when Judy put him in touch with us.

We tried out a few others but Bob was the perfect fit. He was a California dude, brought up in the Valley, who had fallen in love with R&B and jazz. Although he lived abroad, he still had that innate California sunshine in his style. Bob brought vocal harmonies to the band and he wrote with Chris, designing songs around their shared tunefulness. We'd done none of that in Fleetwood Mac before him and it was his idea to integrate the male and female vocals in the band.

It became the blueprint for the sound that Fleetwood Mac is best known for and the origins of it started with Bob Welch.

Bob was seasoned and well-trained, he could talk-sing and he had a precise sense of phrasing and timing. He'd brought us tapes of originals he'd never recorded, so we could see the scope of his abilities as a writer and the potential there. But most of all we all loved his personality. Bands are about the players as people, not just the people who play the parts together. I've met many musical geniuses who I would love to have played with, but they'd never have fit within Fleetwood Mac, because they didn't possess the personality that informs this band's spirit. There's a rapport in Fleetwood Mac that has been there from the start, all of which comes through in the music, no matter which era you listen to. A band is the sum of its parts, not an assembly of individuals. That kind of chemistry is priceless and often overlooked as the key to the success or failure of a band.

Bob's songwriting drove the next phase of our music, elevating us from what seemed like the gritty end into a new beginning. He was a prophet of what was to come, because if we hadn't begun to experiment with the intermingling of male and female vocal harmonies, we might not have been capable of bringing Lindsey Buckingham and Stevie Nicks into our midst so quickly and easily once Bob had moved on.

We spent a while jamming at Benifold until we found our footing, then we booked a summer tour of small ballrooms and clubs around Britain to rebuild our audience and road-test the new songs. It was the first time Bob had ever played most of his originals for an audience, but he rose to the occasion.

We recorded *Future Games* that summer at Advision Studios

in London. Danny and Bob did not write together, so the record was a mix of their songs and a few of Chris's. The album ended up as a blend of styles between Bob and Chris and Danny's more progressive-leaning blues, but it worked. The cover of the album was a photograph shot by my sister Sally, but the back of it marked the birth of John McVie's alter-ego and one of the band's enduring symbols: the penguin.

When John and Chris first got together, before we all moved into Kiln House and then Benifold, they lived near the London Zoo. John loved visiting the zoo and did so nearly every day, usually with his camera. That is where he became fascinated with penguins. He'd shoot photos of them for hours, reading up on the various species to the point that he could name them all on sight. We decided the back cover of *Future Games* should have individual shots of each of us as a way of introducing our line-up. John didn't want to do that and insisted that the record company use one of his penguin portraits instead, such was his love of penguins. Around that time, after a night of drinking, he even went and got a penguin tattooed on his arm. Thus the penguin has been a mascot and an image in Fleetwood Mac's visual legacy ever since.

We spent the next eleven months on tour in America and Europe, through most of 1972. Our album did very well in the States, where we got top billings at venues like the Fillmore, where Van Morrison opened for us. Most of our shows were sold out and we were proud to break the house sales record at many of the venues we played across the country. After so much transition, we were back and that was a wonderful thing.

It hadn't been an easy road and I had to look no further than John and Chris to see the proof, because the stress of it all was tearing their marriage apart. When his nerves were shot and he'd reached the end of his rope, my emotionally-reserved friend would explode. Since they were so close in every single way, Chris bore the brunt of it.

Jenny came on tour with us occasionally, though never for very long. I'd always beg her to come and I loved it when she did, but touring wasn't for her. She did it to relieve her loneliness and because she missed me, but the long car rides with our baby daughter Amelia on her lap, hoping she wouldn't cry and wake sleeping band members, were more stressful for her than being home alone at Benifold. She was never a night-owl like the rest of us and with the baby was even less so. Poor Jenny found more loneliness on the road, waking up early to push Amelia's pram along the streets of Manhattan while I got some much-needed sleep.

Jenny was on a different schedule, which furthered her separation from the group. She was a new mother, which she felt removed her from the rock-and-roll world. Being on tour with us only hammered the point home in her mind. She was always naturally shy, but she was more so on the road, talking to no one other than me most of the time. Inevitably she'd leave the tour earlier than we'd planned, which unintentionally hurt my feelings. She's told me that she always felt as if she had no purpose there, no identity outside of being Mick's wife, and it left her introverted and exhausted.

During that touring marathon we did so much; we opened for Deep Purple, we played with Savoy Brown, Long John Baldry, and many others. We even made time to record an album called *Bare Trees*, our second studio effort in six months. The songs reflected the jaded road-weariness that had overcome us. Chris's 'Homeward Bound' said it best – it was just a simple plaintive wish for a proper night's rest in her own bed. We also scored an American chart hit with Bob Welch's 'Sentimental Lady'.

The album and that song became an FM radio staple, whereas at home in England the press considered the album somewhat of a disgrace. It was seen as the inelegant end of a once great British blues band.

Overall things seemed to be on the up, but that only meant there was trouble around the corner. As 1972 wound on, Danny Kirwan became more and more withdrawn from the band. He slowly alienated himself, growing ever more hostile toward each of us until I was the only one in the band who'd even talk to him. In my opinion alcoholism began to take hold of him. His consumption increased drastically during this period and his character transformed. He became contrary overall and he began to pick fights, mostly with Bob Welch, because that was easy. The two of them were very different as people and musicians. What saddened me most was that Danny had never been a negative guy, but he had quickly become one, which to me was a clear indication of a deeper issue in regard to his drinking.

We did that tour in two station wagons with our gear in a trailer behind us, and by the end of it, I was the only person in our operation who would even agree to ride in a car with Danny. It wasn't that he was oblivious either, he noticed everyone pulling away from him, which made things worse because he did nothing to change it. It seemed only to steel his perception that we were all united against him. This tangible tension came to a head that August at a show we did at a college, I can't remember which one. Bob and Danny had been getting on each other's nerves for weeks; we all felt a blow-up brewing, but we did not expect what happened.

No one in Fleetwood Mac has ever been a sub-par musician and Danny, like the rest of us, was meticulous about his craft and having his instrument properly in tune. He had perfect pitch as a singer and was equally precise as a guitarist. However it began, Danny and Bob got into an argument over Bob's guitar being supposedly out of tune. We were all sitting backstage getting ready to go on, when Danny went off on a rant about Bob never being in tune. Then he got up suddenly, went into the bathroom and smashed his head into the wall, splattering blood everywhere. Danny wasn't the kind of man to do that, in fact I'd never seen him do anything that violent in all the years I'd known him. The rest of us were paralysed, in complete shock, as he came out of the bathroom bleeding, walked over to his Les Paul guitar and smashed it to bits. He then set about demolishing everything in the dressing room that wasn't nailed down as we all sat and watched.

When there was nothing left to throw at the wall or overturn, Danny calmed down. Then he looked at us.

'There is no way in hell that I'm playing with you all tonight,' he said. 'There is *no way.*'

We tried everything but it was no use. And we had no time; we were already late to the stage and we could hear the crowd chanting for us. So we went out there without our lead guitarist. Bob did his best to cover Danny's parts but there was no way he could make do.

We apologised to the audience and told them that Danny had fallen ill. Throughout the set I stole looks at the side of the stage hoping to see Danny with a new guitar, ready to join us. In my heart I believed that the sound of his band limping through its paces without him would bring him to his senses. That didn't happen, which made it clear to me that Danny was truly distraught and that I'd need to have a heart-to-heart talk with him back at the hotel. The last thing I expected when we got offstage was to find him sitting in the dressing room waiting for us.

'Danny? What are you doing here? You didn't go back to the hotel?' I asked.

'No, I sat out at the sound board,' he said nonchalantly. 'I stayed to watch. Yeah, not bad, really.'

That was it for me; I felt betrayed and angry. Throwing a temper tantrum and refusing to play was one thing, it was quite another to then stay to watch us floundering without him. Danny didn't stop there, he turned the knife in the wound.

'There was room for improvement,' he said. 'Especially you could have played a lot better, Mick. You missed some cues and you should have picked up the tempo on a number of occasions.'

'Thanks, Danny, I'll remember that.'

I couldn't believe he even had the nerve to critique our perform-ance, but I held my tongue. My bandmates wanted to fire him immediately, right then and there, but I wouldn't let them. Since our manager was in England, I was the de facto leader, so the decision fell to me. I weighed up the options; if we fired him, we'd have to cancel the rest of the tour. That night, over dinner, I sought the advice of Jon Lord of Deep Purple. Jon listened and then talked me through what had to be done, because there was no other option. Danny had to go. No one had ever been fired from Fleetwood Mac before. Danny was the first, but he wouldn't be the last.

I went to his room, knocked on the door, sat on the bed and fumbled my way through it. I told him that we all knew he wasn't happy with us and that we weren't happy either, and that the best thing would be for him to leave the band. Danny didn't say a word, he just sat there silently. When I asked him if he understood, he nodded, and that was it, Danny was out. I then went upstairs to John and Christine's room and was crying before I even got to the door.

*

The next two and a half years were absolute chaos, there's no other way to say it, and from where we were coming from, that is significant. Our fan base had moved across the Atlantic, because by the beginning of the mid-1970s there was far more of a demand for us in America, where the kind of blues-rock we were doing was in fashion. In England we had two things holding us back. The first was that our die-hard blues fans felt that we'd abandoned them. The second was that the glam-rock era of Marc Bolan and David Bowie had begun, so we really didn't fit in anymore. We could still play pubs, of course, but we'd had a taste of life beyond that and we weren't going back if we could help it.

We needed a replacement for Danny and we found one in Bob Weston, whom we knew from touring when we met him in Long John Baldry's band. We briefly added Dave Walker, lead singer of Savoy Brown, to the line-up, for one album, *Penguin*. Dave did a good job and sounded great alongside Weston's slide-guitar playing, but it was a short-lived affair. When we returned to write new material, Dave was only interested in writing songs that sounded like Savoy Brown. Bob, on the other hand, was a great fit for us and eager to remain in the band. He brought a ton of much-needed energy to the proceedings.

Bob Weston was charming and funny and a great player, too, so he fit right in. That charm also cost him his job and, for a time, our band, because he began an affair with my wife. Jenny first met Bob during one of her stints on tour in America with us. She's told me that both she and Christine used to joke that Bob looked like Stan Laurel of Laurel and Hardy, and was just as amusing. All of us liked him because he was amiable, which Jenny saw too; according to her, Bob was the first of the bunch to pay attention to her. When we were recording at

Benifold, he would stop by and spend time with her as she prepared food or fed our daughter, Amelia. She was pregnant with our second daughter and very much stayed in her own world. He used to drop in and have coffee with Jenny while the rest of us were up in the music room and they developed a platonic rapport that eventually grew into something more, after the birth of our second daughter.

For one thing, Bob and Jenny discovered that they were born on the same day in the same year, which created a deeper connection in Jenny's mind. Bob was a breath of fresh air in her world; he was the first band member with whom she felt she had a friendship, apart from her being married to me. The same thing would happen with Bob Welch, who also made an unrequited move toward her during his time in the band. It all stemmed from Jenny's need to connect and not getting what she needed from me. She was such a beguiling, beautiful little creature that men were always smitten. In her mind, she valued the friendship and needed that connection, but it didn't always mean she wanted to get her knickers off. In the case of Weston, however, it did.

We continued to tour, and later that year Jenny gave birth to our second daughter, Lucy, while we were off in America. I didn't see her until I returned six weeks later. My parents were at Jenny's side and she spent the weeks until my return at their house in Salisbury. A few months after that, we gathered at Benifold in 1973 to record our next album, *Mystery to Me*, using the Rolling Stones' mobile studio, as we had done for *Penguin*. We moved everything out of the two great rooms on the first floor of the house and, set up the instruments and microphones, all connected by thick cables running outside the front door to the truck. The sound in there was amazing, just massive, like a concert hall, resounding off the trees and all through the grounds.

Those songs were my two daughters' lullabies for those weeks and the title of the album came from Jenny. She's told me since that the mystery was how she'd begun to feel for Bob Weston. The two of them would go on long walks or hang out together in the house. I didn't see it at all, to me it looked as if Jenny had found a friend in the band. I was happy, actually. I figured that if she felt more comfortable, she'd come on tour more, allowing us to be together. When Clifford Davis booked our next set of dates, I suggested it to her. We had two daughters now, which meant twice the work for her, so I didn't expect her to consent, but she did.

I couldn't have been happier. I had my wife and children on tour with me. For the first time in what seemed like forever, Jenny began to imbibe and stay up late with the rest of us. When she drank, her shyness melted away and the lovely, smart girl I knew so well emerged for everyone to see. Jenny was wonderful on that tour; she'd have fun with us at night after the show and still have the energy to get up early and take care of the girls.

It was a whole new Jenny, which made me start to wonder what else was going on. I noticed how she blushed when Bob teased her and how they'd sit and chat on their own every chance they got.

'Jenny,' I said to her, when we were alone in our room one day, 'I know how hard it is having me on the road so much. It's not easy. So many people we know are breaking up. Let's try to stick together.'

When we talked about it all again recently she told me that she remembered that moment, but by then it was too late. My sentiment fell on deaf ears. She'd felt lonely for too long. I'd been too aloof, though I'd loved her so much. I'd contributed to her feeling that there was a barrier between my life with the band and my life with her. By the time I said those words the damage was done, her decision made. She'd craved attention for so long and needed to feel, and Bob Weston provided that excitement.

Jenny remained on tour longer than she ever had, spending more and more time with Bob. It was clear to me and to everyone else what was going on. I remember having a few days off in Hermosa Beach and coming out to the hotel pool to find Bob and my wife playing with our children, having a wonderful time. That was too much for me to bear, so I sternly put an end to it. But the fact that I'd been in such denial for so long distresses me to think about it now. How could I have let that happen? I let Jenny get to the point of crying out so much for the attention she needed that she not only found a new boyfriend, he also happened to be my guitar player. It was almost as if I were condoning it, having it occur right there before me, as if we were on a commune where we shared lovers.

I confronted Jenny later that day.

'What exactly is going on between you, Jenny?' I asked. 'The two of you were playing with our daughters as if you are one big happy family.'

'Mick,' she said, shaking a bit. 'I'm falling in love with Bob. I can't be here anymore. I want to go home.'

I was silent for a long time. I didn't want to hear what I already knew to be true.

'Well, Jenny, then you should go. I would never keep you here against your will.'

When we talked about it all again recently, Jenny told me she couldn't believe what she was doing. She was torn. As she saw it, she'd taken a stand, she'd asserted her independence, but she was terrified. She'd been in a daze, overwhelmed with her feelings and fuelled by brandy; she'd taken to drinking too much and eating too little and had lost a lot of weight. I was worried about her, but that didn't outweigh my heart-ache.

I gave her a bouquet of flowers when I said goodbye in the hotel lobby.

'Be careful out there, Jenny,' I said. I held her close and gave her a kiss. Then I got into a car and left with the rest of my band, Bob Weston included.

Jenny was on her own and didn't know what to do. She stayed with Bob Welch's girlfriend Nancy in LA for a few days then flew home to England with our daughters, one of them two and a half, the other just five months. When she got there, Ronnie Wood and his wife, Krissy, let her stay at their house in Richmond, as they were spending a lot of time at George Harrison and Pattie's house in Oxfordshire. Ronnie and Krissy were very kind, even turning a blind eye when our daughter Amelia tipped over and broke one of their Tiffany lamps.

Meanwhile back in the States, I tried my best to soldier on with the tour, knowing that my wife had fallen for Bob Weston. I wanted to honour my commitments and the band's commitments and sort it out with Bob later. That was naive, because by the time we got to Lincoln, Nebraska, I couldn't take it anymore. We had been getting through the shows, but not talking, and it was all too much. I was coming unglued emotionally. I didn't want a resolution, I didn't even want to confront him, I just wanted him gone.

It was horrible because Bob and I were good friends and I think if one of us had initiated an open-hearted discussion, it all might have been all right, since essentially Bob shook up my relationship with Jenny, which was something that needed to happen. We didn't have that conversation. Instead, I told our road manager John Courage to fire him and cancel the rest of the tour because I couldn't handle it. Courage did it right; he sent the crew to Bob's room to get him out and onto a plane the next morning before the rest of us had even woken up. Bob went back to England and he and Jenny shacked up together for three weeks. She's told me that she was such a nervous wreck over what she'd done that she only felt fine when she was drinking. Nonetheless it didn't take long for her to figure out that she didn't love Bob, she loved the part of herself that he allowed her to get in touch with, the child-like part she could no longer access with me. She felt that I'd abandoned her for the band, so she had done the same.

Jenny went to Benifold to pick up some clothes during this time and while she was there, in need of guidance, she arranged to see a psychic from the village. Jenny told me recently about this woman, how she'd described the whole painful situation so accurately. She could see I was in Africa – I had travelled to Zambia – and was a very unhappy man, and then she said, 'You're being used as a pawn by the powers that be. There is something greater that will happen because of this situation, but now your place is with your husband.' Jenny knew she was right. The psychic had given her the guidance she needed. She ended the affair. Bob was very angry and hurt, because he'd felt something more for her. At that point she got in touch with me and told me she wanted to try again.

I had taken off to Zambia, because to say the least, I needed to clear my head. The whole band did; after Bob was fired and the tour cancelled, everyone retreated to different parts of the world for a much-needed holiday, before gathering once again at Benifold. In the interim, our manager Clifford Davis put together a fake version of Fleetwood Mac featuring members of a band called Curved Air that he also managed. He refused to forfeit the money that had been advanced for the remainder of our tour and opted to pass off a bogus version of our band, claiming he owned the rights to the name.

This of course was the last thing we needed. It was also the most preposterous thing we'd ever heard and the greatest betrayal from one of our own that we could have imagined. If there was ever a time to call it quits, this was it. There we were in England, far from what had become our core audience, thousands of miles from our record company and with our band in tatters, as our trusted manager of seven years tried to move on without us. It was heartbreak heaped on heartache for me. Reuniting with Jenny at Benifold was much the same. My feelings for her had remained the same but I was deeply hurt. She'd gone from feeling unnoticed amongst the band to being the person everybody talked about.

It had all gone so wrong, but I wasn't going to let it end. I just couldn't. I couldn't allow other musicians to tour under our name, whoever they were. Bob Welch was my ally in this and I needed his resolve because the others, John and Christine included, were drained. Their marriage was on the rocks and the idea that not only would we need to find yet another guitarist, but also have to fire our manager and fight for the right to our name, was dumbfounding. This mountain seemed insurmountable, even for us.

Bob Welch, the McVies and I would sit round the table at Benifold for hours debating what to do. We didn't have a manager, which to me was our biggest problem. I didn't know how to proceed, because I'd always relied on someone else to book our gigs and handle our affairs.

'We don't need anyone else to do it, Mick,' Bob said one day. 'We can do it ourselves. Between the two of us, you and I have enough experience. We've been gigging musicians for years, we know how it works.'

He wasn't wrong and we'd seen first-hand what could happen when the affairs of the band were left to those who didn't have our best interests in mind. Bob and I decided that we'd manage the band together and do what had to be done legally to reclaim our name from Clifford Davis.

The first thing we had to do was file a lawsuit against Davis and since he was touring the bogus Fleetwood Mac in the States, that's where we needed to file it. We had no idea how far Clifford would take his pursuit of ownership, but if he wasn't willing to settle quickly and the suit went into the American judicial system, we would be required to appear in lawyers' offices and in court; in short we'd be making frequent trips across the pond.

'If we're really going to do this, Mick,' Bob said, 'we should be close by. Every time a paper is filed with the court or we need to sign something, we'll be delaying the process by days or weeks being so far removed. If we are managing the band, we are the representatives and we're going to have to be there.'

'But we have the house, Bob,' I said. 'This is our home. We've made our last two albums here, this is us. I just don't know.'

'I know, Mick,' he said. 'But look at it this way. If we're going to keep going, this band needs a new start. You have to remember, there were good times here but they weren't all good.' He cracked a wry smile.

'You can say that again,' I said and started laughing.

Bob was right. Jenny was back with me but the pain in my heart from what had transpired between her and Bob Weston was far from healed. There at Benifold, reminders were all around. A change would do us good if we were to save our marriage.

Our record company, Reprise, was in America, too, so it made sense that we should be accessible to them during the process of rebuilding our band. Above and beyond all that, our front man

Bob Welch was never really into communal living or our country mansion. He was a California guy and he wanted to go home. He had a life there and he had a girlfriend, whom he later married, and though those were his ulterior motives, he was absolutely right that West Coast sunshine and a taste of the music scene that was evolving in Los Angeles was just what we needed.

As a group we decided that we'd relocate for six months, reclaim our name, get back in the studio and then go out on the road. It was going to be a case of do-or-die; we weren't selling Benifold, we were going to Los Angeles to regroup and start again, or fail trying. The hope was that we'd have our affairs back in order by that time, or at least have the machinations in motion, and then we could make an informed decision about where we wanted to live.

Jenny's affair with Bob Weston inadvertently became the catalyst for a great deal of change. It had cost Bob his job and momentarily broken up the band. It had shaken me so much that I went off to Africa for a month and took my eye off the ball, and when that happened our manager absconded with our name and all that we'd worked so hard for. As a result we moved to LA, and what was meant to be a six-month trip turned into a two-and-a-half-year legal battle and a permanent relocation. I hadn't been paying proper attention to my marriage and I'd allowed someone close to me to take advantage of my distraction. The same can be said of my relationship with the band. Both affairs and all that came from them were wake-up calls for me, so going forward I vowed never to drop my guard again. I knew I couldn't control the future, but I was determined to keep my focus on the band no matter how much my emotions and love life might serve to cloud my vision.

CHAPTER 9

FALLING INTO PLACE

We landed in Los Angeles in the spring of 1974; Jenny and I
with our two children, our close friend Sandra, and the McVies.
John and Chris stayed in a house owned by John Mayall for a
while, until they found their own place, and Jenny and I stayed
at the infamous Chateau Marmont until we found a nice two-
bedroom house in Laurel Canyon. John and I both bought
ourselves used Cadillac convertibles for $1,000 each, mine was
metallic gold and John's was white. I remember driving that huge
yacht of a car through the winding roads of the Hollywood Hills
and cruising along Sunset Boulevard with the top down feeling
immediately reinvigorated. It was a new start for all of us.

It had been months since we'd worked as a functioning band
and it would be close to a year before we would do so again.
We had an arduous process ahead of us, a legal battle that Bob
and our lawyers set in motion as soon as we all got settled. The
meetings and paperwork were endless and Clifford Davis didn't
plan to concede. He believed he owned Fleetwood Mac and
that the name had value in itself, regardless of who played the
music. It made no sense and as we got deeper into the lawsuit,
the degree of deception he had shown us was loathsome.

Once I'd found myself unable to continue playing with Bob Weston and had cancelled our tour to retreat to Africa and heal myself, Clifford Davis had sent letters to the other members of the band inviting them to be a part of a 'star-studded new project' he was putting together. None of them took him up on it. Meanwhile he'd told all of the members of the bogus Fleetwood Mac, none of whom had even played or recorded with us, that Christine McVie and I would be joining them later in the tour. He made similar promises to promoters and the press. When the tour began and his plans fell apart, he told the band that I'd pulled out of the tour entirely and that they'd have to go on with a replacement. Audiences felt duped, word spread fast and ticket sales fizzled. Those guys ended up staying together and renaming themselves Stretch, then went on to score a minor hit called 'Why Did You Do It?' that reached number 16 on the UK charts in November of 1975. The song was a direct attack on me for not showing up for the bogus Fleetwood Mac tour, which I'd never promised to do in the first place, of course. All of it was too bizarre.

We sued Davis, he counter-sued us and on it went. We got an injunction barring the faux Fleetwood Mac from touring. Consequently Davis's side won an injunction barring us from performing – as ourselves – until the legal proceedings had concluded. We could write and record but we couldn't release an album, tour, or otherwise earn money as Fleetwood Mac. Pre-existing albums were excluded so our record company, Reprise/Warner Brothers, re-packaged some singles and material from albums they hadn't released Stateside and put it out as *English Rose*.

As these things do, it took far too long but eventually the court ruled in our favour, at which point John McVie and I established a company called Seedy Management and vowed

Seedy Management: Me and John McVie during a promo shoot for Penguin.
What good are gold records if you can't pawn them anyway?

Gone west: John, me, Bob Welch
and Christine, Hollywood, 1974.

With my daughter Lucy,
Napili Bay, Hawaii, 1975.

Who invited the rabbit? Mo
Ostin, Lindsey Buckingham,
Stevie Nicks, Joe Smith, Me,
Chris and John at the Beverly
Hills Hotel in 1975.

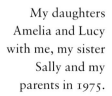

My daughters
Amelia and Lucy
with me, my sister
Sally and my
parents in 1975.

The Rumours crew, 1977.

Here we are in 1977. Lindsey, me, Stevie, Chris and John.

For the sake of the U.S. Government: Me, Mickey Shapiro and Jenny at our second wedding.

At it again! Award show fun, 1977.

Get Tusked: with our gold records for *Tusk*, 1979.

Star treatment: having
our star added to the
Hollywood Walk of
Fame, 1979.

Me, John and
his wife Julie at
their wedding
in LA, 1978.

Best man for
"The Man"!
John and I at
his wedding.

Lindsey and I giving a traditional Maori greeting in New Zealand, 1980.

Staying afloat.

What the hey? In the lotus position during the shoot for the Rolling Stone article announcing my bankruptcy, the Blue Whale, Malibu, 1984.

Fleetwood Mac, 1982.

At the US Festival with Steve Wozniak and Bill Graham in 1982.

John and I beside
a crashed plane at
the side of a runway
we'd just landed on.
From my Polaroid
collection.

Seeing John off after
he'd completed his
parts for the *Tusk*
session. Behind us is
his boat - 'Challenge'
he sailed to Tahiti.

Me with Duane Eddy.
I learned to play
drums to his records,
following the moves
of his drummer Sandy
Nelson. I later played
on Duane's records.

to handle our affairs on our own from that point on. We also signed a new record deal with Warner Brothers and dived into recording *Heroes Are Hard to Find* as a quartet, with Bob and Chris co-fronting the band. It was the first time we'd ever had one guitarist and I don't think it would have worked before then, but Bob Welch delivered. It made me reconsider what Fleetwood Mac meant and what was possible. The new arrangements allowed for more space in our sound and more experimentation with harmony and even horns.

The album was a more sedate affair than our previous efforts with Bob, the result of spending too long in creative limbo, but there are a few standout songs in the collection. Both the title track and Chris's 'Come A Little Bit Closer' are anthemic and melancholy and were among her best to date. Bob's writing was strong as well, on songs like 'Born Enchanter', which was a bluesier variation of the jazzy, esoteric-pop style he'd achieved so well on 'Hypnotized'. The album charted better in the States than any of our previous efforts, reaching number 34, which was a tremendous boost to our spirits and if our record company had questioned whether we still had an audience, it sent a positive message that we most certainly did.

From the moment we set down in Los Angeles, we began to attract a following of interesting fans and friends, among them the great photographer Herbie Worthington. Herbie was, as Jenny put it to me, 'a big bear left over from the hippie era.' He was a bright soul, always smiling, usually wearing loose white Indian cotton tunics that flowed to his knees, with a pair of Jesus sandals. He was a self-proclaimed seeker of the Light, who meditated, and he introduced Jenny to an inspirational book shop called The Bodhi Tree that was a place of sanctuary for her over the years.

Herbie saw what was happening with the band because he

was very in tune. Jenny told me recently just how much Herbie found my eccentricity 'mind-blowing'. I'm flattered, I really am, because Herbie was an artist as iconic as the images he created. He could make anyone comfortable, because he wore his heart on his sleeve and so from the start, he was able to capture fleeting moments in our world. He was the one we chose to shoot the cover of *Heroes Are Hard to Find*, an image that features me modelling gorgeously a pair of lace underpants that belonged to Sandra. I've got my chest puffed-up, which means my ribs are showing, and I'm holding my three-year-old daughter Amelia's hands as she stands on my shoes. He took that photo of us in a three-way mirror, so the final image is three sides, back-to-back.

Herbie was to remain a close friend of the band. In fact, he was the one who took the iconic photos that became the covers of *Fleetwood Mac* and *Rumours*, our first two releases with Lindsey Buckingham and Stevie Nicks. Herbie was such a sweet love child, unprepared for the scene he fell into. Cocaine was particularly inappropriate for someone like him. It was inappropriate for all of us at one point or another, but he became captivated by it and it was a shame. He wasn't suited for that type of world, but that was still a few years off.

We set out on a tour of the States, because our album didn't even chart in England, but we didn't care. Judging by our record sales, our audience had shifted completely to the States, which was fine with us since LA was our new base of operations. We toured nationally and had a great time. It felt like the train was back on the tracks; we made money, we sold out some venues, everything went smoothly and we began to feel like a functioning musical entity once more. This victory was short-lived.

In December 1974, Bob Welch resigned from the band, ending

a four-year period in which we'd finally found an identity and recorded, in my opinion, some of the best pieces of music we'd done since Peter's departure. Bob's exit wasn't like the others; there was no big blow-up, no signs it was coming, no change in his character, and no hard feelings. It was all above-board, and to me, all the more a sad goodbye. I knew things weren't great in his personal life, but I was surprised that Bob wanted to leave the fold, because he'd invested so much. After all, he'd lobbied us to relocate to America and he'd been there with me every step of the way through the tedious legal battle for our name. He didn't have to go those extra miles, but he did. Then once we'd finally won and got under way again, he wanted to go. There was no sense that Bob might turn round and change his mind, the way Peter Green had done, and there was no time for me to try and stop him. His exodus was sudden and the rest of us were disturbed that he hadn't given us more warning.

What he told me was that the touring and the lawsuit had taken their toll on him. Besides, his marriage was on the rocks and creatively he felt he had nothing left to give to Fleetwood Mac. We could do nothing but respect Bob and honour his decision. We all remained close with him, so much so that our company, Seedy Management, managed his solo career well into the 1980s and all of us played on his records.

We lost Bob forever in 2012. In fact the end of 2011 ushered in a year of loss in the legacy of Fleetwood Mac; Bob Welch took his own life, our original bassist Bob Brunning died of a sudden heart attack, Bob Weston died of a gastrointestinal haemorrhage, and Herbie Worthington, the photographer whose iconic images defined the next era of the band, passed away from heart disease.

*

The McVies and I were, once again, a back line without a front end. We had all come to enjoy living in Los Angeles, so we made our relocation permanent. Jenny and I did our best to patch up our marriage in our quaint little house in Laurel Canyon. Finally she had the homestead she'd always wanted. In true bohemian style we got all of our furnishings second-hand from garage sales in the area and fell comfortably into the easy-living lifestyle of Los Angeles in those days. There was a community up in Laurel Canyon that was quite apart from the bustling clubs and nightlife that lay just over the hill on the Sunset Strip. It was night and day from the bucolic solitude of Benifold and she loved it. I could see that it opened Jenny up and I hoped, as she did, that we'd find our way back to loving each other the way we had before.

Things weren't perfect by any means, because we hadn't learned to communicate any better, but each of us tried. I was still hurt and angry, but I did my best to put that behind me. I had the band to focus on. For her part, Jenny sought out the Self-Realization Fellowship, a church open to all denominations, established by Paramahansa Yogananda to teach meditation. She'd been inspired to go by her brother-in-law George Harrison, who had given Yogananda's book *Autobiography of a Yogi* to Jenny many years before. Meditation was very good for her and I was glad she had found a practice that resonated with her view of the world.

We were still in that house in Laurel Canyon when Bob left the band, and on the day that changed it all for Fleetwood Mac, I'd driven my Caddy down the winding road from our place to the Canyon Country Store to buy some groceries. That store has a rich musical legacy. It's where musicians from the Byrds to Crosby, Stills and Nash and Joni Mitchell gathered to jam on the lawn. Jim Morrison lived just behind it and

Mama Cass from the Mamas and the Papas lived in the basement for a time. That is where I ran into a guy I knew from the scene around town, whose name I now can't remember for the life of me, but he was doing some PR work for a new recording studio, inviting musicians he knew to come and check it out. It was called Sound City and it was out in the Valley. That guy is responsible for Fleetwood Mac as most people know it and he should be bragging about it to this day. Maybe he is, because honestly, I've not heard from him since.

'Good to see you, man, what are you doing now?' I asked him.

'I'm good. I'm working for a new studio. You should come check it out, you'd like it,' he said.

'You are? I'm looking for a studio right now. And I've got to get it figured out before the band goes back on the road.'

'Well, come down and see it then,' he said. 'I can get you a good deal.'

I looked at my groceries sitting in the sun in my backseat. 'Let's go right now,' I said. 'Can I put those in your car? They won't last long out in the sun with my top down.'

Sound City was fine; the live room seemed like it would capture drums well and when I met the house engineer Keith Olsen, I liked him a lot. I thought it could be the perfect place to record the next Fleetwood Mac album and I couldn't wait to bring Bob Welch there. I never did, of course, because he quit a few weeks later.

'Do you want to hear something I just finished working on?' Keith asked.

I followed him into the control room and couldn't help being distracted by the fetching waif of a girl we passed in the hallway. It was Stevie Nicks. She was there with Lindsey, who was doing a few overdubs in another room in the studio.

Keith cued up 'Frozen Love', the last track on their album *Buckingham Nicks,* seven enchanting minutes of vocal harmony and dynamic guitar. Keith was very proud of the album; he'd produced it himself and felt that he'd discovered the next great group. I couldn't agree more. I loved what I heard and asked him to play more.

'Congratulations Keith,' I said. 'It sounds fantastic and that guy's one hell of a guitar player. Good luck with it. I'll definitely be calling you to book some studio time.'

After Bob quit, we were in panic mode once more. I called Keith immediately, asking after a lot more than studio time.

'Hi there, Mick, how are you?' he said. 'You ready to book some time? Maybe after the holidays?'

'Well, yes and no, Keith. Bob Welch has left us, so we're looking for a new guitar player. I was calling to ask about that guy whose playing I heard in your studio when I came to visit. I'd like to ask him to join our band. What do you think?'

'You should do it,' he said. 'Lindsey is incredible. But he's a team – his girlfriend, the girl you heard singing with him, is a part of the package.'

'Well, we really just need a guitar player,' I said. 'But I'd like to hear all of their songs again.'

'You should. They're the whole deal, Mick. Take them both.'

When I went back and gave the album more time, I realised he was right, but worried about complicating an already touchy and time-sensitive situation. We couldn't lose momentum and we had to get in the studio. A versatile guitar player who sang and wrote was the easiest fix, because it was replacing Bob. It wouldn't be the upheaval of another different line-up with a new vocalist, and a woman at that. But I wasn't going to be allowed that choice.

'Hello, is this Lindsey? This is Mick Fleetwood.'

'Hey there, how are you doing?'

'I'm well, listen we're looking for a guitar player and I'd like to know if you'd like to come play with us?'

As Lindsey points out when he tells this story, he immediately began using the word 'we'.

'That sounds great, we'd love to,' he said. 'Because my girl-friend comes with me.'

I didn't dare test his boundaries on that subject, it was clear he wouldn't otherwise consider the gig, which was fine with me, so long as we all got on. I'd already begun to think about how well their style could be integrated into our sound. But what I liked most about Lindsey's insistence was that it was in keeping with how we did things in Fleetwood Mac. It was family first, it was loyal. They were like-minded; they wrote together, lived together, loved together. They were very much what Fleetwood Mac was all about.

Stevie was born in Phoenix, Arizona, the daughter of a successful corporate executive, which necessitated the Nicks family moving frequently around the West throughout her child-hood, to Albuquerque, El Paso, Salt Lake City, Los Angeles and San Francisco. Her musical influence came from her paternal grandfather, Aaron Nicks, who was a country singer and taught his granddaughter to sing harmonies with him on classic duets like 'Are You Mine?' by Red Sovine and Goldie Hill when she was no more than three or four years old. Aaron lived up in the mountains of Arizona and played guitar, fiddle and harmonica in saloons all over the state, sometimes taking Stevie along for the ride to dance and sing on stage with him. When she was about five, he wanted to take Stevie on a tour with him but her father refused, which caused a huge family row, resulting in Aaron being estranged from the family for a few years, which Stevie took very hard.

Stevie's family had moved to Los Angeles by the time she was sixteen and for her birthday she was given a guitar, with which she wrote her first song, 'I've Loved and I've Lost and I'm Sad but Not Blue', about a popular boy in school that she pined for. She briefly had a band called Changing Times, but her musical journey didn't really begin until the family moved, yet again, to San Francisco. She attended Menlo-Atherton High School, transferring there as a junior, where she was very popular; she was even voted runner-up for Homecoming Queen in her very first year. As a senior, she met Lindsey Buckingham, a year her junior, at a party. Stevie was there with her guitar and Lindsey was playing 'California Dreamin'' by the Mamas and the Papas on piano, when she walked over and started harmonising with him. The two sang a few more songs, then parted ways and didn't see each other for two years.

Lindsey Buckingham was raised in the upper-middle-class suburb of Atherton and his father was the owner of a successful coffee plant. Lindsey and his two older brothers were all swimmers. In fact his brother Greg won a silver medal in the 1968 Olympics. Lindsey took to water polo but quit that in college to pursue music. He's never taken a guitar lesson in his life and doesn't read sheet music; his gift came naturally and immediately. It was his calling. As a young boy of seven, he'd picked up a toy guitar and started playing along with his brother's records. His parents encouraged him by buying him a small, thirty-five-dollar Harmony, upon which he began deciphering every single in his brother Jeff's collection. He found there a haven of rock and roll and learned from the best; Elvis, Buddy Holly, the Everly Brothers, Chuck Berry, Eddie Cochran and more. As a teen, Lindsey's interest shifted focus. He gravitated towards folk music, which is how he mastered finger-picking.

The combination of those two traditions informs Lindsey Buckingham's playing, a singular style unlike anyone else I've ever heard in rock and roll.

Bands like the Kingston Trio out of San Francisco were a big influence on him and through them he became interested in bluegrass, classical, and all manner of scales and fingering patterns. That method of pick-less multi-finger plucking inspired him, but when he was ready to join a band in his teens, Lindsey's style wasn't suited to the heavy psychedelic sound of the late 1960s, so he picked up the bass guitar and in 1968 he formed a band called Fritz with a few friends from high school. They were missing something, so Lindsey got in touch with Stevie, who was attending college at San José State at the time, and asked her if she wanted to join.

Fritz stayed together for the next three years and became well-liked regulars on the Bay Area circuit. They opened up for amazing West Coast talent including Jefferson Airplane, Quicksilver Messenger Service, Moby Grape, the Charlatans and, of course, Big Brother and the Holding Company. That gig was life changing for Stevie; seeing Janis Joplin's perform-ance, how she poured herself into it and the tangible bond she created with the audience, really affected her. Stevie didn't want to be Janis, or commune in that way, but what she took from that moment was the intensity of the relationship. Janis connected and made the crowd feel every single word she sang and Stevie aspired to do the same.

Fritz got a manager who shopped them around for a record deal in LA, but their music wasn't really a part of that scene. They were a fusion of psychedelic-rock and folk music, unlike anything on the charts or being signed at the time. The big songs of 1970 were the Beatles' 'Let It Be', Mungo Jerry's 'In the Summertime', and Simon and Garfunkel's 'Bridge Over

Troubled Water'. The Jackson 5 had their second hit with 'ABC' and the album *Led Zeppelin III* was redefining heavy rock and roll. No record company A&R guy was looking for a band like Fritz.

By 1971, Fritz parted ways and by then Lindsey and Stevie were romantically involved. They began writing together, eager to continue with their musical endeavours. In Fritz they had more or less been a duo within a band, so becoming a duo on their own was a natural evolution for them. As young lovers do, they agreed to chase their dream and move to LA in search of a record contract. Before they could put their plan into effect, however, Lindsey contracted mononucleosis and was bedridden for the next nine months. They made the best of the situation; they wrote songs, and Lindsey bought an electric guitar and taught himself to play lead. He also bought a professional four-track Ampex tape recorder that his father allowed him to set up in an extra room in the offices of his coffee plant. There, over the next few months, Lindsey taught himself the art of audio engineering. He took to it right away, because the kind of meticulous attention to detail required of a good producer came naturally to him. Working on that four-track for hours, until those early Buckingham Nicks demos were just right, undoubtedly made him the brilliant producer he later became.

Once Lindsey recovered from his illness, the two of them moved to LA. They befriended producer Keith Olsen, who was already working out of Sound City, and he helped them shop around for a record contract. They also got to know Richard Dashut, Keith's assistant engineer. He and Lindsey formed a fast friendship and Richard became Fleetwood Mac and Lindsey's co-producer, our sound man on the road, and our constant creative partner and friend for years to come.

Those early days were tough for Stevie and Lindsey. They had little money; Stevie worked as a waitress at a 1920s flapper-themed restaurant and cleaned houses. They ended up living with Keith, and then sharing a small apartment with Richard Dashut at a place that became a crash pad for their musical friends such as Warren Zevon and Waddy Watchell. It was more of a studio than a home, with Lindsey spending every waking hour on his four-track, perfecting what they were working on.

Their debut album, *Buckingham Nicks*, was released in late 1973. It's interesting for me to think back on 'Frozen Love', the song that had impressed me most of all, because it was the only song they'd written entirely together. It was a harbinger of things to come. Unfortunately, the record-buying public did not see the same brilliance in *Buckingham Nicks* that I did. Despite gigs opening for established acts including Mountain and Poco, they didn't attract a national fan base at all. They were like an invention that sat around for two years until the world discovered them: 'Oh, look, a new way to open a door!'

The only place Buckingham Nicks caught on was Alabama, specifically in Tuscaloosa and Birmingham. It was a freak thing; in those two towns they got radio play and sold out three-to-four-thousand-seat theatres. It was a strange carrot being dangled, because they got a taste of success but only in that one market, with which they had no association whatsoever, and that was frustrating for them.

After *Buckingham Nicks* was released and didn't connect, the duo was dropped from their label, Polydor, and they were devastated. Money became so tight for them that they had to move back in with Richard Dashut, who had moved into his own apartment. Lindsey wasn't giving up; he began working on demos for their next record, right there in the apartment, on his Ampex machine. They had no label and no one in the industry was coming knocking, but those demos held the key. Among other songs, they'd recorded 'Monday Morning', 'So Afraid' and 'Rhiannon'.

To pay the bills, Stevie held down a day job, while Lindsey took a short touring gig with Don Everly's band that Warren Zevon had organised after the Everly Brothers split up. It was brief, but Lindsey got to sing some of Phil Everly's vocal parts, which was a full-circle experience for him since he'd learned to play guitar to those very songs. When the tour passed through Nashville, he also got to meet other idols of his such as Roy Orbison and Merle Travis. The pair were coming to the end of the line, however, because Stevie's family had started asking her how much longer she planned to pursue music. They offered to support her if she came home and went back to school, and she'd begun to consider that a viable option, because she and Lindsey were literally at the point of going hungry.

We all met for the first time at a Mexican restaurant called El Carmen – John and Chris drove up from their place down at the beach and I met Lindsey at my place on Kirkwood Drive, off Laurel Canyon. Stevie was there first, waiting for all of us, still dressed in her flapper's garb, just off a shift at the restaurant. She's said to me more than a few times over the years that when John and I both pulled up in our Cadillacs, we made quite the impression.

Lindsey and Stevie made quite the impression themselves. They were a beautifully handsome couple. Lindsey was gorgeous, like Marc Bolan, with his hair and piercing eyes, and Stevie was stunning. Knowing what those two could do musically, they were like two living sculptures that you couldn't take your eyes off. They were utterly captivating, the perfect bohemian couple. We got no vibration that there were any problems between them, as we know now that there were. The thing that's funny about that meeting is that we weren't really auditioning them, they – Lindsey especially – were auditioning us.

I've thought about this moment many times over the years and the same feeling remains; once we sat down together at that table, I knew something was there, something was right. I knew I'd made the right choice, and because of that I could not stop smiling. Maybe it was years of experience being in a band, being a bandleader by default, and finding a way to play on when it seemed like there was no point. Maybe I'd developed an instinct for finding like-minded compatriots, or maybe the buzz of potential was so tangible at that table that it washed over me and left me grinning. That good-looking couple with all that talent, it would be amazing to have them in the band. The thing is, they are still that couple when they walk out on the stage every night we play – and no matter what they say, I believe it still beguiles them. They've tried extremely hard to be devoid of a connection to each other and they can't do it.

I knew I wanted Lindsey and Stevie in Fleetwood Mac, but the decision wasn't all mine. It would be a tremendous change to have two women in the band, so John and I agreed before-hand that ultimately Chris would decide. We knew that Stevie wrote and sang, and since she didn't play anything, she would become a figure out front, leading the band. We wanted to make sure Chris was fine with that.

'I don't care about sharing the spotlight,' Chris told us before the meeting. 'She can have it. The two of them can. But if there's going to be another woman, I just have to be sure we get along.'

That is why I kept smiling; every time I looked across the

table, I could tell that Chris and Stevie had hit it off straight
away. Over the course of our meal, and a few pitchers of marga-
ritas, I decided that this was it and once it came time for dessert,
I saw no reason to hold back.

'So, Lindsey, Stevie, can I ask you something?' I said. Everyone
else stopped talking and looked at me. I shot looks at John
and Chris to make sure I wasn't out of line, and I wasn't.

'So, would you like to join our band?'

They turned to each other for a moment, beamed, then said,
'Yes.'

Life changing moments can be that simple.

Even though we were ready to have them both, Stevie has
said that Lindsey was the one who took convincing. He wanted
to keep pushing on and doing it themselves. They'd got a taste
of making it in one market, and he wasn't so sure he wanted
to give up on their dream just yet.

'Lindsey, we can still be us,' she told him. 'Let's do our thing,
do what we are, but in their band. We don't have to build an
audience. They have one. This is a stage for us, a stage that
already has a name.'

'Well, yeah,' he said. 'But I just don't know.'

'Lindsey, let's do this. We have nothing to lose,' she said.
'And, hey, if it doesn't work out, we can always leave.'

This was just four weeks after Bob's departure and we were
back in business. I couldn't believe our luck. We hired Stevie
and Lindsey as salaried members of Fleetwood Mac, paying
them $200 a week. In the next month, Chris returned home to
see her family for a bit while John, Lindsey and I began
rehearsing in a garage we rented in Santa Monica on Pico
Boulevard. It was an appropriate start, jamming in a garage,
the way a new band should. Once Chris returned we had learned
each other's moves and had a solid musical foundation for her

to expand upon. We moved our rehearsals to the basement of the ICM building, where our agent at the time, Tom Ross, took it upon himself to subsidise us and oversee our development from the very start.

The first song Chris played with Lindsey and Stevie was 'Say You Love Me' and it was so natural and so powerful when they harmonised with her on the chorus that I could barely keep playing. The three of them became one voice and I could see that Chris felt it too. Bob had backed her up, but this was something else altogether.

It was going to work and we all knew it. Lindsey had never been backed by a rhythm section as interwoven and nuanced as John and me, and his playing positively took off. I knew immediately that we'd never need another guitarist; Lindsey could do it all – leads, rhythm, moving effortlessly between the two, and all while singing, no less. I'm not sure anyone realises just how gifted he is. When you added Stevie to the mix, my God, the combination was positively intoxicating. She was charming, witty, and her gorgeous voice literally blossomed before us in those early days as we figured it all out. Stevie was otherworldly, in possession of a vibrato as haunting as Edith Piaf, filtered through the lens of a cowgirl beatnik poet.

Lindsey and Stevie, for all intents and purposes, were already a band. They didn't join Fleetwood Mac, our two bands became one. They brought their identity into our midst, intact; they were the little machine that got swallowed by the big machine. I recognised Stevie right away as a writer and she reminded me of my dad, because she was writing in her journals all the time. Stevie wanted to bring mysticism into the band, which I supported completely because I do believe that there are many aspects to our existence greater than we are. It was an unspoken thing between us, because we understood each other right away, recognising a fellow drama queen. That said, I think Stevie is often branded as being more heavy hearted than she really is. She is the poet with an interest in the mythological and mystical, but that's a backdrop to her personality. She was, for a long time, thought of as being reclusive and mysterious, but that's only because I don't think she liked doing interviews, so people never saw a snapshot of the real girl. The truth is that she's incredibly normal and grounded and a really humorous person, one just as silly as I am. Without that sense of humour, I doubt that she would have survived all of the trials and tribulations in her life.

Before meeting us, Lindsey knew of Fleetwood Mac because of Peter Green. Lindsey's favourite album of ours was *Then Play On* and he knew it really well. I find it a wonderful coincidence that Lindsey's favourite record of Peter's was the one most like *Tusk*, in the sense that Peter had to do that record his way, to be able to stay in the band. As they say, great minds.

Stevie was a fan of ours as well, but I think she was more familiar with our most recent material. Once she'd joined, Stevie made a point of listening to all of our previous records, to better grasp the depth and width of the legacy she was willingly becoming a part of. After she'd studied everything we'd done with Peter and Jeremy, and all the versions, she told me that the common thread was a sense of the mystic. There was something that we were channelling that was greater than the players. That remains the greatest compliment I feel we've ever been paid.

CHAPTER 10

THE 'WHITE' ALBUM

Out at their beach-side apartment in Malibu, Christine started writing songs for what would become our album. She had an old, worn-in Hohner electric piano set up so that she'd get a view of the Pacific Ocean out the window. That's where she wrote 'Say You Love Me' and 'Over My Head', as well as 'Warm Ways' and 'Sugar Daddy'.

In one day, I heard Chris's demos as well as Stevie and Lindsey's, basically the bones of our debut album. I was completely floored. 'I'm So Afraid' was a track that Lindsey had been labouring over for four years; he'd got the harmony of the guitar parts so in tune they were a virtual orchestra unto themselves. 'Monday Morning', 'Landslide' and 'Rhiannon' were show stoppers, even as rough sketches recorded on Lindsey's four-track.

We worked on all of those songs as a group for a few weeks until they became fully realised. Each day the energy built and the excitement grew because it was like being in a boot camp where everyone was so focused that results happened very quickly. Lindsey and Christine were two musicians who fell in with each other immediately; it was a departure for him, because he'd been used to working only with a poet. Whereas a lot of what Lindsey did for Stevie was interpretation, building musical soundscapes for the stories she told so beautifully in her lyrics, Chris's songwriting came from the blues and got right to the point. Lindsey took that and ran. It was the yin to the yang – and that doesn't count his own songs. Watching him work his way through all of it was inspiring; I hadn't felt that way since Peter Green had been at the helm, and I know John felt the same. It was wonderfully overwhelming; watching Stevie dance around the studio as she worked out her vocal parts, one thought kept pounding through my head: there wasn't an audience alive that wouldn't respond to her when we hit the road.

I'd dedicated myself to carrying the band across the finish line, but it now gave me a fanatical zeal. In just two months, by February 1975, we'd all agreed that we were ready to record. We moved into Sound City and signed Keith Olsen on as our producer. We recorded all of our demos, plus two new songs we decided to do once we'd got going. The first was a cover, 'Blue Letter', by the 1960s country-rockers the Curtis Brothers. The idea came to us literally on the spot; the Curtis Brothers were recording demos at Sound City and when we heard them play the song we decided to give it a go. The other last-minute add was a cover as well, 'World Turning', our reinterpretation of Peter Green's original.

As much as we were excited to work together, there were growing pains. Lindsey had a long list of ideas as to how things should be done and how they should sound. He can play any instrument I've ever seen put in front of him, so it was natural for him to sit at my drum kit and suggest rhythms, which was fine by me. But as I think I've made clear by now, I don't exactly play the way one 'should' play drums; in the same way John doesn't approach bass in a technically perfect style. We do it our way and those ways happen to blend seamlessly.

I still like it when Lindsey suggests drum fills to me, because we think the same about music but feel it differently. Usually I get something from his idea, even if it's just a concept of what I don't want to do. From me he gets a sense of 'vibe', for lack of a better word, that doesn't always click for him right away. In any case, John did not take so kindly to our new bandmate's ideas when it came to his instrument. Very early on in our honeymoon period, he put Lindsey in his place.

'Hang on a sec,' he said, interrupting Lindsey who'd picked up a bass guitar and started playing a rhythm line. 'You realise who you're talking to, right?'

'Well, yeah,' Lindsey said, smiling, a bit unsure.

'I'm McVie,' John said. 'The band you're in is Fleetwood Mac. I'm the Mac. And I play the bass.' And that, once and for all, was the end of that.

Lindsey had been the man in charge in Fritz and in his duo with Stevie, but this was new territory for him. Fleetwood Mac was a unit and though we made creative decisions by consensus, there was a history that he had to respect. He always did so, even when it meant stepping outside of the band to do what he needed to do.

That album was the first time, but far from the last, that we relied on cocaine to fuel the long hours of work. That drug hadn't been in our world much before then, but we soon became quite conversant with it. Let's just say that Sound City wasn't just made of bricks and mortar, there seemed to be white powder peeling off the walls in every room. It was readily available within the boundaries of that establishment. It was part of the culture of that studio and that's how we got into it. We all partook; Keith Olsen and the whole crew that worked there, all of us. We found that a quick blast of rocket fuel gave us the energy to keep at it until we got everything just right. There wasn't going to be a short way round this, considering how many perfectionists we now had in the group.

I never really knew much about cocaine before then. I'd had some and I hadn't really liked it very much. I thought it was like heroin. In fact, I think my first 'cocaine' experience, which was during the Peter Green era of Fleetwood Mac when we played with King Crimson at the Fillmore East, was heroin. Someone was cutting it up for the bands backstage and now that I know exactly what cocaine does, I can safely say that my first time had to have been heroin. All I felt was sick to my stomach, so from then on I refused to do any cocaine when it was offered, because I'd decided I just didn't like it. I guess I'd been a prude – a drunk, but a prude – all my young adult life. In any case, when we started up at Sound City, I'd never bought it before in my life, but oh, how quickly that changed!

I refuse to be romantic in my perspective of drug abuse, but back then, when it was new, it wasn't a problem. It was all about going forth together; it was all new and undiscovered territory. It was a part of the culture of the day. At the time, everyone in LA, at every level of entertainment was doing it. This was the first wave of the tsunami of white powder that rolled in and drowned everyone in that city in the 1970s and 1980s. Whether you did it or not was your choice, but I can say with relative certainty that if you came through the door to record at Sound City at the time, you were going to be offered some as if it were simply another of the available services at your disposal. There was an engineer who would test it for purity with his set of oils. It wasn't like smoking a joint, it was like a chemistry lesson, and I thought it was kind of cool. I got into the ritual of it; I'd do some and we'd all end up talking and bouncing ideas off of each other. It was really good for someone like me who had a lot to say, but sometimes didn't really talk when he probably should have done. On that level cocaine certainly got me talking and I don't think I've ever stopped talking since.

It allowed me to stay up late and be free with my ideas, and we got a lot of productive stuff done that way. Certainly not all of the time, but in the beginning, it was more often than not. Our first album together, the 'white' album, was the signpost at the start of an era from which so many stories of our debauchery have been exaggerated. I'm not here to confirm or deny. It's all so tired at this point. That said, I will share this memory, just to give you an idea.

In a somewhat nostalgic fashion, I remember wanting to keep track of all the bottles we'd consumed while recording, so I sequestered an area of the live room and ordered everyone to deposit their bottles there when they were through with them. I planned it to be a tribute and I called it 'the graveyard beside the battleground', the battleground being the area where we rehearsed and recorded. I had plans to take a photo of the graveyard when we were done with the album, to include on the record sleeve. All manner of dead bottles were buried there; wine, whisky, beer, brandy, cognac – I believe every spirit known to man was represented. Before we were anywhere close to completing the album, the graveyard had nearly taken over the battlefield and had to be scrapped. It became intimidating and it shamed us, and after we agreed that it must be emptied out, I did not begin that experiment anew.

The album *Fleetwood Mac* was completed in June 1975 and I knew it was something special. It felt so good and so right, and I know everyone in the band felt the same. Music is a process of chasing the intangible, something that can't truly be verbalised, because it abides in the realm of feeling. When you are with the right players, connecting those dots, and you create something you all really believe in, as a musician, there's nothing more powerful.

I believed in it so much that I set up a meeting with Mo Ostin, the president of Warner Brothers, to tell him so. I was excited, we were all excited, and to me that meant other people would be too. Mo had become a friend, someone whose taste and experience in music I respected, and still respect, immensely.

'There's some great stuff here, Mick,' he said after listening. He wasn't discouraging, but he didn't share my degree of enthusiasm by a long shot.

To be fair to Mo and to the staff at Warners, they didn't know what to do with us. Here he had this gangly Englishman who was both a band member and manager of a band that did all right, but were somewhat of a pain in the ass. We had frontmen coming and going, line-up changes, tour cancellations. We were an outfit that could be counted on consistently to move between 250,000 and 300,000 records whenever we put out an album, but that was about it. We never did better, we never did worse. Essentially, what we earned covered the expense of keeping us on the label and little more. I used to like telling Mo, and the other staff that worked with us, that we paid for the lights and hot water in their office. They knew we were good for at least that, so they kept us on year after year.

My fervour did make some kind of impression however, because I managed to convince them to add an additional 50,000 copies to the album's initial print run, though they refused to give us further money for tour support and promotion.

For one thing, the band had never played live to an audience, which is something everyone was worried about. Our fan base didn't know Stevie and Lindsey so it was going to be a huge introduction. The first time we did it was going to be a sink or swim situation. I decided to take that bull by the horns, and in the midst of making the album, booked us a series of dates.

It wasn't strictly an artistic decision: the band as a whole needed money and I figured that no matter what I thought of us, there was only one way to find out whether or not this was going to work. I threw us out of the frying pan and into the fire, taking us on the road before we had even officially announced our new line up. It was boot camp for Lindsey and Stevie who had to front the band, playing our new songs, some of their songs, which our audience didn't know, as well as Bob's songs and Peter's songs. Perhaps it was cruel, I don't know. My only regret is that I don't have a quality recording of any of those shows, which to say the least were unique.

Our first show took place in El Paso, Texas on 15 May 1975, kicking off a bare-bones two-month tour of Texas, then the Midwest and Northeast. We opened that first show with 'Station Man' and a few more songs from *Kiln House* that came off all the better through the harmonic vocal filter of Stevie, Lindsey and Christine. When Lindsey played Peter Green's beloved 'Oh Well', the crowd cheered. We did 'Rhiannon', 'Crystal' and 'Blue Letter', all from our forthcoming album, and the crowd was with us.

That night I saw the seed of what 'Rhiannon' would come to mean, very soon, to so many people. Stevie's star ascended with each passing day, in her tight jeans and flowing tops she was our sensuous gypsy and when she did 'Rhiannon' she transformed, taking the song and the crowd with her out into the ether, somewhere far beyond what we had laid down in the studio. It changed every time she did it and it was beautiful to watch. On that tour, I made 'World Turning' into a drum solo, which felt right, because it was a link from past to present, and in that spirit, I came out from behind my kit and played the African talking drum that Peter Green had given me in London years before. It felt like I had him there with me, a part of things, for that moment in the set.

It's always hard to tell, as a musician, which shows are your best and worst, because musicians pay attention to different details than audience members. There have been so many times that I've come off stage knowing that the band made too many mistakes to count, only to hear that we'd just played the best show of our lives according to long-time friends and followers. This show was the first of the tour, which is almost always touch-and-go and with a new band, even more so. Having said that, even after all these years, I have to admit that first show was damn good.

After the first short tour, we went back to the studio and finished the record. We'd had such a great time and felt everything fall into place so naturally that we booked another much longer tour as soon as we were done recording. We didn't care that the album was a few months away from being released, we wanted to get out there and introduce the new line-up to the public ourselves.

On that tour we generally played three-thousand-seat arenas opening for acts such as Loggins and Messina, Ten Years After and the Guess Who. We took in about $3,000 a gig and if we didn't sell out a venue, which happened a lot because people didn't know who we were, and we were essentially a band playing mostly covers, I'd give the promoters some of the money back. That wasn't expected for the day, but I had a plan; I wanted them to remember my good favour and book us again. I wanted to engender loyalty in a business that has precious little of it.

Touring has always been my natural habitat and most comfortable form of existence, as unnatural as it is to the average person. Among all of the bandmates I've ever had, I think I'm alone in feeling that way. Touring has always served to stress the fissures in Fleetwood Mac and this tour was no different. It was a tremendous success, but it brought the worst out in John and Chris's marriage.

They had worked, played and lived together since the start. They were never apart and the years of stress caused by the tumult of the band had done irreparable damage. At some point on that tour, they'd get at each other so fiercely that Chris stopped being able to stay in the same room with John. Neither of them was going to let their personal issues derail the tour, so they kept it to themselves, but as a couple they needed space and on tour there was little to be found.

The thing is, Chris and John were always, and still are, *really* good friends. There's a deep bond of respect there based upon whence they came, so even at their worst they honoured that as best they could. It was tough to watch because they were the perfect couple and perfect for each other.

I tried to talk to him about it but that didn't go well because John has always been the elder statesman in our relationship. And he still is. He's the one to take me aside and ask, 'What the hell are you doing?', not the other way round. The sad part is that there was no one to do that for him, including me. I'd try and be driven to tears, begging him to stop hurting her feelings and driving her away. But that never got through, he'd become defensive and dismissive and that would be the end of that. Often it was the drink talking, though at the time he refused to see it.

Once he realised the damage, it was too late, so my job as John's friend at that point was to help him understand that his marriage was over, and that the best thing he could do to honour their relationship was to put it right between him and Chris and move on. He eventually did, and married his wife Jules and had a beautiful daughter, and has been the most incredible father. But none of that came before much soul-searching. Nonetheless, John was able to handle working with his ex-partner with much dignity but not without much pain.

He was the kind of man who would normally have refused to do so, but he respected Chris that much and he respected our band that much. He was willing to suffer for it and let me tell you, it was hard for him. I respect him immensely for it, because he faced up to it, whereas I would have found some way to weasel through without confronting how I felt. John is a very strong individual, which works both ways. He never asked to go home, but that same strength might have been what made him deaf to hear the advice that he needed to hear.

With all of this drama beginning to gestate, our tour continued to do increasingly well. I was worried that the splintering of the McVies would derail the whole thing, which would have been a shame because the new band was so exciting. Still, we had one problem; we lacked a hit single. I saw so many possibilities on our forthcoming new album but our record company did not agree. I wanted to get something out in advance of the full record, so that our tour sales would be invigorated, allowing us to rise above the opening act slot. We had support from our label but I wanted more of an impact so I hired an independent PR man named Paul Ahearn to get us radio play. Paul was a friend and roommate of Glenn Frey of the Eagles whom I'd met when he was our neighbour in Laurel Canyon. Paul loved the songs, but thought they weren't mixed properly. He said that they needed to be reworked so that they'd sound good on the radio. There is an art to compressing music, to highlighting the elements that appeal to the listener in such a format, and we had not given any of our songs that treatment.

Paul connected us with a guy named Deke Richards, who had produced many of Michael Jackson and the Jackson 5's early hits. He remixed 'Over My Head', priming it for FM radio consumption. His version was weighted toward the high-end and featured a new guitar introduction and different takes of the vocal harmonies. The result wasn't true to the song as written or played, but I was the first to admit that it sounded fucking *hot* when you listened to it on the average system, like a car stereo. We released the single in September of that year and it was an instant hit: within a month and a half we'd sold 400,000 records.

We spent the remainder of 1975 on a tour of colleges, touring as we always had, in two station wagons with our gear in a trailer behind one of them. We drove ourselves and did nearly one hundred gigs between September and the end of the year. I couldn't have been happier, motion is my stasis, and my comfort is what others consider chaos. It didn't hurt to be back on top, and somehow, although Chris and John were very much on the outs, everything went off well and we sounded better with each passing show.

Offstage, we were all becoming family. I adored getting to know Lindsey. I knew he was a perfectionist, but only once we were on tour did I realise just how possessed he was with the music. It was all he thought about: how to do things better, how he could make his role more perfect. He was more at home working out his ideas on tape loops than he was jamming out ideas with a band live in the studio, which was entirely new to me. I respected how much he'd changed his method to work with us, to pursue this shared dream. Honestly, he was so intense in his work ethic and vision, that it was often a struggle to get him out of his room just to have a bit of fun and blow off some steam. He was so committed to what we were doing, though, that I derived much strength from him, as I have done so many times in the years following.

As the tour wound on, I noticed how this trait played out in his relationship with Stevie. He had always been in control musically of her and of their career, but that was no longer the case. Stevie had blossomed into something new, something that Lindsey couldn't control. When we first met them they spoke as a unit and when they spoke about their musical ideas he spoke for them. After a while she spoke for herself. It was a change that I don't think Lindsey really liked. She'd come out of her shell because she now had a multi-faceted set of musical partners and he hadn't counted on that.

Stevie was free to be herself. She spent much of her time wrapped in a shawl, with a cup of tea to mend her chronically sore throat, writing and drawing in her journals. She was, and is, sweet, funny, and witty; she was a soulmate to me immediately. We are both romantic, dramatic souls who have no problem being silly at the drop of a hat. In Fleetwood Mac she found other people to hang out with and make music with and she'd never had that outside of Lindsey. Things had changed for them and it went both ways.

We were now a very different band, led by two women and a man, when we'd always been led by men in what was a very male-dominated 1970s music scene. Stevie, for one, had a hard time with some of the negative reviews she got. *Rolling Stone* magazine was quite unkind, calling her singing 'callow' and saying that if it weren't for Christine we'd be a lost cause. Stevie is very sensitive, a true artist through and through, and those words hurt her deeply. She began to doubt everything about the band, about what we thought of her, about why she was there. What has become a bit of fun onstage banter to us all these years later, about how we only added her to the line-up to get Lindsey, was a very real concern to her back then.

It bears saying again that yes, we needed a guitar player and wanted Lindsey, but we loved everything she did from the start and the audiences loved her even more. They could not take their eyes off Stevie. She became, and has never ceased to be, the focal point of Fleetwood Mac. She was ascending and she had a hard time accepting it at first.

Our tour schedule consisted of four days playing, one day off, which is very demanding, no matter how young and resilient you are. It wore Stevie down to the bone, because she is someone who needs peace and tranquillity and to rest her instrument. Back then we didn't have any degree of luxury in our touring machine; we had station wagons, our crew was in a Winnebago, and the concept of catering was a pipe dream. We didn't eat well, we drank too much, smoked and snorted as well, and it wore the girl down physically. But she wouldn't give in and she didn't give up. I remember telling her that she had to look after her health and that we'd do whatever we could to make sure she ate better and got the sleep she needed.

'Stevie, I hope you understand something very important,' I said.

'What's that?'

'We *need* you. You are a part of this band now. We can't be Fleetwood Mac without you.'

'Well, no one told me it was going to be like this,' she said. 'I didn't picture Chris and I sleeping on top of amps in the back of trucks. I really didn't. But I'm going to make it through. I'm not quitting. I'm not going to let anyone ever say, "Oh, she couldn't cut it. She couldn't cope. She gave up." That's not going to happen.'

My dear friend, that is the last thing anyone, anywhere, of any age, would ever dare say about you, Stevie Nicks.

CHAPTER 11

THINGS FALL APART

It took a year for it to happen but *Fleetwood Mac* hit number 1 in America on the back of three Top 20 singles: 'Rhiannon', 'Over My Head' and 'Say You Love Me'. We didn't expect anything to happen with the album back home in England because it had been so long since anything we'd done resonated there, but we did get an echo when 'Say You Love Me' broke the Top 40. We'd have our day again in the UK, but it wouldn't be until after *Rumours* took over the world in 1977. That was how much we'd fallen off their radar; they released *Fleetwood Mac* in England in retrospect, in 1978, at which point it charted in the UK at number 23.

The momentum achieved by the album doing so well, at that time and in that place, was tremendous. In a short amount of time our circle of friends, well-wishers and fellow musicians grew exponentially. We met some wonderfully bright souls, like the aforementioned Herbie Worthington, who became a good friend to my family and to Stevie. Everyone we came in contact with was so amiable, as if they'd known us for years. At times this wreaked havoc on Jenny's typical English reserve and her need to keep our family unit close together. Many of these new friends were fascinated by me and spoke constantly to her of my eccentricities and quirky ways. This was a strange land to us, not only that, but we were fast becoming part of a huge organisation that was taking over our lives.

I loved living in Laurel Canyon at first, but with all of the activity surrounding the band, I craved a bit more space, peace and quiet. The privacy of Benifold was still in my blood, and I longed for more of a retreat. I found a larger place for us up in the hills of Topanga, about an hour west from Hollywood. It was gorgeous and still very rural and hippie out there and I loved it. The house was situated down in a gully with a steep path that led up to Topanga Canyon Boulevard. Across the road was the old Topanga market, with bare-foot women walking along with their naked children, bikers everywhere and stray dogs. It was like being back in the sixties in San Francisco – bells and beads, and long-haired guys with cowboy hats. The house came with a large dog, named Zappa, that the previous owners had left behind. She became a faithful companion to our little girls for years.

Jenny has told me that once Fleetwood Mac were back on the road, her schizophrenic type of existence began again. Evenings spent at home, quiet and gentle with our children, chamomile tea, classical music, reading, writing poetry and early to bed. When we returned from the road there was a party almost every night, either at the studio, at a restaurant, or someone's house. On these occasions she'd drink and take cocaine to mask her shyness, but once she got over her reticence, she enjoyed the social atmosphere.

When we lived in England, although I hadn't been aware of it at that time, Jenny always had an underlying fear of me becoming famous and wealthy. She believed that if ever that should happen, it would tear us apart. This belief that things would change was heightened when we visited a numerologist together during this period. The woman predicted that the next Fleetwood Mac album would be very big and that I would become a millionaire. That did not sit well with Jenny at all.

Jenny never cared about the money and fame – that wasn't the issue – she cared about how much the public demand for the band would take me away from our family, which was a very valid concern. I was more than just the drummer; I was the ringleader and the manager of the circus. I was consumed with the band and its success and there was little space for anything else. Jenny looked to me for her support and nourishment, while I looked to the band for mine, and we didn't spend enough time looking at each other. It's often the way it goes when one person is distant emotionally or unavailable, that distance feeds the obsessive need of the other to crave what isn't being given them. She yearned for connection with me, while I was better at loving from afar, making sure she and the girls were safe and protected. To me that was the perfect expression of my love, but to Jenny it was incomplete. She needed more.

What she considered my aloofness, she later told me, stabbed at her heart and made her feel I didn't care, and yet she would hold this turmoil inside, while maintaining a cool exterior. Her façade eventually cracked, however, a few days before we were due to go out on the road. We were at our house, enjoying a pre-tour afternoon barbecue for the band and road crew, everyone in good spirits, or so I thought. I was standing next to Jenny in our galley kitchen and was vaguely aware of one of the road crew goading her drunkenly about the affair in England. She'd been drinking and indulging in substances, as we all had, but I was shocked when she wheeled round and started pounding my chest with her fists. She was hysterical, as years of frustration and unspoken feelings of anger, guilt and loneliness took hold of her and issued forth.

I didn't know what to do. Chris put her arm round Jenny, led her outside and tried to calm her down. I carried on with the party, chatting with everyone and hanging out. I was going on tour regardless, so I marked the incident down to her being upset by my leaving.

I found out later, after speaking at length with Jenny the following day, that it was much more serious than that. She'd frightened herself with her outburst, and was fearful of it happening again. She wanted a separation.

'You have a roof over your head, Jenny,' I said. 'What more do you want?'

'A cardboard box would be fine,' she told me, 'if we could be in it together.'

I went on tour as planned and things began to deteriorate between us. When I returned the distance grew ever wider. Jenny could not get the reaction she wanted from me, so eventually she took action and informed me that she was taking the girls and dog and moving into an apartment in town. I was completely heartbroken. This was at the pinnacle of the success of our first album and I was overwhelmed by everything I had to do to keep that ship on course. At the time I felt as though I was giving Jenny and the girls all the attention I possibly could. But I see now that it just wasn't enough and there was no way I could split myself in two. Instead I soldiered on and kept up an air of indifference, when in truth I was paralysed. I gave Jenny money to live on, made sure that their apartment was safe, and that was all I could think to do.

It's been documented to death, so I'll say it briefly, but the making of *Rumours* almost killed us. Physically? Not really. The myths of excess you've all heard are true, and the truth is that we'd all be dead already if we weren't made of stronger stuff. What nearly did us in was the way we handled our emotions as our personal relationships came apart. But we refused to let our feelings derail our commitment to the music, no matter how complicated or intertwined they became. It was hard to do, but no matter what, we played on through the hurt.

By the time we set about writing for *Rumours*, we had all fallen to pieces; after seven years John and Christine called it quits, Lindsey and Stevie's four-year relationship was over, and my marriage to Jenny on its way to divorce. With my family gone from our rental house in Topanga, I found no reason to stay there. I was hurting and wanted a change of scenery, so I granted myself my first rock-star indulgence and bought a house of my own in Topanga, complete with a stunning view of the Santa Monica Mountains on one side and the ocean on the other. I hired a decorator to complete the finishing touches. I would have liked it better if my family was with me, but it had to do.

John and Christine's relationship started to unravel while we were on the road, but it officially fell to bits during a brief break from touring while we were in Florida. The band had rented a house in order to work on the new songs and we had our road crew and our tour manager, John Courage, with us. 'Go Your Own Way' and a few others were written there, but it was hardly a vacation. Aside from the obvious unstated tension, I remember the house having a distinctly bad vibe to it, as if it were haunted, which did nothing to help matters. It was very strange. Some of us were sleeping in the house, and the road crew were there, and that's where Lindsey played some of his stuff for the album. It was rough but it was great, though the setting didn't do it justice. We didn't hear it again until we got to Sausalito.

For some time, John had correctly suspected that Christine was having a fling with our lighting director Curry Grant. The crew knew about it, and didn't approve, so they'd been making life hard for Curry at every turn. John Courage and I agreed that the situation had to be mediated in some way, because it was becoming an issue at every level. We confronted Chris about it, friend to friend, and she told us the truth. She understood that we had to fire Curry, which we did, even though we didn't want to because he did a great job. Getting rid of him didn't make things any better, however. Once it was out in the open and beyond a shadow of a doubt, John was even more upset, because it was clear to him that Chris didn't want Curry to go.

John and I became more inseparable than ever back then, because the two of us were men in pain. After that unpleasant holiday in Florida, we always drove together, spending long hours talking about our lives as the never-ending American highways drifted past the window. At the end of those tour dates, Chris moved out of their house in Malibu and John took up with another girl for a while, but that didn't amount to anything. After that he bought a boat, which had long been an interest of his, and lived on it for a year in Marina Del Rey.

The pressure of being in a band and a relationship tore Lindsey and Stevie apart as well. The fissure had been there before they joined Fleetwood Mac, because it was hard for them to be both lovers and collaborators. For the first time Stevie had other musicians, one of them a girl, to bounce her ideas off. She no longer had to rely solely on Lindsey to help her develop her musical ideas. The same went for Lindsey who now had John, me, and most of all, Christine to work with.

Amidst all of this, Stevie became a star in her own right; a band within our band, which she deserved, but it did nothing to ease the stress between her and Lindsey. The days of their dual identity were done. That came with a downside for her too, because as much as she liked having her own corner of the band and being appreciated for the artist she is, it was isolating for her. She is the only one in the band who doesn't play an instrument, so by default, Stevie was left out of much of the creative conversation. What's more, she'd lost her musical partner to that conversation. She'd always relied on Lindsey to make her ideas take flight, and though he still did, he now had other interests. The two of them were not only apart romantically, he was also a part of a new whole that didn't include her.

Since my personal drama wasn't unfolding at the office, so to speak, I felt it my duty to be even more of a bandleader than ever before. I needed to look after everyone's emotions, to check in with them all and let them air their feelings; I did my best to be Big Daddy. The music was my only escape and I cherished it. It wasn't the same for the others; the music that brought us together every night was, for them, a reminder of how far apart they were offstage. This would, of course, be even more painful for everyone but me once the lyrics to the songs that became our next album were written. But the only way out was to go through it. There was never a discussion of breaking up the band or going on hiatus. We all needed each other. In the case of John, Christine and me, we had been through so much together that we knew we'd be able to suck it up and continue to be a band. For Lindsey and Stevie, they'd finally got their music heard and they didn't want to let that chance go. They could do their music in their own way without the wolves banging at the door, and every musician dreams of a situation like that.

In January 1976, as 'Rhiannon' began to climb the charts and our debut album reached sales of a million copies, I knew there was only one way for this to work. We had to get out of LA and live together, the way we had at Kiln House after Peter left, because once again we were in a critical condition.

I'd heard great things about the Record Plant in Sausalito, across the bay from San Francisco. It came with a house overlooking the water that we could live in while recording. Without a second thought I booked it for two months and in February we made the move up there with various friends in tow to begin recording our second album. That was the last normal, rational decision that was made in regards to creating *Rumours*, because almost immediately things got messy. John, Lindsey and I lived in the house that came with the studio, while Stevie and Christine lived nearby in a rented apartment overlooking the harbour. The studio was a great place to record, but truthfully it was very odd. It had opened in 1973 and was designed to fulfil the expectations of a music industry at the height of excess. It came complete with two custom limos to transport recording musicians wherever they might want to go, a speedboat for their use, and a conference room with a waterbed floor. There were tanks of industrial-grade nitrous oxide on hand and there was 'The Pit', which had been designed by Sly Stone, who recorded the album *Fresh* there.

The Pit was a studio featuring just that, a pit, sunk ten feet into the ground where the engineer's control board was placed, with the idea that the musicians would be above, around the outside of the pit, allowing the engineer to experience the sound in 360 degrees. Everything, the walls, ceiling, floors and stairs of the pit were covered in garish maroon shag carpet which deadened it sonically but made it awful and claustrophobic to stay in for long periods of time. There was also a loft, accessible through a large pair of red lips, with a bed in it and audio jacks next to the bed so that a vocalist could, quite literally, record their parts while lying between the sheets.

The pit itself had a great sound to it, better than the rest of the room, and from what I was told Sly Stone preferred to record there, defeating the purpose of it altogether. While recording *Fresh* he had his organ hoisted down there and apparently even crowded his entire horn section into there to capture their performance. We never made use of the Pit to record, though it did become a hideaway for some of us, myself included, when we needed a few minutes alone. When all seemed to be lost, I'd go down there and pray for the strength to continue. Sometimes I had to find another quiet spot, because as I discovered, the Pit was the type of spot non-working visitors used for holing up with powder and mirror.

We'd recorded our first album in three months and before we started I knew this one wasn't going to come that easy. I did not think for a moment that it would take nearly a year and multiple studios. I suppose it's a miracle that it didn't take longer, considering the state we were in. When we were at the studio, everyone behaved professionally and civilly, if a bit chilly. But again, how could they not be when our songwriters were writing songs about their ex-partners, who were there playing on those very songs, listening to them over and again until we got it all just right? Any outbursts that did occur usually happened after hours or on a break, or when we'd decided to party more than record, all of which derailed things for the day at one point or another.

We'd brought in our own engineer Richard Dashut and his friend Ken Caillat, because we didn't see eye to eye with the Record Plant's engineer and we wanted to have control of the production, as we had with the last album. I've always felt that a band with a real identity should do the production themselves to keep their vision pure. So with Richard and Ken at the board, we dived right in.

Our songwriters had some great material, but we needed to get our musical arrangements worked out. We spent long twenty-hour days over five weeks, most of them full of terse words, members storming out only to return shortly thereafter. As heated as tempers ever got, we all knew that the music was the only solution and would be our salvation.

With John and Chris barely speaking and Stevie and Lindsey completely at odds, we struggled to get any kind of musical foundation laid. Stevie had broken up with Lindsey and he'd taken it very, very hard. I could see him suffering, struggling under this great weight. When he simply could pine no more, he started dating to get his mind off Stevie. That upset Stevie terribly, of course, because she still had deep feelings for him and was very confused about her decision to end it. These undercurrents of tension caused endless thinly-veiled arguments to erupt at a moment's notice.

Things weren't much better with Jenny. Shortly after she moved into the apartment, she discovered that her shoulder blade was protruding a few inches from her back. She was admitted to the neurological ward at UCLA for ten days to undergo tests. They looked for tumours, found nothing, and concluded that the shoulder had undergone some kind of trauma and would eventually right itself. That had occurred during the tour that preceded our move to Sausalito, so for those ten days I had the girls on the road with me and my parents there to care for them. Such was my preoccupation at the time, I had no idea what Jenny had gone through in the hospital and passed it off as a bit of hysterical hypochondria. She's told me that during her hospital stay she felt abandoned, forgotten and at an all-time low physically, mentally and spiritually. She'd heard nothing from me and she missed the girls, as she endured one test after another, with her marriage in tatters.

Towards the end of her stay in hospital, Jenny was allowed out for the day to spend some time with Sandra. They had remained very close and to a major extent, Sandra was a lifeline for Jenny in LA. They used to take the girls to Disneyland and Universal Studios and Sandra, more than anyone else, understood what Jenny was going through with me.

Sandra had just returned from Sausalito, and had done John a favour by driving his car back down to Los Angeles. Cruising through Hollywood, with Bob Welch's girlfriend Nancy beside her and Jenny in the back, Jenny asked Sandra how things were going at the Record Plant.

'It's crazy,' Sandra said. 'Every room I walked into, every time I'd try to find somewhere to lie down, I'd come across Stevie sobbing or one of the others deep in a serious conversation. There was always some kind of drama going on.'

'Did you see the children?' Jenny asked.

'No,' Sandra said, 'Biddy and Mike took them back to Topanga after the tour.'

'How's Mick?'

'He was trying to be the big daddy, of course,' Sandra said. 'He would go from room to room, mediating with everyone and everything that came up. He had his hands full. But the music sounds amazing.' Jenny told me that her eyes positively lit up when she said that.

'There's one thing, though,' Sandra said, looking round at Jenny. 'Mick's been seeing someone else. She's been on the road with him and she was at the studio. I just thought you should know.'

'What's her name?' Jenny asked.

'Ginny.'

Jenny tells me that almost at the very moment Sandra told her, they were hit by another car as they crossed an intersection.

The sound of glass smashing, metal crunching and Sandra wailing about John's car all happened at once. Jenny hit her head against the window and cut her knee badly and was whisked back to hospital in an ambulance. So much for her day off. The two of them were X-rayed, but they weren't injured other than the stitches Jenny needed for her knee.

I remember hearing about all of this and thinking that Jenny was literally falling apart. It made me resolute in my decision that Jenny and I should be divorced. I worried for her and I worried for our daughters; knowing what lay ahead for the band, I would be around even less and it didn't seem to me like she could properly look after the girls.

During one of our breaks in recording I paid Jenny a visit at her apartment and told her of my decision. Her memory of that time is of me looking stern, frightening and all-powerful. I was wearing a dark green silk shirt, an embroidered waistcoat, and smelling of musk and patchouli. She felt she'd lost touch with the Mick she'd known for so long and that her fear of what would happen to me, if the band really took off, had become a reality. It was a surreal moment and I know I felt the great divide between us. Inwardly I was sad, but I knew separating was the right thing to do.

I know now that her unhappiness was overwhelming; she felt so lost in the world we now inhabited, so far removed from the connection we'd once had, and she had finally lost all faith we could find it again. I began divorce proceedings.

The Record Plant, like a lot of studios of the day, was more than just a place where music was recorded. It was a total social scene. For those in the Bay Area music community, from the artists to the hangers-on, the drug dealers, the weirdos and all of their friends and acquaintances, it was like a cocktail party where the house band changed every few weeks. We had our group of friends with us and that was fine, but there always seemed to be a rotating gang of people in and out of the studio, hanging around and partying while we tried to get some work done. The drugs of course were plentiful and we partook in the finest Peruvian flake quite a bit, both to numb the pain and to find the energy to persevere.

Throughout this period, I was still in contact with Jenny, in fact, as the recording dragged on, I asked her to come up with the girls and stay with me. I wanted her to see some of what we were doing and, in truth, I missed her and my family. I hoped that, even though I'd begun to file for divorce, we still stood a chance of staying together. Jenny had been around us when we were recording before and she fell right in as if nothing had ever gone wrong. Nothing had changed on a fundamental level between us, but we were in familiar territory and we got along well. We both wanted our marriage to work; we just didn't know how to do it within an ever-changing and drug-addled world. We decided to try anyway.

When we returned to LA, Jenny and the girls came to live with me in Topanga, as did my parents. I was hopeful that this was truly a new start for us and at times it seemed possible. There were wonderful days, but sadly they were few and far between. Whenever my responsibilities to the band pulled me away, mentally or otherwise, I could feel Jenny's reaction and we were once again at a distance. She can tell me now, all these years later, it was at this time that my cocaine consumption escalated and how painful it was for her to witness the very nature of the drug at work, bringing with it excessive self-confidence and a numbing of the heart. There was no denying that things had changed since Fleetwood Mac became famous, people treated us differently, and I know Jenny found this hard.

It got to the point where Jenny decided it was best for her to move out and return to her apartment, and when she did, my parents stepped in for the sake of the children. They'd known Jenny nearly all her life and they were worried for her. They told her that they would care for the girls and that she wasn't to see them until she'd had some time to get herself together. Jenny returned to England for almost two months, to regain herself and find some much-needed peace and serenity.

Our record company used to check in on us when we were up in Sausalito, and as time dragged on and we had nothing to play for them, the calls came more frequently, the tone of the voices on the other end more concerned. I was in a unique position because as manager, they had to be honest with me, but I was also in the band. I'd go to meetings as our representative and they knew they were never going to hear me say 'I can get them to do that' to make the label happy, and then talk my band into a compromise they wouldn't like, the way other managers did so often. They also assumed appropriately that anything they said went straight to the band. There was no bait and switch to be had. Sometimes I waited to fill the rest of them in on certain things, but I never withheld information.

After nine weeks at the Record Plant, to put it lightly, we were spent. Lindsey wanted to have more control of the process, which wasn't going to happen because there was no control to be had. I remember sitting with him one night in the studio and telling him that as a musician, you're either in a band or you're not, and he needed to decide which he wanted to be. He had it the hardest; not only was he called upon to help Stevie write songs that were inspired by and not always kind to him, but he also had to sing them with her. His songs about her cut the same way and all of that weighed on him terribly.

One night I found him sitting cross-legged in the studio, playing sitar, completely frustrated and distraught, unsure that he could remain in the group and complete the album.

'Lindsey, if it's making you this unhappy, then you don't have to do it,' I said. 'It's not easy, we all understand.'

I thought the emotional strain of making the album had become too much for him, but that wasn't it. He'd begun to wonder if he could be in a band at all, because he found the group dynamic involved in the creative process stifling. Moreover, he had a vision in mind for the band's sound that he wanted to bring to life and he wasn't sure he would ever be able to do it. He got his chance to fully realise it on *Tusk,* but we weren't there yet.

'Linds, I'm hearing you. And I'm here to tell you that some degree of what you want is possible. But you have to remember that you're in a band. It's a compromise. In a band you're never going to get it all your own way. If that becomes a huge problem, then you have to not be in a band at all.'

That made sense to him.

It wasn't easy on Stevie either but, like me, she dealt with the pressure of what we were doing by having too much fun, and I, for one, was ready to be her partying partner. She also had all manner of suitors to distract her almost immediately, though I believe she really just wanted to be with Lindsey.

However hard it was, we all stuck together. I'm thankful that we didn't have outside management, because if we did, they would have circled like sharks and probably broken us up. We didn't need the added pressure; we were such perfectionists that finding the *right* studio with the *right* room to record in was laborious enough.

CHAPTER 12

RUMOURS

After recovering for a spell in Los Angeles, we reconvened to listen to what we'd done and were utterly shocked by what we heard. Nothing sounded right, not one single thing. All of it sounded *odd* for lack of a better word. We tried different speakers; we tried different mixing studios, but nothing made much difference. We were desperate to find a studio where we could get to work on this raw material, some place where the music didn't sound as though it had been played by a band that none of us were in. That place happened to be a small mixing room on a shoddy stretch of Hollywood Boulevard surrounded by porno theatres. That's where *Rumours* was sculpted from a pile of strange clay into the album it became.

More or less all that we kept from the Sausalito sessions in the end were my drum tracks. We took the tapes and stripped every song down to those, then set about overdubbing all of the instruments and vocals. We basically remade the record from scratch, forcing every member to relive all the heartache inherent in those songs that we'd lived and breathed for nine weeks, nearly twenty-four hours a day.

We'd grown obsessive about the album, perhaps because it

had become a diary of our own pain. But we also wanted it to be perfect, and in Sausalito, there were elements that just never came together. For one thing, we couldn't find a piano that would stay in tune. We must have rented every piano in the Bay Area but none of them were ever in tune because of the Looner Tuner, who was the engineer at the Record Plant who tuned pianos. He'd insist they were in tune, but they weren't.

This guy was in his own world and he drove us crazy. He kept tuning and retuning, but clearly his version of sound scale was based on an alien conception that we could not and did not want to fathom. We went round in circles with him for weeks, which was ridiculous because Christine has perfect pitch and can tell when a piano isn't in tune. It got to the point where we even brought in a blind piano player to see if we had lost our minds. We hadn't, he agreed right away that the piano wasn't in tune. In the end we scrapped all the piano tracks rather than wasting any more time with the guy.

That was one of a few things that befell us. There was also a tape machine we called Jaws because of its appetite for destroying fresh reels of tape without warning. We'd jam and get some ideas down only to find that they'd been eaten and were beyond salvaging. Add to that the general obsession with getting every element perfect and it's easy to see just how wrapped up in the process we became. Plus, there was a party going non-stop there, one that we hadn't necessarily thrown.

It was hard on everyone, because what we'd created was a very intimate, very personal album; it said everything to each other and about each other, through the songs. We realised that this album was so deeply a part of us and so revealing about us that if it was ever to come together at all, our next studio sessions would need to be closed. So we shut the doors to friends and family and in March 1976, we got down to work.

Despite our best efforts, by June we weren't much closer to the end, but real progress had been made.

The turning point was 'The Chain', which had taken shape but wasn't complete by any means. I don't know if it was Chris or Lindsey's initial composition, but John and Stevie are the ones who saved it. It is the only song in our catalogue for which all of us are listed as the writers. It was a piece of music we kept returning to but could never take any further. We'd jam on it and it would evolve, but inevitably no words presented themselves to our songwriters and I can't count the number of times we almost threw it out for good. We kept coming back to it and trying it different ways, but it was still headed for the scrap pile until Stevie put words to it. Then it became our rallying cry and a symbol of why and how we'd persevered through the making of the record. It became, and still is, our anthem.

By June, 'Don't Stop', which Chris wrote for John, was still only half-finished. 'I Don't Want to Know' wasn't done either and 'Oh Daddy', which Chris wrote for me as I was the only dad in the band, hadn't quite arrived. We recorded that song in an empty university auditorium in Berkeley, because we wanted the song to sound like Chris was singing it at the end of the night, after a show to an empty house. It needed that solitude sonically.

The way our band works when we write is that we try to stumble towards each other, then work it all out. We wait for our songwriters to come to us with an idea and some words, or a sense of what the song will be about. From there, John, Christine and I get a notion of our parts, and then we begin to fine-tune. John doesn't like to finalise his bass parts until he knows exactly what the song is about. Many times he's gone back in after the song is complete and redone his parts, because he's got an intrinsic knack for placing his bass line where it will best complement the melody, once he's heard the vocal. He comes up with these lovely bass lines that become another song underneath the main recurring theme he plays. He needs to hear the entire song idea to do that properly, whereas I can get started with a vague concept of how the singing will be and the intended mood of the song. I think of my role as more lumbering, just keeping time and establishing a vibe that locks the others in. Later, once I understand the song, I can have fun, adding all of my percussion parts. Those are my fairy dust and how I endeavour to amplify the narrative.

One of the problems we had with completing anything during the writing of *Rumours* was that our songwriters weren't bringing us words. I imagine that had to do with the subjects of the songs quite often being in the room, not to mention that they were working out their feelings on a day-to-day basis. Lindsey, by nature, always holds back on his songs until he feels he's perfected them on his end. Writing this record he was even more private; he crafted his contributions until the very last minute, requiring the rest of us to revise our parts accordingly. My basic drum tracks were usually the only thing that would remain the same. When Lindsey reworked a song, everything from the vocal backing parts to the melody would change, so there was no chance of keeping Chris's original, basic vocal take, for example. The entire arrangement was different so it all had to be redone.

We didn't get that as much from Chris or Stevie, because Stevie knows how she wants to deliver her words, so when she makes adjustments, they're less drastic in terms of the overlying structure of the song. Chris is a blues player and says what she wants to say very directly; she knows the melody she wants and it's all right there, or evolved enough that we can usually get there together pretty fast. But even Chris wasn't doing that this time. Making *Rumours*, all three of them held back on their lyrics to the point that John and I, as blues players who were used to going right to an idea, were on the verge of ripping their sheets of lyrics out of their hands and saying, 'Just give me the shit now!'

But as blues players we also knew how to support our bandmates properly, so we went through as many permutations of an idea as necessary. That was our training; whether it's in increments or wild leaps, if you must go all over the place to get where you need to be, that's what you do.

Even if we'd been on a roll, we had to take a break at that point to do a bit of touring since we'd cancelled a series of spring dates to continue work on the album. There was a great demand because a full year later, *Fleetwood Mac* was still climbing the charts, and when we released 'Say You Love Me' with the B-side 'Monday Morning', we scored another high-charting single. We hadn't played a gig in nearly six months, so when we hit the road, we were like a bat out of hell; all that inward focus, frustration and introspection fuelled us.

We toured through June and into July on bills with bands including Jeff Beck, Jefferson Starship, Ted Nugent, and the Eagles, who had released *One of These Nights* and were riding high.

On this tour, Stevie Nicks really came into her own and I saw what she had begun to represent to our female fans. Stevie was the mysterious mystic, the seductive songstress, the ethereal being who could not be possessed. Her style, as unique as her voice, was catching on everywhere. I will never forget playing on 4 July 1976, on the American bicentennial, with the Eagles in Tampa, Florida. I looked out at the crowd and saw a field of Stevie Nicks devotees; wispy, witchy black dresses, top hats, just everything Stevie incorporated into her stage attire. When we launched into 'Rhiannon' and Stevie said, 'This is a song about a Welsh witch,' the place *erupted*. Stevie delivered and she gave herself up to the music just the way her fans were beginning to do to her, all of them swaying, dancing with their eyes closed. Stevie had found something within herself that she'd poured into performing that number, something that came from deep inside her, something as real and magical as the Welsh witch she sang about.

During this tour, I reconnected with Jenny. Living in London with my sister Sally's family had been a relatively sane and soothing existence for her and just what she needed. It had given her time and stability to think about her future, and to build a firm determination to commit totally to her life with the children and me. She felt that she'd broken the bond between us, so she had to be the one to mend it. The environment and lifestyle had changed us both, and even though we'd legally divorced by then she believed there was hope for us. She was closer to my parents than her own, we had two gorgeous daughters, and she knew we both loved each other, even though in her eyes I didn't show it properly, which caused her a lot of suffering.

She'd thought it through and was ready, so she flew out to Chicago to join me on tour. This was a test, and if all went well, we'd reunite with the girls together at the end of the tour. Jenny says that the moment she got into the black limo I'd sent to fetch her from the airport, she was seized with anxiety. She was back in the life of luxury, as she called it, in the lion's den where the nuggets of gold resided.

I met her backstage, happy to see her. She looked rested, great, and beautiful as ever.

I held her hand and led her down the hall. 'I've just spoken to the girls,' I said, 'and they know you're arriving today.'

'How are they?' she asked tentatively.

'They're good. I told them you'd be with me on the road and they're very excited.'

'How long are we on the road?'

'Another two weeks,' I said.

She stopped walking. 'Mick,' she said. 'I feel nervous.'

'Why?' I asked. 'I'm here. You'll be fine.'

'I'm nervous about what the band will think of me. All of this being together and then breaking up. It makes me feel so silly.'

I hugged her and held her close. 'Don't you worry about that,' I said. 'They don't care – believe me. Come on, let's go find JC and get you some coke. You must be tired. It'll help you stay awake for the show.'

Jenny sat at the side of the stage that night and I remember staring at her throughout the set and feeling like my wife was back. She felt the same. She told me that she felt home once again, on familiar territory. The lights dimmed after every song and she watched our road manager bring a silver tray full of bottle caps of cocaine for the band members who wanted them. She then helped herself to the allocation reserved for wives and girlfriends in the backstage dressing rooms. She got tipsy on vodka and orange juice and thoroughly enjoyed herself. There was always a party after the show in those days and it went on late and rowdy. Jenny remembers the party on that particular evening after the show, because back then we'd developed a habit of pouring glasses of wine over each other, which we did that evening with gusto. We carried on until the early morning, until, at the end of it all, exhausted, she and I walked to our room in silence.

Jenny fell back into our life on the road very well and I remember thinking that we had a chance. She's told me that on that tour she realised that touring provided the type of cocoon she'd been after; she and I were isolated from the outside world. She liked that part, but the problem was that the world we were in was far from normal. She thought a lot about Peter Green saying that we should all have lived our lives as travelling gypsies. For the first time she saw the wisdom in his vision and wondered if we would always have been together if we'd gone that route.

At the end of the two weeks, I thought it best for Jenny and me to have some time together before seeing our daughters again, so I sent my parents and the girls to Hawaii for two weeks. We arrived at the Topanga house, just the two of us. It was lovely to be home with her, because I'd always hoped that house would be our home. Jenny remembers the excitement she felt walking through the house and seeing signs of the children everywhere, all the familiar toys, books and drawings and the sepia photograph taken of us all by Herbie Worthington that hung in their bedroom. To her it was an idyllic family portrait, me in a chair with Amelia in front of me and Jenny at my side holding baby Lucy, and she saw it as both a good token and a reminder of the work that needed to be done to bridge image with reality.

I'd hung a map in the girls' room and placed pins in all the cities I'd travelled to while on tour, so they'd have an idea of where Daddy was, and that warmed Jenny's heart. She had returned renewed and determined to create a home for our children and to commit to our marriage, no matter how crazy things got. The house she came home to was still partially under construction, so with workers there all day, and nothing but a tarp for a front door, Jenny busied herself during the afternoons, usually by coming down to the Seedy Management offices.

We weren't home for long before the pressure to complete our album started coming from Warner Brothers. We blocked out a week off in Miami to continue work at Criteria Studios, where Bob Marley had just finished recording *Rastaman Vibration*. We could tell, because the place smelled strongly and pleasantly of ganja. I flew my parents out there straight from Hawaii, thinking that it would be a more suitable location for Jenny to reconnect with our daughters, which it was. It seemed like we were back together for good.

The first Fleetwood Mac album continued to rise through the ranks, hitting number 1 on the US charts on 4 September 1976, fourteen months after its release, thereby ending the unstoppable ten-week run of *Frampton Comes Alive!* It was great to feel that our work on that record had 'arrived' but it was hard to celebrate with so much unfinished work to do. Our chart success did nothing but increase the pressure from without and within.

To their credit, Warner Brothers were patient, they really were. By that time we'd spent a small fortune, we weren't done yet and we refused to play them so much as a note. This was the advantage of not having a manager, or having an artist as manager. I sided with the band; we weren't going to play them anything until it was finished, no questions asked. A manager who wasn't an artist would have had his mind solely on business. We'd have been urged to finish sooner, to cut corners and to get the product to market so it could start earning. Instead we got to do it our way, and thank God we did. We chose the art director for our albums, we chose the photographer, our crazy friend Herbie. All of these decisions were organic and holistically art-driven. We'd choose to work with our friends, not someone the record company or an outside manager would invariably have chosen for us. We were horribly unpackaged by design at a time when rock and roll was commodified, planned and marketed more than it had ever been in the past.

If we had been attuned and concerned with trying to capitalise on ourselves in that way I don't think we would have survived. Yet in remaining 'unpackaged' we developed an aesthetic, which essentially became our 'brand'. We made money out of just being who we are. We dressed the way we did because that's the way we dressed. If we'd had a manager, I guarantee that we'd have been squashed into a box, or even worse, become a version of the Beatles when they had their mop-tops. That happened to Peter Frampton after the success of *Frampton Comes Alive!* He'd managed to shed his pop star roots in England and legitimised himself by playing with George Harrison and releasing a monster of a rock album, only to allow himself to be packaged once again as a teen idol in America. Things such as that awful film version of *Sgt Pepper's Lonely Hearts Club Band* ruined him and I think he never recovered. By managing ourselves, we escaped that fate.

At the same time we were trying to finish *Rumours* we had to keep promoting our first album, which had also finally broken overseas. The band took ten days in October 1976 to go to London to meet the European press and it was the first time we'd done so in years. We stayed at the Montcalm Hotel, near Marble Arch, and were met with overwhelming enthusiasm, the likes of which we hadn't seen since 1969. We were also met with a sobering surprise when Peter Green showed up at our hotel and stayed in our rooms for a few nights. Peter had let himself go; he was unkempt, his hair long and straggly, and he'd put on a good deal of weight. It depressed all of us to see him that way, but John in particular took it very hard. I tried to find the old Peter in there but it was tough; John was too upset to even try. Peter would stare long, hard, and unsettlingly at whomever he was talking to, when he wasn't gazing vacantly at the nearest wall. There was an aggression in his manner that we'd never seen before and it was disturbing. It didn't bode well and the next time we returned to England, in April 1977, we learned that Peter had been committed to a mental institution for threatening our former manager, Clifford Davis, at gunpoint over sending him royalty cheques that Peter didn't want to cash.

Danny Kirwan paid us a visit, too, and it was equally sad to see that time had not been kind to him either. Alcoholism had taken its toll, and after his short lived solo career, he'd more or less left music behind. He'd spent time doing odd jobs and had been homeless and itinerant for some time. He kept scratching himself and told us that he was living in a shelter and had contracted 'worms'. I've not seen Danny since.

It was great to be in London with my family, to ride double-decker buses with Amelia and Lucy, who by then had become so used to travelling by limo that the buses were a novelty. After going by private plane to a few select European cities, the press tour was over and it was time to go back home.

Another rude awakening awaited us there when we landed. American immigration realised that John, Chris, John Courage and I were British citizens still working with tourist visas from years back. Tourist visas don't exactly allow you to work for American corporations and earn money the way we'd been doing. We had never got around to getting our US permanent resident visas, known as Green Cards, but we were going to have to find a way quickly if we stood a chance of fulfilling our touring obligations. Getting it handled quickly and efficiently proved to be a huge hassle. Some of us had misdemeanour marijuana possession arrests on record back in England, which complicated everything, and since Jenny and I were no longer married, if we didn't take care of it, she and my daughters would be deported along with me.

We did everything we could think of to speed things up, and though we'll never know if this had any effect, we even played a fundraiser for Senator Birch Bayh, the Democratic committee chairman from Indiana. The only catch was that Jenny and I had to be married in order for us, and our children, to be granted Green Cards, so we had a solemn ceremony in the offices of our lawyer, Mickey Shapiro, with Lindsey acting as my best man and our two daughters as our witnesses.

The house in Topanga, which was going to include a recording studio and all the bells and whistles, still wasn't finished, so in November 1976, Jenny and I rented a house in Malibu at the Colony, the famed gated community on the beach. Jenny loved it there, because it was more social than the quiet sprawl of Topanga. In the row of thirty or so houses backed up to the beach, she'd run into Diana Ross, whose children played with our children every day on the Rosses' big trampoline. Diana's husband managed Ronnie Wood, who lived a few doors down with his wife Krissy and their new baby. Neil Diamond lived close by, too, and could usually be found on his front door step, pencil and paper in hand, writing songs.

We wrapped up the work on our second album as 1976 drew to a close and that's when John McVie came up with the title – *Rumours*. John hit the nail on the head as always. By then, given the success of *Fleetwood Mac,* all eyes in the music business in LA were on us and everyone involved in that business pretended to have the inside scoop on the inner workings of our band. We'd been hearing stories about ourselves for months, most of them so outlandish that we had to laugh. According to this grapevine, every combination of male–female intimate relations were on-going, violent fights were common, Stevie was leaving the band, Christine and Lindsey were running off to start a band together, we were all too addicted to drugs to even play, and Stevie's devotion to black magic had cursed us all. It was ridiculous, as rumours always are, yet they still hurt when they come back to the source, which they inevitably did. There were multiple times when we called one another to confirm that what we were hearing wasn't true, such was the tenacity of these stories. John's title handled all that bullshit with a dose of irony and intrigue. It was perfect.

The first single from *Rumours* was 'Go Your Own Way', its B-side a beautiful song by Stevie called 'Silver Springs', and it was released just before Christmas 1976. It became an instant radio hit, going straight to the Top 10. Record stores around the country ordered 800,000 copies of the album for its release in February, based on the popularity of the single, which at the time was the largest order for an album that Warner Brothers had ever received. Our first album had sold four million copies, which was then the company's best-selling album of all time. Conservative bets had *Rumours* doubling that figure before long.

With the excitement of *Rumours* heading up the charts came the endless publicity photographs and press articles. These sessions took place at various photographers' studios, and one of these – for the cover of *Rolling Stone* magazine – continued, as so often, through the night. I remember arriving home early the next morning, just before the children got up. Jenny could tell it had been a night of drink and coke, and I was elated. I described the idea we'd had of being photographed in bed together; me and Stevie cuddled up at one end, with Lindsey and Christine together at the other, and John alone reading the paper. The intention was a spoof on the rumours about our private lives, and yet, symbolically, the picture showed us exactly as we were. All married to each other.

But in the course of the session, as I told Jenny in all seriousness, I had realised something vital. 'Stevie and I have definitely known each other in previous lives,' I said, before going off to sleep. That image of the two of us cuddling, a large satisfied smile on my face and Stevie giggling beside me would later haunt Jenny for years to come.

As the album sped up the charts we hit the road in March, playing a powerhouse set that consisted of hits from both albums, selling out arenas that held from ten to fifteen thousand. *Rumours* went platinum by the end of March and everywhere we went crowds of girls dressed like Stevie sang along with her on every song, hanging on her every word. This was just the start, because the album hadn't even begun to reach its maximum heights. What that album went on to achieve is common knowledge but what is not is the efforts of the sonic masterminds behind it all. Without the patience, dedication and zealous belief in us that Ken Calliat and Richard Dashut shared, *Rumours* would not have come to be. They were the sixth and seventh members of our band, they made the sound that the world knows as ours come to life in the recorded medium. Along with Lindsey Buckingham and to some degree myself, those two changed the way albums were recorded and they deserve more kudos than these mere words can convey.

A tour supporting the album's release was already booked and we rehearsed for it on the Studio Instrument Rentals lot, just behind the Seedy Management office. I was there every day, and Jenny would come down with the children from time to time to see how it was going. There was a real buzz in the air and a whirl of activity as every aspect of the stage show was honed, with people rushing around, finalising all the details. We knew we were on to something big this time, even bigger than the last album. I predicted that sales would reach around nine million, an astonishing number. The whole thing felt so huge, so all-absorbing, that I know Jenny felt grateful when I could spare time to be home from my frenetic routine of rehearsing, getting tied up in the office, or making plans to manage Bob Welch's solo career.

Any moment when we could be like an ordinary. couple, seeing friends at our home, was to be treasured. It was a rare thing for us to invite people round for dinner. The people I wanted to see, I saw every day, and the others I would bump into at parties or backstage at a gig. But one evening, when she knew I'd be available, Jenny invited Ronnie Wood over and he brought his old friend Keith Moon, from the Who. It was the very first dinner we'd hosted for friends and it was really enjoyable, because it was a rare occasion when it felt as if we were truly working as a couple. We reminisced with Keith about old times at the Scotch of St James's club back in the sixties. He told us that night how difficult he found life sometimes. Because he was a funny man, and often very silly, he had built up an image that had grown so large he felt trapped inside it as too often happens to our most gifted entertainers. Everyone expected him to be wild, to be funny, and he couldn't help but play the part. He was more than that, very introspective, but that element of his personality hardly ever got a look-in, except on rare occasions such as this. Keith didn't feel the need to be a clown that evening, and the memory of our talk has become more precious and meaningful to me over the years, for it wasn't long afterwards that he died.

We toured Europe in April of that year. Jenny and the

children came with me to London where we played at Wembley Stadium, our first gig back home with the new line-up. Jenny's sister Pattie came along, with her boyfriend Eric Clapton. It was a huge success. Then we went to Paris, Jenny and the children, my parents Biddy and Mike, and the rest of my family. We stayed at the Hôtel George V, in a magnificent suite with two bedrooms and a huge sitting room, luxuriously furnished with gilded sofas and chairs and enormous French windows. Jenny sat on the window sill, watching Biddy and Mike as they sat beside me, laughing at the almost excessive splendour of the room and then falling about as I pulled two pencils from a pot and knocked one against the other, saying, 'Look at me. I've got all this money because I can hit things with two bits of wood!' It seemed hilarious and set the tone for a delightful stay in the city.

After Europe we returned home to the West Coast for a moment, then we went back out to tour the Midwest and Northeast. We had toured so much by then, not to mention surviving the strain of making the album, that the only way we could deal with the demands put upon us was by opting for first-class accommodations and transport wherever possible. We'd spent years touring in station wagons, long after we were due for an upgrade, simply because that's how we always did it. We were late bloomers. We thought it was cool, actually, showing up in a fleet of station wagons that we drove ourselves, rather than a tour bus. But once we realised that we could have a private jet, well then, by God, we had one. We got a taste for travelling in style that has never gone away and so we earned a reputation for it. Our rider was extensive, detailed, and exhaustive: we had fourteen black limos at our beck and call, for a time Stevie wanted her room to be pink with a white piano (we'd often have to hire a crane to lift the piano in through the window), and the list went on. We were pleasantly out of control. I remember trying to downsize those demands on one tour in the 1980s to maximise our profits. The changes I made were hardly going from a plane to a cargo van; I think I cut the number of limos on call and tried to get that piano off the rider, just the upper echelon of excess. John Courage and I talked to everyone before the tour, telling them that we were running a tighter ship on this run so that we'd all have more money in the bank. Everyone agreed – until the tour started. Within weeks, people were complaining. They wanted a car on call outside the hotel. Stevie wanted that pink room. We got way too much flak to try that again.

For years our 'lifestyle' bills were a corporate expense. When we went on tour we bought cocaine in bulk and everyone in the band and crew would show up each night at the company canteen. Everyone in the operation, no matter their role, would queue up about half an hour after the show was over, and the rations would be handed out. We even listed the time on our daily tour schedule. Everyone who lined up got their packet. Of course, there would be the begging: 'I didn't pick up yesterday, so I should get two today.' Also those claiming they needed to pick up rations for another member of the entourage. Our tour manager heard it all.

I was in the inner circle so I always had a little extra something, but even I queued up every night. I also knew who amongst our big touring family were more gentle than me and thus more likely to be in possession of unused packets. Many a night, as our after party wound on, I'd find one of them and tap their pockets, looking for a packet.

'You haven't fucking used all of your shit,' I'd say. 'Now, give it to me.'

No one ever tried that with Stevie or me, because they knew better. The two of us never had spare packets.

These antics earned me the disreputable accolade 'The King of Toot', according to all manner of English tabloids in the 1980s. One of them listed the top ten spenders in rock and roll and I came in at number one for the amount I'd spent on cocaine. Paul McCartney was number three for some expensive wall or something that he built on his farm in Scotland. My reputation wasn't unfounded, but it all stemmed from a game we played with one of our engineers in the studio one night. We tried to figure out how much cocaine I'd done in my life by cutting out a line of average thickness for me. Using that as a guide, we estimated how long a gram would be at that thickness. Then assuming an eight ball – that's an eighth of an ounce – a day for twenty years, we calculated that one line comprised of all the coke I'd done would be seven miles long. Foolishly I mentioned this in some interview and said that at best it would have measured one loop around Hyde Park. In any case, this mythical line of mine became the fish that got bigger, every time it got away. By the end, it stretched from here to the moon. That was the figure they used in that chart, which estimated that I'd spent $60 million on cocaine.

In the studio, we had a ritual, in which the engineers and band members all started humming a tune – it changed over the years – which would serve as a siren's call for cocaine, specifically the cocaine that I was invariably holding. The most memorable song was Vangelis's theme to *Chariots of Fire*, released in 1981. If I were tuning my drums, say, and anyone in the studio started humming that tune, it would begin. One of them would start, then it would spread until everyone present in need of a toot was humming it and, as if in a trance, I would drop what I was doing and in slow-motion, beckon them over. In homage to the film, I'd make them run to me in slow-motion, then get on their knees and beg, before I'd administer the goods.

My sister Susan, my mother Biddy, me and
my sister Sally in the 1980s.

Lucy and Amelia, Van Nuys, 1983.

In Ghana working on The Visitor.

Africa by bus: Ghana, 1981.

Taking it in,
Ghana, 1981.

Digging their spirit,
London, 1981.

With the totem
that hangs above
my drum kit on my
farm in Maui, 1987.

Backstage with Gary Busey and George Hawkins. We had a band called The Cholos together. Gary Busey would do Buddy Holly covers.

Me and Paul McCartney, late 80s.

Conducting *Tusk*, Dodger Stadium.

Hypnotized: Bob Welch
at the Cotton Bowl,
Dallas, Texas, 1978.

Great balls of fire:
Keith Richards
and I playing with
Jerry Lee Lewis on
television in 1986.

Christine, Rick Vito
and Stevie, 1987.

Me and my sister
Susan in 1988.

Cuffed and stuffed filming
The Running Man in 1987.

I look a bit unwell: my guest spot
on Star Trek: The Next Generation,
1987. I played an Antedean, a fish-like
humanoid who was an assassin. I said
I would shave my beard for the role
only if my character were beamed
onto the ship - he was, to Deck D
where he got thrown in jail.

The longest marriage I've ever had: John McVie and I.

Me with a mandolin.

Hold on a minute!

LINDSEY
BUCKINGHAM

MICK
FLEETWOOD

Announcing our upcoming performance at Clinton's inauguration, January, 1993.

A changed band. Me, Dave Mason, Billy
Burnette, Bekka Bramlett and John McVie.

With Lynn in the 90s.

My daughter Amelia with my
grandson Wolf, 1996.

Anyone in our inner circle knew that if they hummed that song, 'Uncle Miltie' would succumb. They called me Uncle Miltie, after the veteran American comedian Milton Berle, because of my toothy smile when under the influence.

Whatever our means and whatever our demands, none of it mattered once *Rumours* took over the number one spot on 21 May 1977, ousting the Eagles' *Hotel California*. It took seven studios, a full year and just over a million dollars. All of the struggle, the cost, and the hard work were validated because our album stayed there for thirty-one straight weeks in America. During that time we stayed on the road, as one single after another was released and rose to the top of the charts.

I remained the band's acting manager through all of that wonderful chaos and I remember being portrayed by the press as somewhat of a menacing Svengali figure, which was the furthest from the truth. I was the guy who stopped off at the local magic shop to pick up fake blood, or a joke cigar, to keep people laughing when the going got tough. I was the gentle jester, the prankster who kept spirits high, but I understand why the press sometimes saw me differently. I was tired, plain and simple. I was playing two roles in Fleetwood Mac, but I wouldn't have had it any other way. My blood, sweat, and tears was Fleetwood Mac and I refused to trust anyone else with it. Through the years of low record sales and no record sales, through all the ups and downs, this was my way of life and my life's work. I had taken a vow to see Fleetwood Mac through it, come what may. And absolutely nothing has changed. Aside from the fact that I'm more careful about getting my rest.

CHAPTER 13

I KNOW I'M NOT WRONG

The many demands of the band were wonderful, literally everything we'd all been working so hard for, but they stretched my marriage with Jenny to the limit. I had less time to spend with her than ever and it weighed on her. I loved her, I really did, but I was consumed with the band. I was happy to play my role as husband and dad and did the best I could, but I gave equal importance to playing Mick Fleetwood, leader of Fleetwood Mac. I had no problem doing it all in the same day, or trying to at least, but my efforts were never enough for Jenny. Sharing me with the band had long caused a see-saw in her feelings and by extension in our relationship, and once again things had built up to a breaking point. From what Jenny has told me, all these years later, the fact that she got no reaction from me when she tried to elicit emotion drove her to drastic action, typically aided by drink. I didn't make it easy, because I was proficient at ignoring the undercurrents of tension between us until Jenny lashed out.

One night, when her sister Pattie was in town to visit, we all had dinner at Christine McVie's house, after which I planned to head off to deal with some Fleetwood Mac business. It was a warm, pleasant evening, full of conversation and catching up and altogether lovely. I had a wonderful time and I assumed Jenny had, too, but she was quite drunk, and once she realised I wasn't following her home as we walked to our cars, she threw the ramekins of chocolate mousse at me that Chris had given her to take home to the girls. As I crossed the road to my Porsche, they came flying past me, one of them hitting the wheel as I opened the door and got in. I didn't stop and I didn't turn round because I didn't want to acknowledge what was happening. I just drove away. That moment was indicative of how our relationship would end.

The hardest thing about the whirlwind that my life with Jenny had become was the effect it had on our children. They were stuck in the middle of their parents' problems and between the distraction of the band and our lifestyle choices, they didn't stand a chance. If there's one thing I would like to do, it is to make amends for that. Talking about it here certainly doesn't solve it, but I'd like to think that at least they know I'm aware of it. I can't change it, but maybe there's some comfort to be found in my admission and my comprehension of the trauma they were caused. I sure hope so.

That spring Fleetwood Mac went back on the road for a month of outdoor shows with the Eagles, Boz Scaggs and others. I had my parents along on that stretch and I loved spoiling them, even though my father was embarrassed by the extravagance that he saw, from the fleet of limos to our latest outrageous idea, the inflatable penguin. I commissioned it to be built, about sixty feet high, to float over us when we played outdoor concerts and I intended it to be one of our permanent props. Unfortunately it never worked properly, logging just one successful flight at a gig in Florida. My father found this hilarious and pointed out the obvious to me: 'Mick, you do know that penguins don't fly, don't you?'

Our success was wonderful but victory came with greater tension between our band members with each passing day. There were frequent fights because our art, our business, and our personal lives were all the same, and we lived it out on stage and off, every single night.

Our relentless live schedule had begun to put a dangerous strain on Stevie's voice and we were all concerned. She is not a classically-trained vocalist and she sings with her throat rather than her diaphragm, which is how she creates her inimitable, gorgeous vibrato. Midway through the tour we decided to bring Stevie's close friend Robin on the road to look after her, because Robin was a voice coach, and we decided she should be a permanent addition to our tour family. But despite Robin's presence and all the advice in the world, Stevie could not be tamed when the spirit moved her; she'd tear her instrument to shreds in deference to her songs.

We were in Las Vegas in August 1977, when my mother phoned to inform me that my father had been diagnosed with cancer and that his prognosis was dire. He'd never been sick a day in his life, but he'd contracted melanoma, and I can't help but wonder, if he'd had his skin checked regularly, whether he'd still be here today, sitting next to Mum on her terrace in Maui. Dad had pretty much been told that he was finished, no matter what, because his cancer had got into his lymphatic system. Rather than embrace conventional methods of treatment, he chose to fight the disease through holistic methods, which I didn't understand entirely, other than he didn't want to be dehumanised by radiation. That call was horrible to hear and I was devastated, but I had to carry on, because we had a fully-booked tour.

The remainder of our dates saw us through Arizona, the Pacific Northwest, and Canada. We were done by October, at which point every member of our touring family was utterly spent. By then Jenny had moved our family from Topanga to a house in Bel Air that was properly suburban, complete with a pool for our daughters and space for my parents to stay with us, because I wanted them nearby during my father's last days.

That month Warner Brothers released 'You Make Loving Fun', another chart-topping single, resulting in the sale of an additional two million copies of the album. That, of course, meant more live appearances because the wheel did not stop spinning. After a brief ten days at home we were off again to Australia, New Zealand, Japan and Hawaii.

To complicate matters even further, before we departed, Stevie Nicks and I began an affair during our break at home in LA. It was bound to happen, I suppose, because the two of us are cut from the same cloth, but we're more brother and sister – soulmates, not romantic partners – which is why it didn't last. We are so much the same that we fell into each other's arms, albeit at the worst possible time.

Lindsey predicted it, years before, in a moment that to this day he insists he doesn't remember. It was just when the two of them had joined the band, and we were down South in Memphis, staying in the first Holiday Inn ever to have been built. I don't know if he and Stevie had ever stayed in one, but in any case it was a milestone of sorts for us all. That night after our show I ended up in Lindsey's room, where we shared a joint and got properly stoned.

We were relaxing, sitting there, when out of the blue, he said, 'So . . . it's you and Stevie, isn't it?'

'What?' I said. I was sure I'd heard him right, but wasn't sure what he meant. 'What do you mean? She's your girlfriend.'

'Yeah . . .' he said, giving me an odd look. 'It's you and Stevie.'

It freaked me out completely but I neither reacted nor said anything else, because I was in shock. What he'd said hit me in the gut, amplified all the more because I was stoned. As off the wall as it was, I felt terrible that he'd thought that about her and me even for a minute! At the time, I'd not given it a thought. Of course I found Stevie attractive, I don't think there was a man or woman who didn't, but nothing more. She was Lindsey's girlfriend. This conversation took place years before the spark of anything between us began, but the irony is that Lindsey was right. It was pure intuition, because his interpretation at the time was incorrect, but his premonition that there was something powerful between Stevie and me was entirely correct. What he felt finally manifested itself; eventually I fell in love with her and it was chaotic, it was on the road and it was a crazy love affair that went on longer than any of us really remember – probably several years by the end of it. What else can I say, other than Lindsey has always been ahead of his time.

When it actually did start between Stevie and me, no one really knew at first. We met in secret, because I was with Jenny and Stevie had a boyfriend. Only Stevie's closest friends knew and just a few people in my life knew. Lindsey didn't know and neither did John or Chris. I'd adored Stevie from the start, but until then it wasn't romantic.

It does make sense that things happened when they did, because we were both stretched so thin from the exhaustion of the road, and the unhappiness in our private lives, that we found solace in each other and in all the ways that we are alike. It was the great escape, we'd sneak away and take long drives through the Hollywood Hills. The clandestine nature of it was romantic and it was even more so on tour, in our world within a world, where we could do as we pleased. In New Zealand, after a show, we spent the night driving up to a crater to see the sun rise. A light rain started to fall and we huddled close together on the ride back to the hotel, and afterwards we spent the entire day in bed together without a care in the world.

When we returned home from that tour, my relationship with Stevie was something very real. I was in love with her, and she loved me, and it was not something passing in the night. We were both in love with each other. So I went to Lindsey's house and I told him about it. He and Stevie had been broken up for a very long time, but that didn't matter. I felt a responsibility to tell him, because I knew that there was still something between them, that is still between them. Whether it's enjoyable or some kind of purgatory, they will go to their graves being connected, like it or not.

I went to see him, the day after we returned from tour. We made some small talk until I could delay no longer.

'Lindsey, I have to talk to you,' I said.

'Okay, what's going on?'

'I need to let you know that I'm seeing Stevie. I'm not quite sure how it's going to end up but I don't feel right having this going on without you knowing.'

'Okay,' he said. 'I understand.'

'I'm not asking your permission, I just don't feel right that you don't know.'

I don't recall exactly what he said afterwards other than he appreciated me telling him. I'm glad I made the effort, and also glad that I waited until I knew that I was in love with her to do so.

Sometimes I think about what would have happened if Stevie and I had agreed to make a go of it. We got distracted; she had a boyfriend and I was still hemming and hawing with

Jenny, so it never happened, but there was a moment when it could have. I remember that time distinctly. I wanted it to be more than our circumstances allowed, I wanted it very badly. I wanted to let my family know how I felt for her and I wanted to tell them I was going to try and make it work. It would have been utter madness, just so complicated because of our other entanglements, from our bandmates to our significant others, to everyone else in our lives. But I assure you that there was a time when all of it seemed worth the suffering to me.

Stevie and I used to slip away and go on adventures after gigs, which was an easy way to get away. After the band played a show in Hawaii, we went to Maui and drove up to the land I'd bought in Olinda and we stayed with a chap called Steve Cafferty, whose house overlooked my property. While we were there, Mo Ostin and his wife Evelyn, who were on the island for the gig, sent a helicopter for Stevie and me and that was very romantic. We had wild crazy times; we drove around Maui and found a house that we fantasised about buying. It's one of the most beautiful houses on the island to this day, on fifty acres and just huge. The place is a gorgeous, Victorian nineteenth-century estate owned by the Baldwin family, who were one of the earliest missionary families to settle on Maui. It needed a bit of fixing up, which made it all the more romantic. That's what Stevie and I would do, we'd dream. Today that house is owned by the Coca-Cola family and has been restored to perfect condition. Shoulda, woulda, coulda!

Anyway, things were hot and heavy between Stevie and me. At one point on tour, when my mother and father were out with us, we were in Santa Barbara after playing a show there the night before, and Stevie came down and joined us for breakfast. Jenny wasn't there, just my parents and my daughters, and I remember wanting to say something to them, come what may. I had to fight the urge to blurt it out, because I wanted my parents to know that I was completely in love with Stevie. It would have been such a scandal, because of Jenny, so I remained mute, but just barely. Sometimes I ask myself what would have happened if I'd laid it all out on the table that morning. Whether it would have changed things or not at all. I wonder if Stevie and I could have made a commitment to each other, and if our love would have grown, or if it would have been torn asunder by the circumstances.

None of that happened, so it will always remain an unfulfilled love, but in terms of the intensity it was a proper Hollywood affair on a par with Richard Burton and Elizabeth Taylor. In terms of our relationship with each other, we still have the same connection to this day; we just love each other in the true sense of the word, which transcends passion. I will take my love for her as a person to my grave, because Stevie Nicks is the kind of woman who inspires that devotion. I have no regrets and neither does she, but we do giggle together sometimes and wonder what might have transpired if we'd given that passion the space and time to blossom into something more. We'll never know, because we were moths drawn to a certain type of flame for a while. It was exciting, it was romantic, and our lives met behind closed doors. It suited something in our make-up for a while and we were each other's perfect playmates. That's not all it was, but that's what we needed and what we needed it to be. It was the perfect fantasy.

With my father dying, I did all I could to retreat into the world of the band, and spending time with Stevie was all part and parcel of that. When the band wasn't on tour, I'd spend long nights out, doing all I could to work with the artists on Seedy Management's label, or planning Fleetwood Mac's next moves, or anything work-related to avoid the reality unfolding at home. Jenny and I grew further apart, even more so since she'd stopped drinking and devoted herself to helping my parents find holistic doctors for Dad. I couldn't face what was happening to my father, so I usually found myself drunk and in tears whenever I tried to spend quality time with him.

I didn't know which way was up really; I loved Stevie but I also loved Jenny and my family, so the two of us took a vacation to the island of Bora Bora in the South Pacific, in an effort to grow back together. We were still on the see-saw, trying to make it work, but knowing it probably wouldn't. Regardless, in that tropical paradise, we discussed whether we should remain married and both of us acknowledged how great the gap between us had become. We were open with each other, but I was still unable to tell Jenny of my feelings for Stevie. I wanted to, but words failed me.

I was in a bind; I wanted my married life to work but clearly it wasn't going to. And I was in love with Stevie. I held out for the hope that something would happen, a lightning bolt to strike and show me the way down one path or the other.

In May 1978, we began work on the follow-up to *Rumours*, the album that became *Tusk*. The explosion of the punk movement had changed the musical landscape and the popular conception was that bands like ours, Led Zeppelin, the Stones, Elton John and everyone else from our era, were a bunch of dinosaurs who'd lost touch with the real world. That wasn't true, of course, we were in touch and aware of all those changes in culture, Lindsey most of all. He was intrigued by punk bands like the Clash and lots of New Wave artists such as Talking Heads and Laurie Anderson, and he wanted to follow that muse creatively. The issue for him was whether or not he was going to be able to do that with the rest of us.

The expectation, as far as our record company and the general public was concerned, was that we would continue in the *Rumours* groove, which was something we had perfected and obviously become quite comfortable with. The band would have been just fine carrying on as before, because together we are a creative enough group that we could have elaborated in that vein without running out of ideas. But that didn't happen on *Tusk*. There are songs which sound stylistically like the band who did *Rumours* and those are the songs we approached as a band. They are peppered, in a very conscious and deliberate way, with stuff that throws you off the scent, and those elements were created purely and exclusively by Lindsey.

Tusk was a bit less 'we' than any other record we've ever done because it was Lindsey's vision. Today the album has all the power, and has received all the kudos, that it deserves, which is what Lindsey wanted when we put it out, but that didn't happen at the time of release. The record was certainly not a failure, but neither was it the celebration of the quantum leap we felt we had taken.

Lindsey wanted to produce and record this record differently than we had the last two and I don't know if he thought I'd fight him on it, but I do know he was careful about approaching the subject with me. When he did, I was all for it, I thought it was a great idea. And what he may have not realised is that John and and I had been through a similar journey with Peter Green when we made *Then Play On*. When we began work on that record, Peter started playing six-string bass, so John didn't play on a couple of songs, and Peter did his timpani thing so I wasn't always doing percussion. On that album we suddenly went from being a blues band to a group with flutes and cellos all over the tracks. Lindsey saw us making the same degree, if not the same type, of musical departure. I was up for it, as was everyone, because we wanted to do for Lindsey as we had with Peter. We were happy to follow their lead out of a deep respect for their creative genius. He wanted to record a lot of things on his own at home and use much of those completed demos as was on the album. The rest of the band had to go through a slight education at first, because they weren't used to hearing tracks and being told that it wasn't me on drums, it was Lindsey banging on a Kleenex box. Once the die was cast, however, we were all on board and had lots of fun making the album.

I was still the acting manager of the band, though my days were numbered. By then the other members had got their own business managers and advisors, all of whom had opinions on how their money and our band money should be spent, which is why one of my last scatterbrained ideas as manager never came to be. I wanted us to invest in building our own studio and I even had a partner who would underwrite much of it. It would be done completely to our specifications, so we wouldn't have to waste time moving ourselves between a handful of locations over the months we typically spent recording. If we built a studio, it would be ours; we could own it and it would be our home for years to come. When we weren't using it, we could rent it out. My partner in this idea was Jordy Hormel, one of the heirs to the Hormel meat fortune. Jordy was a patron of the arts and a close friend of the band and he was willing to go into business with us to see this vision through. Jordy owned the building where the Village Recorder studios were housed, allowing us to gut a pre-existing studio and rebuild it.

Unfortunately my idea was not supported by the band. No

one else wanted to take on the responsibility of owning a recording studio, so in the end Jordy bankrolled a full renovation of Studio D down to every single one of our specifications, then rented it to us. It was completely taken down to the bones, then re-floated so that it was sonically balanced in every corner. We had our choice of wood, of sound panelling, and all of it still exists. When you walk into Studio D at the Village Recorder you are seeing the vision that Richard Dashut, Ken Calliat, Lindsey and I had. We designed the place blow for blow as if we were going to be partners, and Jordy, God bless him, is a true visionary who understood completely what we were doing, so he paid for it all. The irony is that if we'd gone into business with Jordy we would have saved money, as I predicted. We worked there for a year and a half, over which time we racked up bills that exceeded what our investment would have been. Not to mention the income stream we lost by not being partners in the studio; eventually it would have paid for itself and continued to earn for us.

I understood why I was being met with resistance – why build a studio to make an album? But I knew how we made albums and I knew that this one, with all that Lindsey was striving for, might take even longer than the last, which it did. Regardless, that place became our home base, and it is still special to us. In fact, we've returned to it for what I hope to be the next Fleetwood Mac album. As of the writing of this book, Lindsey, John, Christine and I have been laying down the foundations for that album in Studio D, and I can honestly say that it sounds even better than I remembered.

CHAPTER 14

JUST TELL ME THAT YOU WANT ME

Being back in Studio D again reminds me of the duality of *Tusk*. The album contains some of the greatest 'band moments' in our career, as far as I'm concerned; songs like 'Think About Me', 'Sara' and 'Sisters of the Moon' are as much our sound as anything on *Rumours*. When we worked through them, jamming until we figured out the arrangements and ultimately recorded them, it was the same process that we employed doing 'Oh Daddy' and so many other songs. There were just other pieces of music on the album that were approached very, very differently. It's been fun being back in that studio together, there are memories there that will never fade. There's a corner of the studio that makes me smile every time I walk by it, because I remember working with Lindsey, just the two of us, on 'What Makes You Think You're the One'. We set up my drums there and recorded them with a Sony boom-box so they'd be consumed by all that lo-fidelity compression.

At the time I was living in my house in Malibu, Chris had bought a beautiful mansion in Coldwater Canyon, while John split his time between his sailing-boat, which was moored in Marina Del Rey, and his home in Beverly Hills. Stevie had a home in Phoenix, as well as a gorgeous Tudor-style house above Sunset Boulevard. Lindsey had moved into a very nice house in which he'd installed the home studio that he used throughout the making of *Tusk*. He and Richard Dashut spent hours there listening to all of the great achievements in production, such as the Beach Boys' *Pet Sounds* and Phil Spector's Ronettes records, and they'd analyse how it was all done.

We broke from recording during the summer of 1978 to do a stadium tour, where we were supported by acts like the Little River Band, Steve Miller, and Bob Welch, whose album *French Kiss* was a huge hit that year. What should have been a triumphant run for us on all fronts was not, however, because my father died during that tour. We were in Philadelphia, when I got a call from my sister that the end was near and I flew directly to Washington DC, then boarded the Concorde to get to England as quickly as possible. I got there in time, thank God, and I saw my father on the last night he was alive. He was sedated but lucid and I'm so thankful that I was able to say goodbye. The next day I flew back and rejoined the band, despite being utterly destroyed by the loss.

At this point Jenny and our daughters were living in England, because we'd grown so far apart, and with me on tour, recording and being utterly entrenched in the band and my lifestyle, she didn't want our girls around me. The day they left me in California a few months earlier had been very hard.

I hugged my girls and I hugged Jenny.

'Take care of yourselves,' I said.

Jenny has told me that she was only an instant from staying. If I'd said, 'Please don't go,' she would have stayed and she would have tried. But I didn't, because we didn't know how to talk to each other. It's incredibly sad.

My girls waved to me out of the window of the car as they

pulled away. They didn't know quite what was happening, they just knew they were going to England. Jenny has told me that she did this to make a point; it wasn't that she wanted to be apart, but she hoped her absence would provide the impetus for me to take a look in the mirror and change my lifestyle. Quite the contrary; it only made it easier to spend time with Stevie. But I did miss my family when they left and I did want to do all that I could to make it work with Jenny.

So that summer when I visited England, I took Jenny on a trip to Ireland. We had a wonderful dinner in a Dublin restaurant, getting reacquainted as our daughters played under and around the table. It felt like we were a family once again. That's when I asked her to come back to California. It was another turn on the cycle of parting and coming back together. It seemed to me that the only way to get my family back was by a grand gesture that symbolised a new beginning. I wasn't self-aware enough at the time to realise that I was just repeating a familiar pattern, nor that my relationship with Jenny was still fundamentally the same, and therefore doomed to suffer the pitfalls of the past once more. I had very romantic notions about it all just working out.

'You don't have to live with me,' I said. 'I'll get you a house by the ocean. You'll be close enough that we can think about our future and figure it out together. You'll have space to do that on your own.'

'We can't live with you in your state, Mick. Not with the drinking and drugs.'

'I know and that's why I'm not asking you to. Please consider my request. I want my family back.'

'Yes,' she said. Jenny was willing to give us another chance.

We left our kids with family friends and spent the last few days of our holiday on our own, in a quaint, cold room above a rowdy pub. Ireland had worked its magic and it was like

Jenny and I had never been apart. Devoid of distractions, we were completely comfortable, joking and marvelling at the surroundings, taking in the world together the way we used to.

I got them a house in Little Ramirez Canyon in Malibu and after they'd settled into their new home, I had to come clean to Jenny. If we were going to stay together, I had to. By the time the night came round, I couldn't take it anymore. Jenny and I had been relatively sober together in Ireland, but the weight of what I had to reveal to her was too much to bear. I started drinking vodka, because that was all we had, and after a while I pulled out a packet of white powder, much to her dismay.

'How are you?' she asked.

'I'm fine,' I said. 'Lots going on.'

'What's going on?'

'The usual stuff. The next record, meetings with Warner Brothers, I've got to sort things out,' I said. I took a long drink from my glass.

'Well,' Jenny said, 'have you had any more thoughts on us? I guess we'll just take it as it comes?'

'Yes, Jenny,' I said, and took another drink. 'There's something I ought to tell you.'

Jenny slumped back on the sofa.

'I've been having an affair with Stevie for the past few months.'

Jenny told me that she didn't understand the words at first. She was in shock. Then once she took in the meaning of it all, she felt sick.

'How long has this been going on?' she asked. 'While we were in Ireland?'

She stared at me and I said nothing. She's told me since that a paralysing anger came over her. She wondered why she was even there and didn't understand how I could have neglected to mention it before deciding to move her back.

Jenny has told me that she felt so stupid, all she could do was search her memory for signs. She remembered that *Rolling Stone* cover we did, the one where the band was all in bed, and how Stevie was next to me and when I came home from the shoot, I told her, 'Stevie and I have known each other in another lifetime.'

Jenny stared at me, I stared at her. I'd come clean and that was all I could hold on to. Jenny was in a different place.

'Mick I'm tired,' she said. 'You need to go. I'm going up to bed.'

'Jenny, wait,' I said, taking hold of her arm. 'Don't do that yet.'

'Why not, Mick?'

'I'm confused,' I said. 'I don't know if I want to be with you or with Stevie.' It may be hard to understand, but I was torn. I was in love with Jenny and the family we shared, but I was also in love with Stevie. It's not logical but I was entirely of two hearts.

Jenny looked at me, stunned. 'Mick, are you staying here or going home? Choose one. You can sleep on the sofa. I'm going up to bed.'

I wasn't content with that, so I followed Jenny around, trying to get her to talk to me as I drank more vodka and dipped into my envelope of powder. There was nothing left to say but I spoke anyway, quite literally until both of us were exhausted. By the time the sun came up we both knew it was finally over. Jenny returned to England with the girls shortly thereafter – this time for good.

By early 1979, most of the songs for the album were in states of semi-completion, and we found that we had more than enough for a single album, so we decided to release it all as a double album. To us, the music was a break from what was expected, but releasing a double album was the type of grandiose, yet intimate gesture that was expected of us. The title track symbolises that message in every way.

The song 'Tusk' took quite a while to develop and it nearly didn't make it out of the studio. We used to call it 'the riff', because it was something we would play before shows in the few minutes we had in the dark as we were being announced, so that our sound man, Richard Dashut, could get his levels right. Lindsey had that riff and I would play softly along on the drums, with John on the bass, and that was the origins of what became 'Tusk'. The original refrain was something we'd play for less than a minute. But we did it the same way every night because we liked it, so we tried to make it into something more in the studio. Richard even created a loop of it to get the ball rolling, but nothing ever came of it. In the end, the inspiration that made 'Tusk' the song it is now came from a very unexpected place.

After my father's death, my sister Sally took my mother to Barfleur, a beautiful fishing village in the north of France that Mum always loved. We all missed Dad, and I was looking forward to joining them and spending time with Biddy; it was the first occasion I'd been able to do so since Dad's death. When I arrived off the long flight from Los Angeles to Paris, I was at the pinnacle of my rock star excess so, naturally, I hired a long white limo to drive me to this very small, quiet village. I'd had my share of drinks on the plane and continued to imbibe throughout the remainder of the journey, which is just shy of four hours. By the time I arrived, I was pretty well gone and I remember being taken by the full moon that night, and walking around taking Polaroids of everything.

When the exhaustion of the trip and all I'd had to drink hit me, it was quite late, so I went up to my bedroom to sleep. I drifted off for what felt like five minutes. Perhaps it was, because I was awoken early in the morning by a brass band playing directly under my window. I had a bracing hangover, so I was relieved when the band moved along and the sound of their horn section faded away. I'd just got back to sleep when, lo and behold, there they were again, before once more drifting off into the distance.

I slipped back into sleep, hoping that it was all some kind of jet-lag-fuelled bad dream, until I was woken up yet again by their return another thirty minutes later. I now realised that this band was very real and they weren't going away, in fact they were probably returning every half-hour, on the hour, until the end of time. Since I couldn't beat them, I did the only sensible thing and joined them.

I opened the shutters, winced at the light, and went out to the veranda. A few feet below me, I saw the entire village dancing in the streets. They were following the band. It was a festival for a local saint and everyone was involved in the party; generations of families, from the elderly in wheelchairs to the children, all of them dancing, the adults drinking Calvados and wine. The brass band was the Pied Piper that no one could resist. I was completely taken, and I was an outsider; I grabbed the remainder of my bottle of Beaujolais from the night before and went down to join in. We did loops round the town along the one main road for the rest of the morning. Each time we did a circuit, we gathered more people, until there was a proper Mardi Gras in the street.

That joyous, irresistible cacophony is what I heard when I listened to that loop of 'the riff'. I wanted to capture the energy, that sense of community, and the gala created by that band in Barfleur. I realised that brass was exactly the catalyst that would make 'the riff' a proper song. Beyond that, I saw greater possibilities. This needed scope, it had to be vast, and it needed a natural echo. It also required a sense of communal elation. Here is how I saw it: we needed a huge marching band and we needed them, and the song, in Dodger Stadium. Visualising even further, after we committed that to tape, I imagined us recreating it on tour every night via a local marching band in each city. My bandmates thought I had lost my mind when I shared my plan. They had no idea why I would want to take 'the riff' to that extreme, but they let me try.

Our dear friend Judy Wong knew someone who worked for Dodger Stadium and from that inroad we made plans to record 'the riff' with the USC Trojans marching band. We had 112 players playing it live in an empty stadium, capturing the loco-motive emotion of that piece of music in all its glory. We filmed it and it's all right there in the video we released for the track. My favourite quirk of it all is that John McVie wasn't present, but he was there. He'd recorded his part, so beautifully as always, and was done and gone. John is a perfec-tionist and in my opinion one of the greatest bass players alive. He's under-rated too, because he's English and humble and he'd never brag. I'm not joking; I've seen him come close to assaulting one of our producers for complimenting him on his playing to a degree that he deemed inappropriate. But I'm going to do it and he can come at me anytime he likes. John McVie is one of the elite. He's up there with the best of all time; he's one of the most sublime, gifted and nuanced bass players anyone could ever hope to hear. James Jamerson, John Paul Jones, John McVie – I can't think of anyone else who deserves to be in that class.

Because John is so good, he'd done all his parts on *Tusk*

and had made plans to sail his boat to Hawaii and then the South Pacific by the time we got round to filming in Dodger Stadium, so he was off and away. In his place, we had a life-sized cardboard cut-out of him, and Christine and I took turns walking him around and placing him wherever we went. I do wish John had been there that day, because we had so much fun. The marching band did their thing, Stevie did a baton performance, and it could not have been more over-the-top. It was musically and emotionally the absolute mirror of what we were doing and who we were.

Apart from the inspiration for *Tusk,* that Barfleur trip was also meaningful to me because I had dinner with my mother at a little restaurant on the harbour, just the two of us, and for the first time we spoke about my father, not just as Dad, but as the man he was. We talked about his life and about all that he accomplished, as well as the many things he bemoaned not doing. For the first time, I realised just how much I am like him in that way, and it wasn't an easy revelation.

I torture myself; in fact, in my mind, I'm still fighting things that I've claimed have long been put to bed. My father was like that. He didn't appreciate what he had done to the degree that he should have and he focused too much on what else he could have done. I've often felt that what I've done in Fleetwood Mac doesn't amount to much and that I could have done more. Along those lines of logic, I tell myself that I know I've played on the songs and I'm a part of them, but I didn't write them. I've woken up feeling as if I've done nothing compared to my musical compatriots. I don't have a song that I can point to. But in recent years I've realised that I do. All of it, everything I've done for the band, is the song.

*

In the end, $1.4 million later, we delivered our twenty-song master mix of *Tusk* to Warner Brothers, at which point they completely freaked out. Mo Ostin and the team told us flatly that we were insane to want to release a double album and from a business standpoint they were right; in the wake of punk, music fans had started spending less on records. High fidelity wasn't as important and swapping tapes, rather than buying records, was more in vogue. Warner Brothers weren't sure they could sell our album at a price high enough to recoup our advance and move the kind of units they wanted to sell.

I say this without hesitation; as a band we really didn't give a shit. Not at all. By then we had committed to our vision and the ensuing record and no one was going to change our minds. Our record company came up with a few advertising and marketing plans to try to draft *Tusk* into the existing Fleetwood Mac image and story, but none of them really worked. They had to accept that this was the record we had made and we were going to support, in the way we wanted to do it.

Tusk came out in September 1979 as a double album, priced at $16, which was very steep for the day. The label figured that we had to sell about 500,000 records to break even. In the end we sold four million, but not before *Tusk* was considered a commercial and critical failure. Keep in mind that any other band selling that many would have been considered a unanimous success, but given *Rumours'* sales were then into the double-digit millions and still climbing, four million seemed anaemic. Not to us; we were completely fine with it. Considering the artistic leap of faith involved, I saw it as a huge success.

Personally, I think we would have sold more if our record company hadn't agreed to let Westwood One radio broadcast our album in its entirety in England on the day of release. In my opinion, that allowed it to be recorded on cassette and duplicated – essentially it was avowed piracy long before digital media was even a spark in the eye. I can't be angry about it, because I know exactly what I would have done if I were a fan. Given that chance to capture the album for free, or go buy it the next day for well above the average price of a record, the choice is clear.

Tusk itself proved to be an album way ahead of its time. Most of the critics who panned it, and didn't understand it, have come back and admitted they were wrong, and a generation of musicians half our age single out that album as a defining inspiration, alongside albums like *Pet Sounds*. *Tusk* is unique and honest and singular of vision.

I know I've thrown kudos Lindsey's way every chance I get, because he deserves it and he needs to hear it. For years he didn't receive enough credit and I'm not talking necessarily about *Tusk*. I'm referring to all the work he did crafting Stevie's songs, watching her become this iconic creature within our play, as he remained the workhorse in the background, when he must have been thinking, Bloody hell, doesn't anyone realise who is *really* doing this? I know it was hard for him, continuing on that way after he and Stevie had split up, and he has bemoaned it in plenty of interviews over the years.

Lindsey had to wear two hats in the band and I, most of all, understood how hard that was because I did, too. Similarly, I often wondered if any of the others even noticed or understood what I'd had to do to get us to where we were and to keep us there. It was tough, because it felt inappropriate to admit that to them; I felt like a child craving attention, and though I was aware of this irrational need, that knowledge didn't make it go away. My unrewarded labour was more academic though, while Lindsey's was more creative, yet I always had empathy for his position because I felt myself to be in the same boat.

Tusk has become a legendary song and one that served to establish the sense of community that I hoped it would, though not in the way I originally planned. The marching band element has remained the connective tissue, however, because from time to time I have gone and marched with the USC Marching Band at the invite of Dr. Bartner, the musical director of the band. We also had the band there when we recorded the song for The Dance at our reunion show. But nothing was better than the first time we played *Tusk* – we did it live with them at the L.A. Forum and it was a spectacle. We were on the stage and we had the whole band up there with us, as the white horses that escort them onto the field at home games came galloping down the aisles. It was complete lunacy, with baton twirlers making their way through the audience and these gorgeous horses galloping in full stride. We'll be playing the newly renovated and reopened Forum on this upcoming tour I'd love to see the USC players join us there again, though I'd wager that recreating that original spectacle falls quite outside the rules and regulations of the freshly manicured facility.

We have good memories and a wonderful relationship with the USC Band, and that song of course, though I did nearly blow it completely. In 1998, Dr. Barnter asked me to come down and join the band, as I'd done before and I was happy to do so. USC was playing Notre Dame, which is a long standing rivalry and an annual college football tradition. And that day, completely oblivious, I showed up with a green sweater on, which is the team colour of Notre Dame, not USC. I was quickly informed but there was nothing I could do really, I had no other clothes with me. So off I went, leading the home team's band onto the field where we did a stirring rendition of *Tusk* while wearing the opposing team's colours. Lynn, who found the entire episode endlessly entertaining, told me recently that footage of this moment can be found on YouTube for those of you interested in seeing this gaff in all its glory.

The entire day was a comedy of errors, really. Like an inappropriate jester, I lead the band in the wrong colour, then figured things would turn around because Lynn, my manager Carl and his wife Erica and I were promised 'excellent seats' by Dr. Bartner. The other three had been seated while I did my thing, so after I was done, I left the field, escorted by someone from USC, excited to meet them and at least enjoy the game. Following this guy, I began climbing. And climbing. And climbing. And climbing. After a ten minute ascent, during which I was convinced I'd have a heart attack, I arrived at our seats, which were, and I'm not exaggerating at all, in the very top row of the L.A. Coliseum. That arena holds 100,000 people, was built for the 1984 Olympics and is one of the largest stadiums of its type in the country if not the world. I went from being on the field to being five thousand feet in the air, barely able to see it, piled in with the sold out masses. I sent Carl on a mission to procure better seats but it wasn't happening, there were literally none to be had. We all had to laugh, because I'm sure it wasn't intentional, but it felt like I'd been penalised for turning up in green. I've learned from my crime and have since struck Notre Dame green from my wardrobe altogether for fear of making that mistake again.

We set out on a year-long tour of North America, the Pacific and Europe in support of *Tusk*. We wanted to play in the Soviet Union, but that wasn't to be. That tour, in my opinion, was the very height of our touring at the top of excess. We had a team of karate experts as our security guards, a full-time Japanese masseuse, our catering was supplied by top-notch California chefs, and it usually went uneaten. We had our own airliner and we booked the best hotel suites around the world. We had rooms in those hotels repainted in advance of our arrival, specifically for Stevie and Christine. We had a huge cocaine budget and the usual fleet of limos waiting for us at every port of call. It was fabulously expensive, wonderful, and sometimes depraved. But in the end, it wasn't a good time because more than ever, our musical family was as distant from each other offstage as our music was intimate on stage. To be frank, that tour nearly killed the band.

When we set out, it was to a mixed bag of reviews. In England the song 'Tusk' went to the top of the charts, but not so in America and elsewhere. Our performances were great, because the music was, but at every turn the press asked us the hard questions: 'Are you breaking up after this album?' 'Is Stevie making a solo record?' 'Who is Sara?' And on and on they went. I played my role the best I could, as the spokesman, typically after a sleepless night or three.

We toured the album through until spring 1980, and our shows, especially by the end, were the best and worst anyone would ever see of Fleetwood Mac. By then we were dead tired, burned-out and just sick of it all, but doing our best. We would run the gamut from inspired to flaccid each night and we never knew quite which it was going to be until we got a few songs in. By the end of it, Stevie's voice was a ruin and Lindsey had pulled his back out so badly that he needed a spinal tap. During the last shows of that tour, Lindsey told our audiences that it would be a long time before we toured again. Boy, was he right.

CHAPTER 15

A STRANGER IN A
STRANGE LAND

The end of the *Tusk* tour was the end of an era. We needed a rest and some of us – Stevie and Lindsey mostly – needed a hiatus from the band in every way. Each of them had plans for solo projects intact by the end of the tour, and both agreed that they would return afterwards but they needed to chart their own course for a while. Regardless, I still worried that their forthcoming journeys would make it ever harder to get Fleetwood Mac rolling again.

My personal life had undergone a transformation during this period as well, and it was just the beginning. During the making of *Tusk* I'd started seeing Sara Recor, wife of Jim Recor, the manager of Loggins and Messina. Never in my life had I ever considered pursuing another man's wife, but that is how strong the attraction was between us. To make matters worse, Sara was also one of Stevie Nicks' very closest friends. In the hypothetical stage alone, this relationship was a complicated mess, even for me.

I knew it wasn't right, but I didn't care, and I confided in my dear friend Judy Wong. I was falling head over heels for Sara, and Judy, who was a little matchmaker and my white witch mentor all the years I knew her, went to bat for me and found out that it wasn't a closed door. Once I knew that, I couldn't help myself; I made my proverbial moves and that was that.

I was still living at my house in Bel Air when Sara and I started seeing each other. She didn't move in completely but she was there most of the time. That is when I ended the on-again, off-again relationship I had with Stevie. I wrote her a letter explaining what was happening, and knowing my grasp of written prose, I imagine it was horribly composed, which I'm sure made it all the more hurtful to a soul who feels the power of words as deeply as Stevie Nicks. As I learned later, that letter was more hurtful to her than I could have ever imagined. In truth, Stevie had been in and out of other relationships the entire time we were together, so I didn't realise that she was as emotionally involved as she was. In fact, I'd spent much of our ongoing affair feeling like I was more committed than she was, because after Jenny and I had parted for good, I hadn't been seeing anyone else but Stevie. So it surprised me that she was so hurt, but then again, she wasn't expecting me to take up with her best friend.

My love with Stevie was convenient; it was the perfect underground liason. We didn't have to reveal it to anyone, and though we never allowed it to evolve into a fully-realised, committed relationship, it was a true love affair. She and I joke about it to this day; there was tremendous passion. Then the game was called off. I wonder what would have happened if I had started seeing anyone other than Sara; I suppose I could have had my cake and eaten it too, the same way that Stevie did. She couldn't help but ask, 'Really? It had to be her?' Stevie wasn't wrong, but love is not a rational thing.

This was pretty out-there behaviour and I'm not proud of it, from being with Stevie while still trying to patch it up with

Jenny, to being apart from Jenny and only with Stevie, then taking up with Stevie's best friend. I still had so much guilt about carrying on with Stevie behind Jenny's back, leaving that poor girl pretty much in the dark, like Princess Diana, with me telling her I wanted to be married to her while I was seeing someone else. I'm not sure which decision of mine was worse, because what I stirred up by seeing Sara was a maelstrom. Stevie wouldn't talk to me and my other bandmates expressed their disapproval. Sara's friends completely cut her off and sided with her husband, so she was stuck with my circle, one of whom was the best friend she had betrayed. I'm not sure there could be a worse start to a relationship.

Sara, and this whole turn of events, was the inspiration for the Stevie Nicks song that bears her name. Stevie's original version was much longer, nearly sixteen minutes, and told more of the story. It's for Stevie to unmask the meanings and intentions behind all of the lyrics, but I do know that the 'great dark wing' mentioned in the song is a reference to me. That is what she and Sara thought my black Ferrari sounded like when it came up the drive to Stevie's house.

The end of the *Tusk* tour also officially marked the end of my time managing the band, because both Stevie and Lindsey had acquired their own managers, and both were vocal about how the band's affairs had been handled during our last year on the road, primarily that we didn't make enough money. It all came out during a meeting to recap the final leg, which was a European tour, and that occasion became an analysis of my entire term as band manager. It wasn't pretty, but there's no need to rehash it here in great detail. In retrospect, I think all of us agree that during my tenure I was more the indulgent father-figure than a hardline number-cruncher, though I must point out that I managed the band throughout our most successful era financially. In any case, it meant more to me to keep my bandmates happy and to keep us creating, to make sure we lived our dreams, even when I knew those dreams cost more than they should. When a team of accountants asked me why we didn't make more money on that tour, I asked them if they knew just how much it cost to find a hotel chain that allowed you to paint their suites pink, and have pianos present, waiting for our leading ladies, all across America. They just stared at me and I suppose they should have. The answer, since they needed to hear it, was that only posh hotels accommodated such singular requests and those requests cost money – lots of it.

Our expenses were massive on the *Tusk* tour and, as I've mentioned, when John Courage and I tried to cinch the belt and cut corners, we were met with uproarious complaints, so much so that we didn't dare keep that up. Being both band member and manager had its advantages, in that everyone felt comfortable talking to me about their feelings and their needs, making it easier to keep everyone happy. This was wonderful when it came to our creative direction, but in terms of the bottom line, it made it impossible for my bandmates to talk to me about money.

Going into the tour, we'd all committed to a vigorous number of dates to support a record we believed in, and that effort paid off. The *Tusk* double album reached number 4 in America and we sold five million records by the end of our run. That was nothing close to *Rumours* numbers, but we didn't expect that. *Tusk* was a difficult album, which is exactly why we took it to the streets, so to speak. We sold it live and clearly we connected. That bigger picture was lost on the number-crunchers and the lawyers brought in by some of the members at this point. The new parties saw only that as a manager, I should have ensured there was more in the band's bank accounts after that much time on the road. They also ignored that, for my efforts, I took only ten per cent of the net profits, post expenses and not off the gross profit, which is what every other manager takes typically. I received no piece of the publishing on our songs and yet I worked every day to further the band. So to me, that percentage seemed fair, and my bandmates had agreed all these years. But that changed and I suppose it was bound to, once we reached the level that we did. Since that day, we've been a band ruled by democratic committee, sometimes for better, sometimes for worse.

When the workings of the machine came up for review, after a decade of devotion, John Courage was released as the tour manager immediately, and I was released as manager shortly thereafter. I took that news hard because it felt like a rejection, despite my bandmates gathering round and assuring me that it wasn't. There would be no changing things, but that didn't matter, because there wasn't going to be a Fleetwood Mac to manage for quite some time.

That was one of a litany of problems that required my attention. I also had a tax issue with the IRS and I'd stretched myself thin financially buying properties in Los Angeles, as well as a massive farm in Australia that I discovered to be haunted, first-hand. The place had such otherworldly energy that I and others who visited the farm with me could barely stand to spend the night. I was forced to sell my house in Bel Air, the one I'd come to love so much, in order to become a resident of Monte Carlo, in Monaco. My business manager at the time assured me that this was the best way to avoid handing over the majority of my holdings to the United States government. The apartment I purchased was fine – nothing special – and I figured my mum would enjoy it during the months I was on tour. My plan was to split my time between Monte Carlo and Los Angeles, without being a US resident.

With Fleetwood Mac on break, I was keen to find something to do. This seemed the perfect time to fulfil a dream that I'd had for a few years. Back when Jenny and I had broken up, I had gone to Africa to be somewhere completely *other*, where I could be alone with my thoughts. While there, I took in so much, I felt so much and I smelled so much; Africa healed my soul, but I was in no state to do it justice. I was inspired, though, and I vowed to myself that if ever I had the means, I would return and delve into the rich musical culture I felt all around me, every single moment I was there. Now was the time to do so, and I set about planning to go there to play and record with the greatest drummers in the land and the best singers and players I could find. I wanted to bring what I found in Africa to the rest of the world.

In December 1980, my friend and lawyer, Mickey Shapiro, and I decided to fly to Ghana to sort out how to do it. On my way over there, I stopped off in England and stayed with Jenny in her cottage in Surrey. We had been in touch, of course, because of our daughters, and though I'd been living with Sara for a year or more, I missed Jenny, always. I even told Sara that there might be a time when I'd reconcile with Jenny and that she should be wary of that. I was at Jenny's house when we learned that John Lennon had been murdered and it threw the both of us. Jenny lay down and pretended it hadn't happened, and I wasn't far behind her. But it had happened and we were heartbroken. It inspired a walk down memory lane, as we recalled all the times we'd spent with George and the Beatles in our youth in an effort to comfort each other. The whole thing sent the two of us into yet another cycle of wanting to get back together again.

Our second divorce had just been finalised, but we didn't care. Being there, together in the cottage with our children, just felt right. One Sunday we went over to Jenny's mother's house for lunch and met up with her sister Pattie and her new husband Eric Clapton, as well as Jenny's brother Boo's very proper in-laws. After lunch and a good number of brandies, everyone gathered in the sitting room. Eric, who was well gone by then, sat on Jenny's mother's knee and started teasing her, his face right up against hers.

'Oh, Eric, don't be so silly,' she said.

'Come on, Mumsie,' he kept saying. He was doing it to test the stiff in-laws' limits.

I didn't think it was proper, so I grabbed him by the scruff of his neck and marched him out to the garden.

Later that evening, Jenny went home with our girls and I spent a few hours getting properly out of my mind with Eric and Pattie. By the time the night was over I was hopelessly jet lagged and drunk and got completely lost attempting to navigate the five minute drive home to Jenny's cottage. As close as it was I was far too spaced out to navigate the maze-like English country lanes, which quickly became a surrealist puzzle akin to an MC Escher sketch to my addled mind. I'd rented a beautiful Jaguar and I kept going round and round for hours, to the point that I noticed my fuel gauge tipping toward empty. I had no idea where Jenny's was and I no longer knew how to get back to where I'd just been, so at that point instinct kicked in and I did the only thing that made sense and headed to the nearest large town, Guildford, which was about 25 miles in the wrong direction.

My plan was to find a phone and call Jenny, get more petrol, and get myself home. The only problem was I realised I didn't know her number. When I rolled into town, there was just one hope for me, and that was appealing to the authorities. I found the local police station, and still completely off my head, went in and asked them to help me phone Jenny. It's nothing to be proud of but in those days I was able to keep up appearances when situations demanded it of me, and this night was probably my greatest performance. Legally the police couldn't give me Jenny's number, but they did let me use their phone, with which I called my mother, who was back home in the States, to ask her for a mutual friend's number in England who would know Jenny's number.

Finally I got Jenny on the line and she gave me extensive directions to get home. She said she'd wait up and in about half an hour she'd come outside so that I'd be sure not to miss her house. That was all fine and well, but by then my buzz was wearing off and I was in dire straits. I had no drugs to keep me up and my entire consciousness was getting fuzzy. To make matters worse, when I emerged from the Police Station I saw that an early morning fog had descended, cutting visibility in half. I felt myself unravelling and I wasn't sure I was going to make it. As I walked to the car I saw a guy on a motorcycle about to set off for work and I more or less cornered him.

"Listen," I said, handing him the address, "I need to get to this place and I can't make it on my own. Will you escort me? I'll give you 20 quid. I just don't think I'll find it."

He looked at me like I was crazy, which I certifiably was, but he was gracious and agreed to lead me all the way there. When we arrived I invited him in for tea and he declined, nor would he take the money.

"Not to worry," he said. "It was my pleasure."

I turned to see Jenny waiting there at the front door in her nightgown and that is when all the strength that remained in me left my body. I literally crawled up the walk to her and fell into her arms, exhausted. Honey, I'm home, indeed.

A day or so later, Mickey and I left for Ghana, because that was the pride of West Africa, being the first nation on the continent to achieve independence from its European sovereign nation. We figured Ghana would have it together but what we found was complete turmoil. There had recently been a coup that had been overturned. Civil rule had been reinstated a few weeks before we touched down, but that didn't mean much. The infrastructure was in shambles and nothing worked. Upon checking into our hotel, we learned that the elevators were broken and there was no telephone or telegram service, because the workers who ran those services had yet to be reinstated. There were no taxis or rental cars, and the American Embassy was only a non-existent concept.

We had one contact we could count on, an American drum scholar named Craig Woodson, who had been there for a while. Craig was intent on recording local drummers in order to map their rhythms into a computer program. Mickey and I were completely freaked out by the state of affairs, even more so when we discovered that Craig wasn't in Accra, the capital, where we were. He was up in the hill country, in Kumasi at a gathering of drummers.

'We're going, Mickey,' I said.

'Yeah?' he asked. 'Are you sure?'

'We're going.'

We found a local guy to drive us up to the town to find Craig. On the way there, we learned that he was a gold smuggler. We also learned the hard way that he was a very reckless driver. We didn't have far to go but the roads were horrible, which burst my bubble; I'd dreamed naively of taking a mobile studio to the various locales of the country in order to record musicians in their villages. That clearly wasn't happening.

We met up with Craig, who told us that the only way to make the record I had in mind was to work with Faisal Helwani, the kingpin of the music scene in Ghana. He had the only functioning, professional recording studio, as well as a night-club, a bordello, and a casino in Accra. Faisal was a character and he saw our project as an opportunity to work to his advantage, but in the end he came through. For a donation to the musicians' union, he got us all the musicians I wanted to record with and he made it happen.

We agreed to create a record with African and Western musicians playing together, accompanied by a concert and a film, that would be captured by a team of both African and Western engineers. Mickey and I put together a budget to fly over the necessary personnel and equipment and it came to about half a million dollars. Mo Ostin and Warner Brothers passed, but we heard that RCA was looking for content to fill out their emerging VideoDisc technology. The timing was right and so we secured a deal to finance *The Visitor*.

I hired Richard Dashut to record everything and he bought with two sixteen-track tape machines (one to serve as back-up if the other one broke), and hired a five-man crew of assistants. I asked Bob Welch to join me but he declined, so I invited my friend George Hawkins to come and play bass and sing, plus Todd Sharpe, who had been in Bob Welch's band, to play guitar. The three of us were the nucleus of a band that featured a rotating roster of Ghanaian pop and folk musicians.

Richard and I spent a night on my farm in Australia on our way to Africa. At that point I knew beyond the shadow of a doubt that I was going bankrupt and that this would be the last time I'd see that farm. And as if on cue, as Richard and I pulled away, the skies opened and the most horrific thunderstorm I'd ever seen nearly swallowed us alive.

I was very much in denial and defiance of the fact that my rockstar lifestyle was coming to an end, and was not happy to hear that my credit card had been cut off during our layover in Singapore. My accountant had told me it was going to happen, but still I wouldn't hear it. Richard and I got on the phone and somehow extended my credit line, with which we had a truly wild night that I topped off by buying myself a gold Rolex in the duty free shop at the airport. And with that, we were off to Ghana.

When we landed the band and crew had already been there for five days, and we'd been sending telegrams back and forth. Faisal, who was keen to impress us, met us at the airport. Knowing I had a taste for cocaine he had procured a few grams of medical grade stuff through his connections at a nearby hospital. It wasn't something he or the Ghanians did, but he knew it would please me and he couldn't wait to give it to me.

That night we had a proper welcoming party, and I sampled his wares, which were very, very pure. I was overcome by the generosity and the spirit of all the Ghanians around me and at the same time struck by how little they had yet how gracious they were. The reality of the excessive life I was living and all that I was running from back home hit me full force and in the moment, disgusted by myself, I smashed the gold Rolex I'd just bought on the bar. It made an impression on this gorgeous African girl who decided that she was going to come home with me for the night. She did come back to my hotel and in the wild spirit of the evening she decided that she wanted to be white like me, at least for the night. So we got a bag of flour and mixed it with water and covered her in it and she put on my top hat and paraded around the room. We didn't have sex but we did sleep together and as she wished, we went to bed, both of us white.

We spent seven weeks in early 1981, recording, throwing huge parties and having an extraordinary time. We procured a Mercedes bus and drove to musicians' homes to audition them and record the sessions for possible inclusion on the album. The entire country was in such dire straits financially that everyone asked us for money, most of all the bureaucracy we had to deal with at every turn. The people themselves were so kind and giving to us that it all worked out in the end.

The hotel we stayed in was more of a compound arranged by Faisal, who was a bit of a crook with his finger in every pie. It was very raw and rugged, which we learned quickly. Luckily we brought Jim Barnes an old rigging guy for Fleetwood Mac and ex Vietnam veteran who had seen just about everything in his lifetime. He and our guide at the hotel taught Richard and I to properly slice the throat of a goat and how to cut off the head of a chicken. They do, by the way, run around at top speed after you do it. It was dramatic to me, but it was just what the doctor ordered. I needed to get out of the lap of luxury and away from the rockstar life that had me used to someone waiting for me with an 8 ball on the runway wherever I went. On that note, Faisal, as much as he wanted to impress me, never could top that welcoming package. I did ask for more of course, and rather than tell me that he couldn't do it, he ended up bringing me a bag of what can only be called sugar powder that literally created frosting up your nose.

I learned so much during those seven weeks. I learned that all of the material things that had been so important in my life, particularly on that last Fleetwood Mac tour, meant nothing. I learned that I didn't need phones or paved roads to be happy – in fact, I needed very little to satisfy my soul on a daily basis. I needed music and food, energy and community. I managed to heal myself and mentally prepared for the financial troubles that I knew awaited me back home. I became sensible, and even kept that Rolex and got it repaired. I wore it for years afterwards, never forgetting how the huge dent in the back had gotten there. Years later that watch was stolen from me by a woman in a whorehouse in Amsterdam. I was so crushed because by then I'd grown so attached to it. Christine McVie heard me talking about how it had been stolen and the next day, without a word she gave me a new one. I have a feeling that she might not have if she knew exactly how I'd lost it.

I also learned a new universe of rhythm in Africa. I was born and raised on the 4/4 beats of blues and rock and roll. The Africans play in a twelve-beat style, one that is buoyed by constant improvisation; in a typical five-man drum circle, one, maybe two talking drums will improvise, while the rest play secondary beats on drums or bell instruments. I was only capable of playing support in that scenario and was happy to do it. By the end of my time there, I felt the spectrum of that rhythm in my soul.

African and rock rhythms intersect in funk, of course, and so most of what we recorded met happily on that common ground. We cut a new version of 'Rattlesnake Shake', with a children's drum ensemble backing us up, and along with a group called Adjo, we cut a few tracks including a cover of Buddy Holly's 'Not Fade Away', and 'Walk a Thin Line' from *Tusk*. The title track to the album was a collaboration with the Ghana Folkloric Group, who were capable of some of the most beautiful vocal harmonies I've ever heard.

We made an incredible album and we played a concert to two thousand people that went on all night long, to the point that I thought I might collapse from playing so long. Then we returned to England to mix it all. I wanted to use George Harrison's studio, but it wasn't available, so we used Jimmy Page's and decompressed from our African odyssey. George did contribute some guitar to 'Walk a Thin Line', however. I also got in touch with Peter Green, who was in great spirits, and convinced him to sing on the new version of 'Rattlesnake Shake', as well as a few other tracks. It was amazing to see Peter and to work with him again, however briefly. It was to be the last time I'd see him for years.

We ended up spending every bit of the half-million-dollar budget we'd been given and the album didn't earn back one cent. I didn't care, because I'd learned more about the world and myself than money could ever buy. My record company didn't feel quite the same way.

Back in England I'd reunited with Jenny once again. She threw a party for me; her brother Boo and his wife were there, as were Eric and Pattie and a few of Eric's friends, including a very charming, unassuming chap named Phil Collins. It was a great homecoming in true English style. A few nights later we went to a costume party at Pattie and Eric's, and Jenny and I dressed as schoolchildren, which was an honest reflection of who we really were to each other. I wore grey flannel shorts and a cap and Jenny was in a short skirt; we'd spent the entire day trying to find clothes to fit me.

Jenny has reminded me of Pattie and Eric's costumes. Pattie was Minnie Mouse, in a short red-and-white polka-dotted skirt with black stockings, and black gloves she held to her mouth as she giggled, and Eric was something else, in one of Pattie's see-through dresses with his Y-fronts showing underneath and short black socks and shoes. He had a sponge on his head, made to look like an old lady's tight perm, and he had lipstick spread across his face. Phil Collins had something equally daft on, wearing knee-length trousers, braces and a knotted hand-kerchief on his head. It was a great time and a warm welcome home. I loved being with my family, but it was all just for the moment – our happy time together was as joyous and as short-lived as putting on that costume for the party.

CHAPTER 16

ISN'T IT MIDNIGHT?

By this point, there was much media speculation about the state of Fleetwood Mac, mostly saying that we were through. But that couldn't have been further from the truth. In fact, after *The Visitor* was completed, it was time for me to meet the band in France to begin recording our next album. My bandmates were empathetic to my tax issues in America, and they'd agreed to record abroad so I could avoid the IRS coming after my earnings. We settled on a mansion in Herouville, about sixty miles from Paris, where Elton John had recorded *Honky Chateau*. The setting was beautiful, and in typical Fleetwood Mac fashion, we did everything top-notch, including redecorating the rooms occupied by the girls to their specifications.

We were back and ready to recreate the *Rumours* groove, which we did in a modernised style on the album that came to be called *Mirage*. Our writers showed up in France in 1981 with great material. Christine already had 'Hold Me', which became our first single. She'd written the song about her relationship with Dennis Wilson, which had ended a few months earlier. Chris had loved him with all her heart, but she couldn't keep up with him and couldn't make it work and she'd had to part from him, because it would have been the end of her if she hadn't.

Stevie had 'Gypsy', a song that she'd saved for us during the recording of her solo album *Belladonna*, which at that point had sold ten million records. That was one of her leftover tracks, and some leftover it was – it's a perfect portrait of the people we were at the dawn of the 1980s. It has a wise world-weary melancholy that's as poignant as anything off *Rumours*.

Lindsey had songs too: 'Can't Go Back' and 'Eyes of the World', and he quickly wrote 'Book of Love', 'Empire State' and 'Oh, Diane', shortly after arriving in France. He was different; he'd done what he'd needed to do on *Tusk* and was eager to get back to recording as a band, with the band. His new-wave stylings were gone as well, in fact his playing and approach was back to basics and called to mind his appreciation for early rock and rollers. For me, the return to the fold was invigorating to my very core.

We recorded everything as a band, much of it live, then spent the next seven months perfecting and overdubbing. That was our tried and true process. In the meantime I moved back to America, into a house in Ramirez Canyon in Malibu, with Sara. I dubbed the place the Blue Whale, because it had a huge pool and was something I'd fantasised about owning since the first time I laid eyes on it. It was just down the way from the little house I'd found for Jenny three years before and I had watched it being built at the time, complete with a guesthouse that I thought made it the perfect spot for entertaining friends. I wasn't even sure I could afford it, but my business manager said I could, and that was all the encouragement I needed when in pursuit of a dream. So I bought it and over the next few years turned it into a decadent playground that suitably reflected my life.

Mirage was a commercial, critical and artistic success; we had two huge hit singles in 'Hold Me' and 'Gypsy' and we quickly sold five million albums. The success of Stevie's solo career did much to boost our sales and the birth of MTV in 1981 didn't hurt us at all. If American fans had forgotten about us, or a new generation had never heard of us, a channel broadcasting our videos regularly twenty-four hours a day made up for lost time. Our album went to number 1 and, as it always was, it was good to be back.

This was the first time that the band did not tour extensively in support of our new material, however, and I can't say I was happy about it. Stevie's solo career was in full swing and she didn't want to commit to a marathon Fleetwood Mac tour while her star approached its apex. As a compromise, we did an eighteen-date run, centred by our headlining slots at two big outdoor dates, one of them being the historic US Festival. All in all, we toured *Mirage* for about a month.

I felt like a fish out of water when those dates ended. It wasn't that I felt more comfortable touring; I just had a very hard time accepting that my band's album was in the top of the charts and selling well but we weren't on the road. Without that effort on our part, *Mirage* died after just five weeks at number 1.

My bandmates were preoccupied with their solo projects, so I dived into my own. I had a deal for a few solo records with Warner Brothers, so I made my house a crashpad for all of my musician friends, with the intention that something would come out of it. The place became a rock-and-roll boarding house where ten people lived at any given time. Dave Mason of Traffic (and so many other bands) lived in my guesthouse for a while, and I recorded the album *I'm Not Me* in the Blue Whale. That record inspired what I came to call Mick Fleetwood's Zoo – a coalition of my friends that I took on tour throughout the next few years. The Zoo was George Hawkins on bass, Steve Ross on guitar, and Billy Burnette on vocals, with a few others coming in and out. It all began with the grand idea of going to Brazil as a follow-up to *The Visitor*. I bought a portable studio for that purpose but in the end used it to record at the Blue Whale. Both Christine and Lindsey played on the album, which was a mix of oldies, covers and new songs. I liked the final result a lot but it stiffed completely. I wasn't really sure what I was doing wrong, because the players and the music were great, we just weren't connecting with the record-buying public.

That didn't keep us from touring throughout America in the old-fashioned way, by bus, wearing tuxedos and sometimes playing bars. It was a lot of fun but it wasn't glamorous; we'd arrive to small, nearly empty rooms and often it felt like we were there just playing for ourselves. I didn't care, because living on the road in my comfort zone kept me from facing the cold hard facts of life. I was in dire straits financially, I wasn't doing my job as a father to my daughters, and the band that bore my name was in flux. I didn't worry if no one showed up to the Zoo shows, because in my mind if I was playing, I had a purpose. My band, however, was embarrassed for me.

Despite the severe change in scale, there were highlights. At one gig Stevie came down and did 'Rhiannon' to a dinner theatre, and after a radio station found out she was coming, three thousand people showed up, mobbing the streets. That was a rare show for the Zoo, however, so after those two albums, RCA released me from my contract. I'd earned nothing in sales so they'd earned nothing as well and as much as they liked me, I don't think they wanted to see me have another go. I didn't either, really.

*

By 1984 I had to file for bankruptcy for the second time and though I knew things weren't on the up, it still came as a surprise. I'd hired a young, eager business manager who had a 'live for now' strategy which of course was fine for me, but didn't seem to plan enough for the future. Then somehow it all fell apart. I was forced to sell the Blue Whale as well as all of my cars and my recording equipment. I lost Sara in the process: she moved out, broke it off with me and went back to work in the 'real world', because I couldn't support her. Meanwhile I moved into a house with Richard Dashut and laboured to put my life back in order. Thankfully no matter how dire things seemed, I was never in danger of being completely on the street. I was grateful to always have the royalty income stream from Fleetwood Mac to keep me afloat. That is essentially how I settled all of my financial problems. At first that left me little else to get by on, but eventually it caught up and the monies I received from record sales of the catalogue enabled me to be comfortable. Cosmetically most people never even realised that I'd gone broke, not once but twice, because the thing I'd devoted my life to developing had served to save me.

I continued to play gigs with the Zoo but all I cared about was getting Fleetwood Mac together again. The problem was that I was the only one eager to do so at the time. Stevie was enjoying a huge solo career and her second solo album *The Wild Heart* had sold into the millions. Lindsey was working on his third solo release and Christine had scored a hit with 'Got a Hold on Me'. Meanwhile John was relishing his semi-retirement, sailing his boat wherever he pleased and playing the occasional gig with John Mayall and the Bluesbreakers.

It all came down to me pushing the buttons again but my efforts to do so didn't work. In the end, Christine was the accidental catalyst. When her single did well, she called John

Courage out of retirement to assist her in making an album in Switzerland and also to manage her solo career. Christine had been asked to cover Elvis's 'Can't Help Falling in Love' for the film *A Fine Mess* and she wanted Richard Dashut to produce it. Richard knew how huge an Elvis fan Lindsey was, so he suggested that Christine ask him to play on it. Then John Courage asked John and me to play rhythm and so, in August 1985, all of us aside from Stevie found ourselves working on this song for Chris. We had fun, we really did. I don't think any of us, besides me, showed up thinking about making another Fleetwood Mac record, but once we were in the same room how couldn't we? That is how our next album, *Tango in the Night*, began.

Time apart had created distance, and the ways we used to come together were gone. Now there was a committee of lawyers and managers whose approval must be sought. Lindsey was deep into recording an album with Richard Dashut, so we thought it best to hire an outside producer to allow Linds to feel that he wouldn't be diverting his career for the band. We met with Nile Rodgers but that didn't work, then Mo Ostin sent us Jason Casaro, who had just produced a huge hit album for the Power Station, but after a week or so we realised that he wasn't right either. We needed to find our groove again, but an outsider wasn't going to get us there; only we could.

In the end Lindsey and Richard decided that they would produce the album themselves, because we weren't going to be happy with anyone else. It took eighteen months, which was in the ballpark of our typical recording schedule, but this time the working conditions were drastically different. We started out in a studio in the Valley but soon moved into the studio Lindsey had built in the garage of his house. That is where we mixed and did our overdubs, and truthfully, it was the nexus of where that album was made. It wasn't a proper studio by any means, but it was where Lindsey felt at home, and he was in charge. There were no lounges and secluded corners to hang out in, because Lindsey's house was his home, so John Courage brought in a trailer and parked it in the driveway, enabling us to carry on as usual without disturbing the peace. He had to, because I was still very much drinking and drugging and out of deference to Lindsey, needed a place to carry on.

That said, it was clear from the start that Lindsey had changed. He was all about the music and had no intention of tolerating any indulgent late nights. But it was more than that, the whole thing was a very different session for us. First of all it wasn't really a studio; it was Lindsey's home studio. There were a lot of drum machines and it was all a bit clinical and boring. I always hung around during recording so I spent a lot of time with Lindsey but more often than not I'd find myself holed up in that trailer in his driveway, waiting for drug dealers to pay me a visit. I'd go to work and be lonely because there was no partying going on, then I'd go back to Malibu and have these wild times with a collection of characters I'd befriended, from Gary Busey to Robin Williams to Nick Nolte. I found it ironic that my "day job" of being in a rock and roll band had become boring and my extracurricular socialising more exciting. It was a different experience. In the end I became a fly on the wall watching a brilliant mad scientist working in his laboratory, and that I really enjoyed.

It was fine once we all settled in, but it took the rest of us a while to adjust. John, for one, had barely played in the past two years, so it took him a short while to get his chops back. Christine gave us some of the best work she's ever done: 'Everywhere' and 'Little Lies', which became huge hit singles. Lindsey played his role as producer as well as he did band member, contributing 'Big Love', 'Caroline' and 'Tango in the Night' from his now-postponed solo album.

When we started recording, Stevie was on tour in support of her album *Rock a Little*, and in the summer of 1986 I joined her touring band, alongside heavy hitters such as Waddy Wachtel on guitar. I could see that she was working herself into the ground, between the drinking, the cocaine and her relentless schedule, and I worried for her health more than I ever had before. She had been walking a taut high wire for years and had always managed to keep from falling. But now she was in serious danger, and she knew it, too. After her tour wrapped up, Stevie checked herself into the Betty Ford Center and detoxed, and after that, she joined the rest of us in the studio in early 1987. Her nerves were understandably raw, and she felt distant from the proceedings, which in truth she was, because she'd barely been there during the creation of the album. But we worked it out and she managed to join the party just in time, contributing 'Seven Wonders' and 'Welcome to the Room, Sara', to the final cut.

Tango in the Night came out in the spring and jumped into the Top 10 on both sides of the Atlantic. In the UK it even reached number 1 and sold more than two million copies. The next logical step was to tour the record. Everyone was ready to go, except for Lindsey. He wanted to stay home and finish his solo record, which ostensibly would put an end to this cycle of Fleetwood Mac.

Like Stevie, Lindsey had disconnected himself from the Fleetwood Mac universe. He'd done a few solo albums and attained complete freedom in his creative process, devoid of the band politics that had drained him so. Success didn't matter to him, the independence to follow his muse did. It was entirely his choice to come back and do *Tango*, and looking back, it was a huge gesture for him; much bigger than any of us real-ised at the time. As he has told me in the last few years, recording that album was very painful for him. He wanted to do it for the band, for all of us, but it was hard.

I think midway through the process he had buyer's remorse once he realised that nothing had changed; particularly that Stevie and I had not changed with regard to our lifestyle. If anything we'd grown worse. But it was too late for Lindsey by then; he'd dipped his foot in and he'd committed to producing and performing on the album. By the end of it, though, the prospect of doing any more with us, no matter how proud he was of the music, was impossible for him. He considered being in the band a danger to his personal survival, because he'd changed his ways. It's daunting to me now to think about what he must have been going through, for him to walk away from us at that juncture. He didn't want to see Stevie and me destroying ourselves with substances and he didn't want to be dragged back into the drama of all that came with Fleetwood Mac. He told us quite directly that he just couldn't do it. We were all furious, of course, because by the time he let us know, we'd already booked a huge world tour and expected that he'd want to be a part of the great record we'd made together – a record that he'd produced in its entirety.

Tango was the first time Lindsey was truly at the helm as producer and performer, and celebrated as such by the rest of the band. As a guy who felt he'd not been given proper kudos for his efforts in the past, I expected him to be overjoyed. *Tango* is so entirely crafted by him, from the solo material that became many of the songs, to its pristine production. I expected Lindsey to view the album as his baby, so I never imagined that he would walk away without taking his work on the road.

I think Lindsey would have been happiest at that point if

we'd been like the latter-day Beatles, making albums and not touring, but that has never been who we are. I figured that if we called his bluff, he'd change his mind, but he didn't. We even gave him an ultimatum and that did not go down well at all; at a meeting, all of us, in no uncertain terms, told him that we were going on the road with or without him.

Historically that was not a happy day. Lindsey walked out of the band and was gone in no uncertain terms for thirteen years, longer than anyone seems to remember – including me.

In any case, Lindsey was gone, and I didn't expect him to change his mind and come back any time soon. Having said that, when he did come back, he came back completely and unconditionally. Today he has total commitment to what we are doing and in that respect I have a true partner in him. Everything he's doing and that we're doing together is about crafting the future of Fleetwood Mac, for however long it lasts. Lindsey feels that he spent his years apart from us doing what he had to do, making the music he had to make. He was never concerned with fame or money, he was on a journey of self-discovery. Pursuing that path was the only thing that enabled him to return to us eventually and to be truly happy doing it.

When Lindsey walked away, however, the rest of us were shocked. We had a great album in the charts and a fully-booked tour, so I had to think fast. Without hesitation I called Billy Burnette, who I'd worked with before, and Rick Vito, who is a great guitar player, and assured the rest of the band that we could pull it off. We went into rehearsals immediately and the two of them brought that tour to life. It was hugely successful. I can't speak for him but Lindsey must have felt like Brian Wilson of the Beach Boys, sitting at home while the great album he'd made was out there, being performed by the rest of his band.

Rick and Billy deserve a huge thank you for taking up that slack, because they had tall boots to fill. Rick doesn't play anything like Lindsey, but he and Billy together found a style that worked very well without stomping on Lindsey's toes. No one should try to pull off what Lindsey does; it's forbidden territory. The real stars, of course, were our two ladies; they carried the day and kept the spirit of Fleetwood Mac intact. Together we found a new incarnation and we had a happy, crazy tour – the crazy part of which Lindsey Buckingham would not have enjoyed at all. Billy was already my well-established drinking partner and I was still very much living that life. It was a hefty world tour, with a lot of highs. We played to ninety thousand people at Wembley and in that moment I completely forgot that Lindsey wasn't with us. We'd shared so many moments like that together, it was strange to walk out and take a bow and not have him within arm's reach.

CHAPTER 17

THERE AND BACK AGAIN

For most of that wild ride supporting *Tango* I was with Sara, which was a circus unto itself. There was a lot of passion in our relationship and we did love each other very much, but our lifestyle was like two intertwined rollercoasters. We would break up and get back together all the time and have these terrible rows. It was just substance abuse. When either of us was far gone and stretched thin, anything at all might start a fight, after which she or I would go off and disappear for three days and just crash wherever.

Aside from always thinking that I might reconcile with Jenny, to me it was never about other partners; it was Sara or no one, and I don't think there was much unfaithful behaviour on her part either. But eventually Sara did go and hook up with someone else, which happened at the end of the tour, and at that point I thought I'd lose my mind without her in my life. I was determined to try and get her back for good when I returned to California. I met up with John at a Fleetwood Mac band, crew, and family softball game, a day or two after we returned, and he told me that Sara was staying at his house up on Mulholland Drive with her new boyfriend, who was one of the techs on our crew. John spilled the beans because he felt bad about it. He knew we'd broken up, so it wasn't anything illicit, but he realised I still had feelings for her so he had to tell me.

The guy she was dating was someone Sara had known before she and I started seeing each other, so it wasn't completely random. In any case, I ran off the field, went straight to John's house and found them in the bedroom. A few minutes later, Sara came out in a robe and, right then and there, I asked her to marry me. She thought I was crazy, but she agreed to come home with me. It was a case of history repeating itself; the only way I saw to get her out of that relationship was to ask for her hand in marriage. I'd done the same with Jenny more than once to get her back.

Sara and I married in 1988 and divorced in 1995 and much the way it had gone with Jenny, marriage did nothing to change the way we got along. Our marriage was a bandage that couldn't bind the wound. If there is anyone in my life that I wish I could make amends to, it is Sara, but unfortunately it's too complicated because she's had a very hard time finding her way in life. I didn't support her as a partner in the way that I should have. We both had our issues with substance abuse, but Sara was drowning and I didn't take it seriously enough. I treated it like a joke, by which I mean I had no intention of changing my ways, even when she changed hers. Sara eventually sobered up on her own and I was proud of her for that, but I never shook off the guilt, because I felt that she got damaged on my watch.

Whatever role I'd played in her issues with substance abuse, I did my best to remedy things for her after we parted. My instinct is to try and fix situations that I've been a party to, and that is what I did for a good while, but it came to a point where I'd done all that I could, yet nothing was ever enough. Trying to make up for my inattention of the past with indulgence in the present veered into a narcissistic school of thought that assumed I was capable of changing someone else's life. No one can truly change our lives but ourselves.

There was even a period when my third wife, Lynn, had to take up the gauntlet for me and be a caretaker of sorts for Sara. I last spoke to Sara four years ago, and Lynn has spoken to her a few times when she has been in crisis, suffering from the same old demons, and that wasn't fair to Lynn either. Some doors close and must be kept closed – even if you don't feel good about it.

Fleetwood Mac without Lindsey obviously wasn't the same, but after the *Tango* tour we were on a roll, so we went into the studio to record *Behind the Mask,* the only album we did with Rick Vito and Billy Burnette. It wasn't hugely successful but the touring was great, because as a unit we pulled it off, thanks largely, of course, to our two leading ladies. Critics, such as those at *Q* magazine in Britain, praised the new music and line-up. We played more sold-out shows at Wembley, and when we ended our run of gigs in Los Angeles, Lindsey joined us on stage for a number. That was a nice moment of connection between us all but it was short-lived, because by that point, Stevie, Chris and Rick Vito had all let me know in no uncertain terms that this would be their last road show. Stevie planned to return to her solo career and Rick planned to launch his own, while Chris, whose father had died while we were on the road, wanted to retire from touring altogether. Both Chris and Stevie assured me that they would contribute to the band's future studio work, but neither would commit to the live dates that would inevitably follow.

Thus began a strange lost period of the band and I take full responsibility for it, because I refused to give up. In truth, my decision making was off; this is the one time I should not have soldiered on. It all started in 1993, when Presidential candidate Bill Clinton chose 'Don't Stop' as his campaign song, won the election, and requested that we, the 'original' members, play it at his Inaugural Ball. It was a request we were more than happy to oblige. Getting us all back on stage didn't spark a reunion as many, myself included, had thought it would, but it was inspiring enough for me to want to make new music. We came to call the resulting group 'the mini-Mac', featuring John and me, Chris, Billy Burnette, Bekka Bramlett and Dave Mason. The album we did is called *Time* and it was the first one since 1974 that did not feature a song from Stevie Nicks. It was also our least successful album commercially, and the only one since the early 1970s that didn't even chart in the US.

Time wasn't a bad album, but it was too unfamiliar for the fans and, to some degree, for us. I didn't take any of these possibilities into account before diving in. We ended up with a band of talented people playing good music, but they should not have been touring as Fleetwood Mac.

I was convinced that since Chris had agreed to record with us on *Time,* she'd rescind her vow not to tour and would join us. But just as Lindsey had done on *Tango,* Chris helped to the degree she could and then, for her own survival, she couldn't do one bit more. Our new group undertook a world tour in support of *Time* over five months in 1994 and another five months in 1995, playing on bills with Crosby, Stills and Nash, REO Speedwagon, and Pat Benatar. We took the opportunity to revisit Fleetwood Mac's 1960s catalogue and in Tokyo we even got the chance to have Jeremy Spencer join us on stage for a few songs. We toured all over the world and it was hard, because when we weren't a support band, or playing mini-festivals, we headlined at small venues.

We never should have done any of it. It was naive of me to do as I'd always done, to play on and immediately record an album and go back on the road, just because that is what had always kept the band alive in the past. There were too many essential pieces missing from the machine this time. We were a totally different band, with only the original drummer and bass player, and our original name. Had Christine remained, there would have been three of us and that would have been defensible.

I should have known my vision for this endeavour was flawed when it became clear that Dave Mason and Bekka Bramlett did not get along whatsoever. I thought they would, as Dave had worked a great deal with her parents, Delaney and Bonnie. Bekka had known Dave since she was a kid and I imagined there would be a real chemistry between them, because he had been around their house, probably singing songs with her parents as she looked on, like one big, happy, musical family. Apparently not. That tour was heavy on free-flowing substances of all kinds, which didn't help matters, but still, there was real bad blood between them. I was a wreck with drinking and carrying on, but as the tour wore on, I found myself having to play mediator for them almost every day. I'd completely misread what I thought would be a quaint and historically perfect collaboration. Bekka had no time for any kind of collective, connective, band-family stuff on the road at all, and like her mum, she did not mince words. Believe me, you don't want to have Bekka or Bonnie Bramlett unload on you, but that is what started happening to Mason regularly.

All along I'd thought Mason was the right choice for several reasons. He came from the same era and the same side of things as John and me, and he was also a friend, who had lived with me out in Malibu, and I saw this as an opportunity for him to get back in the saddle and put his career back on the map. None of that really worked out either. Dave is a happy-go-lucky character and it seemed to me that he didn't really care about any of those things at all.

So there I was, the captain of a failing band with a volatile personnel situation, and it just wasn't worth saving. I have to say that we did go out and put on a great show each night, regardless of the feuding and shouting matches. We did a lot of Dave's stuff in our set and a lot of R&B classics that Bekka was great at performing. But that really wasn't what the thousands of people who came out to see Fleetwood Mac were after. As fun as it was, it just wasn't right historically. In the end, everybody got a letter of disengagement, which probably wasn't much fun for them but I didn't know how else to pull the plug, so I just pulled it.

John and I weren't out of work for long. A few weeks after announcing that Fleetwood Mac had officially disbanded, we found ourselves working with Lindsey again, playing drums and bass on material that he was assembling for a solo album. In truth, I saw it as a new band that I would be forming with Lindsey. But before I knew it, Chris had joined us in the studio, and then Stevie, who wanted Lindsey to write with her on a song for the soundtrack to the film *Twister*. We were all in the same room, and without me even willing it. Once more a Lindsey Buckingham solo album had got our band back together. It felt good and the chemistry was very apparent. From there, my manager and long-time friend of the band, Carl Stubner, masterminded the reunion; he went out and got us a record deal and booked a tour. We decided to do a live recording of our greatest hits, plus a few new songs from each of our songwriters, and we recorded it all on a sound stage at Warner Brothers. The album became *The Dance*, which was our first major chart-topping record in fifteen years and the first that line-up had done together as a unit since *Tango* in 1987. It debuted at number 1 in the States in August of 1997, and spent seven months in the Top 40, selling over five million albums. The timing was right; it came just as *Rumours* turned twenty, and we embarked on a forty-four-date tour.

At the end of the tour, however, Christine left for good. She wanted to return to England and retire from music and the band altogether. Throughout the tour we knew this was going to happen, but refused to admit it, because it was so great to be back together and on top of the world. We hoped that she'd change her mind and I kept telling her not to be hasty about her decision. One night toward the end of the tour, one of the last chances I'd be able to spend time with her alone, I went to her hotel suite and I realised just how much her mind was made up. Before I could even steer the conversation towards asking her if she'd reconsider, Christine stopped me cold.

'Mick, don't ask me,' she said. 'Please . . . don't ask me.'

Christine knows me extremely well, like a sister does a brother. With those few words I knew that she was gone and done with Fleetwood Mac.

'Chris, I promise you,' I said. 'I will not give you the speech and I will never ask you again. You have my word.'

And I never did.

In fact, during that tour, and especially in the years that followed, the one who most pursued Chris about returning was Lindsey Buckingham. He is a very up-front guy and all those years when I'd be trying to convince someone to do one thing or another, he'd always tell me I was out of my mind. Then, when I would make it happen, he'd just shake his head and say, 'I don't know how you do that stuff!' But we experienced an unusual role reversal on that tour because Lindsey became the one serenading Chris, right up until the end; he'd take limo rides with her and try to win her over, long after I'd stopped. To his credit, he never lost faith.

'I think she's going to change her mind, Mick.'

There was me, playing his part. 'You're dreaming, Linds, she's made up her mind.'

He believed there was a chance, up until the moment when she left after the last date of the tour. He wanted to believe, because his relationship with Chris is stronger creatively than people realise. Lindsey can do his own thing, but Chris is a huge anchor and inspiration for him; she is his true musical partner in the band. Lindsey had never been in the band without Chris – and he didn't want to be, if he could help it.

We carried on without her and recorded *Say You Will*, which was a definite seismic shift in the group dynamic when it came to recording and songwriting, because of her absence. Chris did stay in touch during the making of that record and there were times when it was clear to us that she missed being in the band. She spoke to me and to Lindsey, and I believe she made a few phone calls to Stevie as well, during all of which she alluded that she might like to contribute to the album. I always pictured her sitting at home in England, sipping a glass of wine, wondering whether she'd like to write a few songs and record. That, however, would be opening a major can of worms and the rest of us knew it. If she wrote songs, then she would have to rejoin the band and really do it, because at that point we were halfway toward re-establishing ourselves without her.

After one of those calls from her, I'd always tell Lindsey: 'I got another call from Chris, have you? She's called me a few times, throwing around the possibility of writing for us.'

Stevie and I at
the premiere of
Twister, 1996.

Blues Brother: With Dan
Ackroyd at the Rolling
Stone covers party, 1998.

Rock and Roll Hall of
Fame Induction at the
Waldorf Astoria, New
York City, 1998.

At Bill Clinton's farewell
party at the White
House, 2001.

Amelia, me, Lynn and Lucy about
to board the tour plane, 2003.

With Bill Wyman at a sale of Beatles
memorabilia in 2001 at Wyman's
Sticky Fingers restaurant, London.

With Stevie on our plane during
the Say You Will tour, 2003.

My close friend and manager
Carl Stubner and I at the
Phoenician in Scottsdale,
Arizona on the Say You Will
tour, 2003.

Stevie, Lindsey, me and John,
Australia, 2004.

A visit from Peter Green. At
Wembley Arena, 2003.

My car Lettuce Leaf beside a Spitfire at Goodwood
Racetrack, Chichester, England.

Madison Square
Garden, 2009.

Tessa and Ruby and Lynn getting up
close and personal with a wombat
during an off day on the Fleetwood
Mac Unleashed tour in November, 2009.

My girls Ruby and Tessa and I
say goodnight to the audience
in New Zealand, 2009.

With Tessa and Ruby backstage
in Chicago, 2009.

Pattie Boyd and I standing before a picture of she and George at an art exhibit in Sydney, 2009.

With Jenny Boyd at her book launch in London, 2013.

Playing the talking drum at a fundraiser for Japanese tsunami victims in 2011.

With my daughter Lucy at a benefit for Haiti in Los Angeles in 2010.

Lynn and I playing with our daughters Ruby and Tessa in Lanai, May 2010.

There's nothing like sunset on Maui, the island I call home.

My co-author Anthony and I donning a pair of my bowler hats during a stroll on my farm in Maui, 2013.

With the girls of Fleetwood
Mac at the premiere of
Stevie's documentary In
Your Dreams, London, 2013.
Chris hadn't agreed to
re-join us at this point.

With my girlfriend Chelsea Hill
in Sardinia, 2013.

Fleetwood Mac, 2014.

Step into my office!

'Well, she's not. She's gone,' Lindsey would say, without hesitation.

All the same, I know that Lindsey started to believe that Chris might return, particularly during the early stages of recording *Say You Will*. He and I disagreed completely on this, however; I knew how serious Chris was about the change in her lifestyle that departing the band represented to her, while Lindsey thought that she wasn't serious and it was just a momentary phase. In the end, I was right.

Lindsey has taken responsibility for *Say You Will*, in the sense that he brought to the studio a lot of musical ideas and pieces that he had already developed at home. This harkened back to the *Tusk* days, and his self-sufficiency proved to be a bigger problem for Stevie than he could have imagined. It made her feel apart and a bit of an outsider when it came to writing. As the only other songwriter in the band, Stevie had thought she and Lindsey were going to have a new and closer creative partnership. But instead, she felt separated from the proceedings, and that was not good. In retrospect, Lindsey has said that he brought in too much of a preconceived vision and if given the chance, he'd not do that again, because it alienated her. Although Stevie never felt a part of the process during that album, at the end she did jump in and write a bunch of cool songs. But for the first time, she felt alone while doing it.

Lindsey now knows that his creative relationship and his friendship with Stevie have to be balanced just right, and to do that, their bond has to be approached delicately. It wasn't as right as it could have been during that record. Considering that it was our first album without Chris, the misfiring of their creative union could have derailed things completely. To his credit, though, Lindsey had a vision for the direction he saw the band going in without Chris, and to explain it further, there is a fever pitch to how Lindsey works, especially when he knows what he wants to do. I think the reality is that he wasn't taking over and imposing his vision, as much as Stevie thought; I think he was holding out in the hope that Chris was coming back. If she had, what he was doing would have been the perfect template for the band to resume in the way we were used to. Once the writing was on the wall, however, he made the necessary adjustments and he and Stevie did their thing and did it well.

We released *Say You Will* in 2003 and it set the musical precedent for us for the next ten years. Lindsey and Stevie handled the lead vocals, and after that first outing, they found their stride fronting the band and writing the songs. Lindsey began writing differently than he had in the past; he would bring us and Stevie demos that were spare ideas, recorded simply, allowing plenty of space for all of us to contribute. It also left room for a new story to be created between the two of them, or an old one to be picked up again.

Lindsey's vision for Fleetwood Mac without Christine became fully realised in the decade after *Say You Will*. He and Stevie have been able to resume where Buckingham Nicks left off, and in some ways revive what was subsumed by Fleetwood Mac. Without Chris in the band, their performance style changed, and their vocal harmonies grew closer to how they were in their early days together. I think the *Extended Play* EP and our 2013 tour showcased just how much the band has grown into that groove, which has been a wonderful connective bridge for Stevie and Lindsey to explore. That is one of the reasons why we opened our 2013 shows with 'Second Hand News', a song that has come in and out of our sets through the years. It was written with Chris, but the subject matter is very much Lindsey and Stevie. Beginning the show with it set the tone, because the concerts we played on that tour were very much a celebration of Stevie and Lindsey, and the tremendous musical and personal journey they've undertaken within this band.

New versions of songs like 'Second Hand News' and 'Without You', an old Buckingham Nicks demo on the EP, have had the effect of getting Stevie and Lindsey out front and centre, literally and symbolically in every way. It has been a proper revisiting of their dual vocal style, and Lindsey in particular has been exploring this return in the past ten years. He wrote a number of songs for the EP that didn't make the final cut, but all of them were designed with Stevie in mind; to sing on, to put words to – all of them expressly for her. Of the songs that did make the EP, the most poignant of his, 'It Takes Time', was a homecoming to their story because it's entirely an apology to her, which is beautiful and heartbreaking.

Overall, the last few years have been a wonderful return to form. I was hoping that we would take this new approach even further on the last tour, and have Stevie and Lindsey do songs together that Chris used to do on her own, and reinterpret them through the lens of Buckingham Nicks. We used to try and do that but the efforts always got dumped. I understood why; Lindsey and Stevie felt they were trespassing in Christine's world. Had we pushed, they would have found a way to bring them together, but that didn't happen. I've even thought about what it would be like if they sang songs together that they usually sing alone – imagine Lindsey joining Stevie for 'Landslide' or Stevie coming out when he plays 'Big Love'? If that ever happens it will be one for the books.

I'll consider that my version of 'producing' a Fleetwood Mac track all by myself.

CHAPTER 18

⟨◈⟩

MY PARTNER, MY FRIEND

Things have been coming together and coming apart for me lately. Here in the twilight of my sixties, I feel I've learned so much, and yet I still have so much to learn. I've taught myself to undo some bad habits and I've begun to see recurring patterns in my life that need to be addressed. It's been a time of flux, because just as my musical family is finally reuniting, the nuclear family I've known and cherished for the past twenty-three years is coming apart.

As of this writing, my third wife, Lynn, and I are going through a divorce. Lynn is a wonderful woman, and the mother of our gorgeous twin girls, Ruby and Tessa, twelve. It was a long time coming, I suppose, and in that way it's all the more heartbreaking, because neither of us did anything wrong other than grow apart.

Lynn and I met in August 1989 in Los Angeles, through our mutual friends, Colin and Jill Stone; he was a friend and a Fleetwood Mac roadie, dating back to the 1960s, and Lynn knew Colin's wife on her own. Lynn was invited down to the studio by Colin and Jill while we were recording *Behind the Mask*, but she didn't go, because, as she told me later, she wasn't a big fan. She owned *Rumours*, and she knew who Stevie Nicks was, but the rest of us were a mystery to her. A few days later, Colin and Jill brought her round to my house to hang out. Sara was out because by then we were heading toward divorce and had begun living in separate bedrooms.

It wasn't a set-up, it was just friends coming for a visit, but I was taken with Lynn immediately. As she reminded me when I asked her about it while writing this book, I spent the entire afternoon more or less staring at her, which everyone else present noticed, to the point that it became quite creepy. We hung out for a bit and then went to lunch at Carlos and Charlie's in Malibu and we ended up sitting next to each other. As Lynn has told me, she noticed how I kept getting up to use the bathroom and powder my nose. Guilty as charged.

Lynn was working in PR at New World Pictures at the time and I recall it taking a few days after that lunch for me to get in touch with her, because her boss's son had died tragically in a car accident. When I spoke to her next she sounded exhausted and distraught, so I suggested that we spend some time together, if only to take her mind off things. At the time, she lived about five minutes from the studio, so I dropped by later that day. She has said I was drunk and showed up with a water bottle filled with some kind of alcoholic beverage. It was probably something mixed with brandy, which was my drink of choice at the time, that I called 'beef' as in 'Where's the beef?'

Lynn and I just hung out that afternoon, holding hands and talking, and I felt very close to her immediately. I spent my dinner break from recording with her and comforting her, and when I left I wanted to see her again. She felt the same way, and so began what became a beautiful friendship, because she is the type of woman who loves to understand what makes people tick and I presented her with quite the study, apparently. I began to visit her several times a week during our daily dinner breaks and after we were done recording for the night. I'd go over and get into bed with Lynn but nothing happened between us. We would just lie there together, watching David Letterman, talking and sharing things about ourselves, and then I'd go home. It was the start of a deeply emotional connection.

Lynn had ended an unfulfilling relationship and was still hurt, and I was going through my break-up with Sara. We were there for each other and we became great friends, who were clearly attracted to each other but didn't have any kind of intimate relationship for a few months. It was all very tender and sweet. There were a few hiccups along the road, because I was still married and understandably Lynn had misgivings about getting involved, but after we parted for a time, we missed each other. So we came back together and at that point we were intimate. After a while, when Lynn didn't see my divorce from Sara proceeding, she told me she had to protect herself and needed to stop seeing me. She was falling for me and understandably didn't want to be the other woman. She said quite simply that I had to figure it all out with Sara and if it didn't work, then I should call her.

I stayed in touch with her during the first months of the *Behind the Mask* tour, which began in Australia in March 1990, but I didn't see her in person, because essentially Lynn was a secret. Sara and I had separated but we hadn't divorced, and although everyone knew it was coming, it was still too soon for me to be seen with Lynn publicly. I did spend thousands of dollars in phone bills calling Lynn from all over the world, however, and between the various legs of that tour we spent every moment together, almost entirely in her apartment in Westwood. That became our lovely little bubble. When I was gearing up to go back on the road after the holidays that year, there was a great sadness, because it seemed like the distance might be the end of us, but in our case it only made our hearts grow fonder. We'd stay on the phone endlessly, sometimes for ten hours at a stretch.

By the time the *Behind the Mask* tour returned to the US towards the end of 1990, Lynn and I were very much in love and so I brought her out on the road with me. It all had to be done in secret, with her in a different hotel room checked in under the name Justin Case, since we had that extra room, 'just in case'. Billy and Rick Vito knew about her, as did John Courage and the other lads, but the girls didn't know a thing. Though Lynn had to hide, sitting in a seat in the audience at the show, or at the soundboard, we did have fun and I think she enjoyed her first experience touring with a rock-and-roll band. We usually had Lynn arrive at the next city before the band, checking in early so she could relax and avoid being seen by the others, then when I arrived with the band she'd come down to my room. It was definitely tumultuous, because I was still carrying on with my old habits and Lynn didn't drink alcohol; in fact, she didn't partake in booze or anything else during the whole of our marriage. During that tour, on a stop in Phoenix, we were staying in a beautiful suite with a balcony. It had been about a year since I'd met Lynn and we were sitting there sunning ourselves, listening to George Harrison's *Cloud Nine* album, and I looked at her and started to cry.

'Mick, what's wrong?' she asked.

'Nothing at all is wrong,' I said. 'I love you, Lynn. That's all.'

Eventually, at the end of 1990, Sara served me with divorce papers. She'd gone to the Betty Ford Center and got sober and she remained so for a really long time. I did not get sober and

I wasn't very respectful of it, which made it truly impossible for her to stay with me. So I moved out of the house and into the Malibu Inn and for a few weeks I didn't talk to Lynn, because I wanted to be sure of how I felt about her, about Sara, and about all of it, now that I was off the road and back into reality with divorce papers in hand. It was hard on Lynn because I simply disappeared. But afterwards, we were free to take up with each other openly and starting in 1991, we were never apart from then on.

Lynn still had her place in Westwood and we lived there together for quite a while. Things were great, but my drinking was becoming a problem. Lynn never gave me an ultimatum, and she wasn't judgmental, she just didn't drink because she didn't like the taste. She'd tried it, of course, and had experimented with drugs and still took the occasional pill here and there, but drink wasn't for her. So she never came from a high and mighty position about it, but obviously she enjoyed me better when I wasn't blind drunk. The thing about Lynn is that she could keep up with people drinking and carrying on and be right there with them the whole night through.

When Lynn hung around with our lot, partying well into the night, I think our lunacy rubbed off on her and swept her up with us. She didn't have to be drunk to throw caution to the wind and she didn't have to do a pile of blow to stay up all night and party. She pulled it out of herself, or absorbed it from the people around us, and I found it astounding and wonderful. It was perfect for me; I never had to worry about her, she was up for anything and she looked after me. I couldn't have been luckier.

Lynn did, however worry about my health and she should have because by April 1992, even I realised I'd been going at it a bit too hard for too long. It had got really bad; I'd bloated up, I didn't look well and I'd begun to embarrass myself. This was after my work with the Zoo, who were a hard drinking lot. So I decided to quit alcohol altogether. Lynn booked us a vacation that we agreed would be my time to kick the booze and just be with her and straighten out a bit.

But old habits die hard and at the last minute I told her I was going on that trip with Billy Thorpe, the great Australian singer-songwriter who had played with me in the Zoo instead and that I still intended to get healthy. To Lynn's dismay Billy and I went to Maui and did anything but that. Eventually I patched it up with Lynn and flew her down, promising that we'd have the trip we talked about. It was her first time in Hawaii and she was really excited about it. But I didn't exactly get round to curbing my drinking.

It wasn't an easy trip for Lynn: Billy was sore that my girl-friend had showed up and ruined our boys trip, and while she was there we went to see Bob Dylan and ran into my ex-wife Jenny backstage, who was uncharacteristically rude to Lynn. Like many others, Jenny was wondering what the hell a young girl like Lynn, who was 26, was after with a guy like me, who was 43. For the record the two of them are great friends today.

I definitely smoothed it all over with wine, to the point that Lynn decided it was time for her to go. She said that she couldn't see me do this to myself and it made her too sad to be a party to it. But we still proceeded to have a lovely last night together in our room, just having silly fun, with her doing stuff like drawing little faces on my toes.

As the night drew to a close, I told her not to go.

'Lynn, I'm going to need to spend the day in bed tomorrow,' I said. 'I'm going to be sick, I'm going to be hungover and I'm going to need to repair myself. But I will wake up after that and I won't drink. Please, please don't go.'

Truthfully, the threat of losing Lynn wasn't my only motivation to clean up my act. For the first time in my life, I was worried. It was easy to see how I'd deteriorated and that I wasn't invincible. I was also shaken by the fact that my sister Susan had been diagnosed with cancer. It was time to put things in line.

'Mick, I'll stay,' she said, sceptically. 'I'll wait and see how it is when you wake up.'

I stayed true to my word. I slept the day away and when I woke up I didn't have another drink for a decade.

From the start, Lynn and I were the best of friends, and she was every bit my co-pilot on a series of unbelievable adventures; from the time we began to be officially together, through to the end of our marriage. That aspect never changed: Lynn was always ready, bag packed, to go wherever fate – or me – might take us. And good thing she did, because starting in the early 1990s my life away from Fleetwood Mac became very interesting, indeed.

After I'd been relieved of managing the band, I strove to flex my flair for entrepreneurship in other areas, because I've always had a interest in business and the possibilities it presented me. This lead me to open a restaurant and music venue called Fleetwood's L.A. Blues in Los Angeles on Sweetzer and Santa Monica in 1991. It was a gorgeous restaurant and more or less the blueprint for the House of Blues which opened its first location just a year later. Along with my business manager and close friend Joe McNulty, my partners and I raised millions to open this fabulous place. One small problem was that my partners, unbeknownst to me, happened to be connected to the Gambino crime family. They were descendants and weren't directly linked to any illegal activity, but they were close enough to the action that I was summoned to a hearing by the FBI to let me know exactly who they were and that they were under investigation. The FBI also let me know in no uncertain terms that because of them, our business would never be granted a liquor license. We had been operating under a catering license, which I thought was odd, until I suddenly found out why.

It was too late by then because we had already opened and every night we kept telling people that we'd be getting our liquor license any day now. We'd started out with a bang, too. We had all manner of musicians and celebrities in attendance; John Lee Hooker was there, arriving in a huge Cadillac with two gorgeous women on his arm. My blues band played and the party was quite a sensation. We had the recipe for success; we'd built this incredible restaurant and performance space, our chef was top notch and we got rave reviews from the LA Times, but without the ability to serve alcohol, there was no way the place was going to survive. It was all of the stuff I'd dreamt of in one perfect venue, but it was doomed to die on the vine. It ended up closing just a few months later which was a huge disappointment to me.

During the time it was open, I met Christopher Rocancourt, a conman who went by the name of Christopher de Laurentiis, Christopher de la Renta and many other fake names in his day. If he were speaking with Hollywood or music industry people he'd claim to be the son or nephew of famed film producer Dino De Laurentiis, if he were speaking with fashion industry people he would claim to be the nephew of famed designer Oscar de la Renta, and eventually when he fled to the East Coast and began to swindle socialites, old monied families and Wall Street financiers, he referred to himself as Christopher Rockefeller, claiming to be an heir to the most powerful family of industrial, political and banking magnates in American history. When I heard about that I found it hilarious that none of those people who believed him to be a Rockefeller ever questioned the fact that he was French and spoke with a thick French accent.

By the time I met him, when he was in his twenties, Christopher was already a successful lifelong conman. From what I understand he had made over a million by forging the deed to a building and then selling it to someone illegally in France. He then came to the United States where he used that money and dozens of aliases to create a mirage to swindle countless people out of a tremendous amount of money, before he was caught and thrown in jail.

He would convince rich people to invest with him, promising them a quick return and double their investment, by spending tons of money on lavish dinners and cocktail parties for them. He always paid in cash, was very likable and charming and was always very well appointed so everyone believed the lie.

We met him at the restaurant, and soon he was serenading my parters and I, saying he wanted to buy the place and save it so that we could get our liquor license under a new corporate entity. He was residing at the Beverly Wilshire Hotel in the most unbelievable suite and was driven around in a succession of Rolls Royce limousines. Whenever we would go by the hotel to see him, we'd find him entertaining all manner of high profile actors and directors at the bar, having meetings about various projects of theirs he was interested in producing. My partners and I got completely stung – we even asked after him with the maitre d' and manager of the hotel all of whom verified that he was Dino de Laurentiis' son. After that we never questioned him.

Eventually it all came out but to the end, the guy always had a story. At the time I wasn't very well off, after my divorce from Sara and two bankruptcies, so I wanted to believe all that he promised me. Christopher would tell me, 'Mickey, you're going to have everything you want. You'll have a big apartment. I have one on Wilshire Boulevard – you can live there until you can buy your own.'

He took me down there in his big Rolls Royce to show me the place, and it was gorgeous, so I told him that Lynn and I would love to move in. I even met the people who were moving out of the apartment, but of course nothing ever came of it.

The entire time, until Christopher fled LA for the East Coast, I was schmoozing him, believing that he was going to save the restaurant and my financial situation as well. He and I became friends and spent a lot of time together, going shopping and having dinner and as you do when you want to woo someone in business, I picked up the tab more often than not, to show him my good intentions. This of course was all part of his plan and how he got things from people. One day we were out in a shop and I saw that he loved this eel skin briefcase and so to gain good favor I bought it for him. The amount of money he was planning to put in the restaurant was massive, so this was a trifle – although for me at the time, it was an issue. I could hardly afford to be buying eel skin briefcases at the drop of a hat but anything he wanted I got for him.

I also ended up paying for a trip to Austin, Texas that he and Joe and I took, ostensibly to scout locations for a second branch of Fleetwood's once he bought it. When we got down there he had a helicopter on stand by and a few real estate agents present to show us spaces and then afterwards, farms and mansions since he insisted that I'd need to live down there during the opening. So off we went to tour these mansions and see a few massive farms outside of town from the comfort of the helicopter. One of them was absolutely stunning and Christopher said he'd buy it and just let me live on it as long as I liked. I thought I was in like Flynn.

As these things do, his con came apart eventually. My partners at the restaurant tired of the endless excuses as to why the money we needed to keep going wasn't arriving from him. Christopher was always about to get the cheque, waiting for it to be approved by a bank in Switzerland or waiting for his father to sign off on it. We'd get concerned, have a meeting with him and he'd tell us it was just a small delay and that he'd bring us some cash to float us in the meantime. This went on for months. One time, Joe McNulty was supposed to receive a large brown bag full of money, and waited literally ten hours for it to arrive. Christopher's con was very extensive and I don't know how he did it, but he had Joe on the phone with all manner of people in Switzerland supposedly at his bank, confirming everything he was saying. It was unbelievably clever.

That bank scam is how he got his operating money I'm quite sure. He was duping loads of wealthy people and then using their money to live on and keep the scam going. One of the last times I saw him, when I began to suspect that it was all over and that he'd never invest with us, I was driving him back to the Beverly Wilshire and he picked up these Armani sunglasses that I'd bought for Lynn who had left them in my car. At this point I still believed that Christopher was who he said he was, but didn't believe that he wanted to invest anymore. Lynn really loved those glasses and they were a present from me but I was such a whore, holding out that we may still have a chance through Christopher. So when he picked up the glasses and said he liked them and that they looked good on him, I told him he could have them. I figured I'd just buy Lynn another pair.

Lynn wasn't okay with that, she loved the glasses primarily because they were a gift from me, and she said that if I bought her another pair it wouldn't be the same. So to make amends I promised her that I'd get them back. It had begun to get a little strange with Christopher, not just with us but with other people around town from what we were hearing but he was still keeping up appearances. When I got to the hotel and went up to his suite however, he had a guy sitting outside that looked like a Mafia hit man. He was there alone in the hallway and I could see that he had a gun in his jacket, which wasn't quite a garden-variety thing in the Beverly Wilshire. The thuggish guard let me into the suite, which was this marble Scarface type ordeal. I couldn't see Christopher so I called out and from the bathroom he beckoned me to come in. I entered to find him in a bubble bath, smoking a cigar and sipping a glass of champagne like Marilyn Monroe. He hopped out completely naked, got into a robe, went into the living room and launched into a maniacal rant about my partners. They had threatened him, and having the connections that they had, I'm quite sure Christopher was taking it very, very seriously. He blamed me for it and kept saying, 'Mickey I thought you loved me.' Then his tone switched like a light and he began to tell me that he wasn't afraid of them or of anyone because of all of the guns he had and how tough he was. I tried to be like a father figure and calm him down but it didn't work. All I wanted was the sunglasses back, but there I was with Christopher going mad, raving on about this gang war he intended to have with my partners. Before I knew it he'd pulled out a .357 Magnum from the top drawer of the dresser, and I glimpsed a collection of other guns in there as well.

'I've got the shit, too, I'm not afraid of them,' he said. 'I don't need to hear shit from anybody! All of you can shut up and leave me alone!'

That was my cue to exit, and for the record I never got the sunglasses back. Christopher went to jail of course, but he was the kind of guy that if I saw him again I'd probably forgive him. What he did was so out there that it bordered on genius the way he had everyone going. I got what I deserved. I believed that money was going to drop out of the sky for me in my time of need, so I was the fool. I was ripe for the picking.

While the restaurant was open we also met some of the first Russians with money to come over to LA and get into business. It's debatable which side of the line they were on but Joe and I were interested in talking to anyone that might be able to help us save the restaurant. One was a business man who invited us over to Russia to meet his people in Moscow and to be involved in a few ventures they had going, the primary one being the import of pure bottled glacier water from the mountains of Tajikistan. Another was to start a club and restaurant for the well-to-do in Moscow because there wasn't anything like that there at the time. That is where we came in because we had a degree of expertise in that area. Expertise wasn't exactly necessary for the various transactions we were being offered, however. The Russians we met asked us to broker all manner of deals. They wanted us to sell military submarines to a few of their South American contacts. Not exactly a continent known for it's military power, I can only surmise that such vessels would have been used for, shall we say, clandestine transport of goods. We were also offered tanks, jets, and just about anything else that a carpet bagger businessman with money to spend might want.

Before I knew it I was in Moscow. In those days the Russian government allowed American currency to be used there so the dollar was king and many entrepreneurs went over to test the waters at that time, Joe and I being two of them. We spent weeks in Moscow and had incredible adventures just when the place had opened itself to the rest of the world. A lot of it felt like spy stuff because most of the businessmen we met were ex-KGB. It's a well known fact that Putin is one of them, because all of those guys still run the country and it's no different than it was before.

Back then there was at least an aspiration to do things differently. Every business plan was a joint venture, as they called them, with the Russians providing the markets and the foreign entrepreneurs providing the products and experience. One of the businesses we were made moves to start was a Tajik airline. We even found a 747 up in moth balls in Santa Barbara for the Russians to buy. We had Tajik Airlines printed on the side but that was as far as it went. Neither the plane nor the business ever left the ground but we had that plane for a while because we believed we were going to start an airline there in Tajikistan.

I remember going down back streets in Moscow to meet people who could 'make things happen' who took us to see properties that would become a club where foreign and local businessmen could meet. Of course it's now common knowledge that doing business in Russia is treacherous. They tend to do business with foreign partners and then tell them to fuck off, keeping their money and shared assets. It's still happening; there are very few people who survive doing business with Russians.

But there we were, in some kind of Klondike Gold Rush, this one just as dangerous, though we didn't realise it to the extent we should of. I remember on one occasion being in one of the few existing businessmen's discotheques and that place was wild. There were women of the night everywhere, whatever you wanted was available for purchase, and there was a tangibly present criminal element. Joe and I were sitting at a table with our guide who warned us to keep to ourselves no matter what happened.

Joe got really drunk and I did too and he is the most friendly person in the world, even more so after a few rounds. We were sitting near these girls and one of them told Joe her handbag had been stolen. Joe rightly figured it was the guy next to her, and was about to intervene. I told him not to get involved, but he wasn't about to listen. Before he said anything, the girl got a better look at the guy and realised she should just leave it. She told Joe not to ask for it back but he wasn't listening to her either. I took a long look at the guy and could immediately tell he was pretty fucking heavy, plus I had a clear view of the gun in his belt. I nearly leapt across the table, got in Joe's ear and told him he'd better back the fuck off because the guy had a gun. That sobered Joe up and he let it go. But the guy had noticed us talking about him and began to get pissed off. He made a scene giving the bag back to the girl, and stood there boldly as she opened it and found it completely empty. No one said a word. Mick and Joe, welcome to Moscow.

One thing I intended to do on that trip was visit an antiques market I'd heard of because at the time the Russians were selling valuable art work and ancient religious icons to anyone interested. These were pieces that had been taken from churches and at first that wasn't considered a crime by the government.

I found out where to go and a cab driver from our hotel brought me there and waited for me while I did my shopping. We had been advised to always keep our valuables close, including our passports and visas, so I put all of those documents plus about five thousand dollars in cash in my rucksack and went down in my full length fur coat to buy some art, hardly fitting in, looking like a rockstar I'm sure. I found a stall full of antiques in this open air flea market manned by all these young dudes. I thought it was a bit weird that this group of young guys had collected all of this great art, and even weirder that they all spoke perfect English.

I started talking to them about the religious icons in their collection and the next thing I knew they recognised me, saying, 'You're Fleetwood Mac!' They were all about 22, so it was pretty wild that they even knew the band, having grown up when the country was Communist and entirely closed to the West. It was even more awesome and bizarre when they began referencing the Peter Green years. I was amazed and thrilled and really taken in – which I suppose is what they wanted – because as I now know, while I was distracted and talking, one of them was relieving me of the contents of my rucksack.

I can only assume that my driver had tipped them off as to who I was, but I still don't know how they knew about Peter Green, because they really knew their stuff, naming songs and albums and everything. In any case, I bought a couple of icons from them which I still have, and I'm lucky that I got them when I did because soon afterwards the government shut that down and made the possession and export of such objects punishable by jail time.

I wandered around a bit more, and by the time I was ready to leave, finally realised that the load in my sack had gotten much lighter. I was like a lorry driver in a cartoon who doesn't realise that his cargo is falling off with each and every turn until he arrives at his destination. That was me, blissfully parading around, losing precious possessions with each passing minute. For the sake of security I'd brought all those things with me, only to have them pilfered inside of an hour right under my nose. I can't say with certainty that the cab driver was in on it, but when I told him what had happened, he went into the market and got my passport and visa back quite quickly. Well, at least I got my icons.

I'd learned to travel young and obviously I don't like to ever be bored. I was used to a high level of drama being in and running the band, so to me, stories like these explain who I am. I was never frightened to go on the craziest of adventures. I don't know what the motivation is exactly, but it's there within me and it certainly is poetic at its best, foolish at its worst. I consider it akin to going on hunting expeditions, or mountaineering, my drive has the same adventurous spirit. I've just always liked to pick up and go on trips that no one in their right mind would go on.

When we were first together, Lynn and I lived in a home in Encino. She worked for Orion Pictures, but in reality she spent more time looking after me and my life, and eventually she left her job to do just that. We were very much equal partners, because while I paid the rent, Lynn was paying her own way. I was still in the process of being divorced from Sara, but it wasn't complete. There was a time when Sara harassed Lynn by calling our home, leaving messages for me from 'your wife', and saying cruel things about Lynn on our answering machine. Sara was hurt and felt betrayed, after she found out that Lynn and I had been together when she and I were separated. It was hard for me; I understood Sara's distress and out of guilt, I let the calls happen. Eventually, Sara stopped lashing out and the calls ceased.

Lynn started to wonder if our relationship would ever grow or if it would simply remain in this type of limbo. She didn't think I was emotionally through with Sara, so she broke it off with me.

'I don't know what it is, Mick,' she said. 'Maybe it's that Sara got sober and you didn't, and now you are, but you're hanging on to something. You're not even divorced. I can't be with you until you've figured that out.'

I was in Las Vegas playing a show with the Blue Whale, my blues band with guitarist Ron Thompson, bassist Bill Campbell and percussionist Oliver Brown, when I made up my mind and called her.

'Hello?' she said.

'Lynn Frankel,' I said. 'I want to marry you.'

'Really?'

'Yes.'

There was a long silence.

'There's something we have to do first,' she said.

'Anything.'

'We have to date.'

'What do you mean, sweetheart?'

'We have to date. We never dated. You have to pick me up and take me out, then take me home and go back to your hotel. We never had a courtship, we spent it all in my apartment. You have to date me and I have to date you.'

'Well, then let's do it.'

So that's what we did: I'd pick her up and drop her off and sometimes not even go inside. We had a lovely, formal courtship. It lasted only a few weeks, but it was important and it was a lot of fun. Our relationship deserved it and things felt different between us immediately. It erased whatever trust issues Lynn had about my feelings for her and allowed us to begin anew.

We moved back in together and set about planning our wedding. At the time I was in the throes of the mini-Mac, and since we were going to be in Europe, Lynn and I decided we'd marry in Italy. She got all the paperwork sorted and we chose a city, but then she came down with a horrible flu and couldn't fly. So we looked at the tour dates again, and the Blue Whale was booked to play the Harley-Davidson Love Ride Convention at the Colorado Belle Hotel in Laughlin, Nevada. We thought that would be perfect – too kitschy to be true. The hotel had a riverboat for weddings that held eighty people and came complete with a minister, plastic flowers, the works.

Lynn told her family, and her mother and brother made plans to come out, as did her biological father. Lynn thought her father wouldn't be able to make it, because it was short notice and he was in the middle of a very intense business negotiation. So I called him and asked properly for her hand in marriage, and told him how much it would mean to Lynn to have him walk her down the aisle. He agreed to come and Lynn was incredibly happy.

We got to Laughlin and did the gig to throngs of all these Harley people and it was wild. We made the mistake of checking in under the name Fleetwood, which resulted in calls up to the room all night from fans carrying on downstairs in the hotel bar. Eventually we had to ask the front desk to hold all our calls, so we could get some rest before the ceremony. Everything was in order on the boat and just as we were walking back to the hotel to go to our separate rooms and get dressed, we saw Lynn's brother out in front of the hotel, crying. Lynn's father had flown to Vegas the night before, but had suffered a heart attack and passed away during the night. Time stopped. We literally did not believe it to be true.

We were eventually married a few months later, on 26 July 1995 when the mini-Mac came to New York City. We had an afternoon ceremony at Tavern on the Green in Central Park and it was lovely. Then we set about building our life together, which continued to be a non-stop series of adventures that left the two of us both awestruck and giddy.

One such adventure, for which I can thank the Clinton administration, was the trip I took to Cuba with the Music Bridges Foundation. My partner Todd Smallwood who wrote and sang on the Mick Fleetwood Band album *Something Big* helped organise the event and he did a great job. In the end a really wild and creative bunch went down, everyone from Burt Bacharach, to me, to Bonnie Raitt, Gladys Knight, Woody Harrelson and Don Was. It was truly, as the event intended to be (and probably why the Clinton administration okayed the venture) a bridge between the two countries on a purely artistic level. Art, music, writing and poetry can make those connections regardless of politics, and that is exactly what happened. The premise was that artists from the U.S. and Cuba would meet for two weeks and collaborate, which we did. Lynn and I and the rest of the American cultural emissaries were put up in this fabulous old Havana hotel, a gorgeous place that had retained all the grace of Cuba's heyday in the 40s and 50s. Each of us musicians were paired with a Cuban counterpart, with whom we wrote music and recorded it in this portable studio they had installed in a few suites at the end of the hall. The culmination of our efforts was a concert, and the celebration of yet another bridge between the US and Cuba: baseball. The Baltimore Orioles were flown in to play against a top Cuban team as part of the festivities.

It was an extension of the olive branch by the Clinton Administration and it was very profound. We got to watch the game, have an audience with Fidel Castro, the whole lot, and my wife Lynn was there with me through all of it. She was the greatest partner in that way: no matter what kind of crazy scenario I volunteered myself for, she was my co-pilot all the way, ready to pack her bag and go with me at the drop of a hat.

Cuba is just 80 miles away from the US and it amazed me how much their culture has remained untouched, even after the United States' direct influence and intervention into their country. Somehow it's all survived, perhaps a little worse for wear, but completely intact and out of time. It's one of the most romantic and musical places I've ever been and the spirit of the people there nearly took my breath away. Havana was full of old and glamorous hotels, gorgeous classic cars from the 50s and music literally oozed from every nook and cranny. I'd drive by school kids, impeccable in their uniforms, waiting for their bus, all of them singing songs together, some of them banging on whatever bit of metal or wood lay nearby by way of percussion.

It was everything I'd imagined it to be, and what I'd envisioned when I read Ernest Hemingway's works. I made a point to visit the hotel where he lived while writing in Cuba and I was allowed to see his actual room, which is closed off from the public. My guide even left me there for a few minutes. I closed the door, looked out the window at Ernest's view, then lay on his bed and did my best to absorb that moment. Of all the things I've been allowed to do on account of my renown with Fleetwood Mac, I consider that one of the greatest.

Again, that trip wouldn't have happened if it weren't for President Clinton, with whom Fleetwood Mac has had a long-standing and wonderful relationship. When President Clinton

left office in 2001, Fleetwood Mac was asked to play a surprise
going away party that the First Lady had planned for him. I'll
never know if he knew about it or not but it seemed like he
didn't. We agreed to play of course, since we'd played the
inauguration, and we were meant to be yet another surprise
on top of the surprise party.

We arrived that afternoon with our touring crew and friends,
all in all an entourage of about 30, and to keep us out of sight,
we were escorted to the West Wing and given complete run of
the place. It was a huge honor, too much fun, and to say the
least quite surreal. We were allowed to wander all over ostensibly the most important and powerful halls of any building
in the world. The lot of us couldn't believe it; we took pictures
of bedrooms, meeting rooms, and my manager Carl and I snuck
around and opened every single door we encountered. Behind
one of them was a remarkable library-like sitting room lined
in portraits of all of the former Presidents. We had to take a
moment and sit in there, just soaking in all of the history and
majesty of where we were.

Our group being a traveling rock band, I have to admit that
events occurred that I'm quite sure do not fall within the White
House code of conduct for guests. Rest assured that nothing
was damaged, defaced or stolen, but suffice to say that some
good-natured naughtiness was had by a few of our troupe.
And though we felt like we had complete freedom and were
utterly on our own, we most certainly were not. Spend any
time at all in the White House and you'll learn quickly that
there are cameras everywhere and everything is observed – if
tolerated – at all times. There's no knowing what else those
cameras recorded, and I for one will never tell.

The tents and tables for the festivities were set up outside
on the lawn, and after we got dressed in the West Wing we

were brought around behind the main tent so that no one would see us. The party got under way, there were speeches and we were kept out of sight, our instruments hidden behind a second curtain that concealed the stage. The proceedings were running behind schedule which was fine, we were all ready, me looking like Mr. Rumours with my balls and my tights on. Then a bit more time passed, until finally we were told that stage time was just a few minutes off. The only problem was that I'd had a few drinks during the delay and suddenly realised that I'd never make it through the set without first taking a pee. I looked around for a portable toilet but saw none, and gathered that returning to the White House, which was a few hundred yards away, wasn't an option.

The closest toilet was only accessible through the audience, but that was an impossibility because Fleetwood Mac playing was intended to be a surprise and no one was going to miss me, at my height, winding through the audience like a wandering minstrel with wooden balls hanging off my crotch.

Not knowing what else to do, my manager Carl walked over to the nearest guard, who was in fatigues armed with a machine gun.

'Sorry to bother you, but Mr. Fleetwood has to pee and we don't see a bathroom back here,' he said. 'Do you have any ideas?'

It didn't look like it but clearly the guy was mic'ed, and home base was listening. He never acknowledged Carl, just looked at him briefly. Then he put his finger to his ear, and said: 'Mr. Fleetwood is clear to piss on the White House lawn, sir.'

The guard then escorted me to the back of the tent, took me outside and let me do my business, free as a bird in the wind, out into the night on the most famous lawn in America.

We went on stage as soon as I returned and it was a great

evening. President Clinton was thrilled and that time along with every other experience I've had with the Clintons has been fantastic. They came to see us in St. Louis on our last tour and before the show ended I made sure to acknowledge them and say goodnight because I knew they planned to leave before the encores. Over the years, Bill Clinton has sent things to us to sign and we sent him some gold records to decorate his office after he left the White House. He always responded with gracious letters of thanks in return, which I treasure. Several times over the years I've also sent him drum skins that I've asked him to sign, and he always has, returning them with another little letter. We book ended his administration and I could not be prouder to have done so for such a great man. Above and beyond him being President, I don't think I've ever met anyone as intelligent, focused and charming. He is the type of person who always remembered everyone's name, the names of their children, and details of the last time that he has seen you. It goes above and beyond any preparation that his staff can do for him, it is just who he is. As a parting gift, the Clintons sent everyone in the Fleetwood Mac family a framed platinum record plaque that contained every single album that the band ever put out, with a notation of total sales and a letter from Hilary, Chelsea and Bill thanking us for being a part of the Clinton White House. I can't think of anything more indicative of who they are as people than that.

As much as we loved our adventures, Lynn and I wanted to settle in one place and start a family, so we moved from L.A. to Maui and in 2002, we had two beautiful twin daughters, Ruby and Tessa. Though we are parting now, Lynn and I, as much as we possibly can, remain the best of friends, with our gorgeous girls as our main priority. We were partners and co-conspirators and the times we had were unbelievably and impossibly fun. The stories I've shared here are but a small sample, believe me. And though what we are going through now is hard, I hope that the best of us is what we both carry forth in our hearts in the years to come, because what we were together deserves that.

CHAPTER 19

IT'S GOOD TO BE BACK

As of now, the most famous line-up of Fleetwood Mac is together and creating again. And it's different this time. It's better. It really is. If you don't believe me, take it from John. Unlike me, my dear friend is a man of few words. He chooses them wisely and well, and he isn't one to gush. That said, after we got together in April 2014 to work on music with Chris and Lindsey, and after John had successfully undergone treatment for colon cancer, he sent me a very uncharacteristic email. He had received a clean bill of health from his doctor and was excited to get his boat all outfitted to sail from LA to Honolulu. He planned to captain it himself and couldn't wait to get going. He emailed me this note before he went: 'Hey Mick, how you doing? I hope well. Don't get too stressed out. Listen . . . it's all different now . . . isn't it? It's fun.'

But wait, before I get ahead of myself, let me tell you how we got here.

It was Christine's return to the group that changed everything. After she left us in 1998, she made one solo album that she will be the first to say was the wrong idea. Not musically, but because she was unable to promote it due to a paralysing fear of flying. In fact, none of us realised just how deep-seated her phobia had become by the end of her tenure with Fleetwood Mac. For years afterwards she would not go near a plane. She ended her time in the music business altogether, because that meant air travel, and spent the better part of seventeen years in the English countryside. That was part of her plan, to have a gorgeous country house and spend her days hunting and fishing and driving her Rover and raising her dogs.

We would see her from time to time; I probably kept in touch more than anyone else. We'd go out to dinner whenever I was in England and we would talk about what she was doing. She was detached; she'd made a concerted effort to leave music and all that she'd known, but in the process she became alienated from life itself. She spent a lot of her time on her own, alone in her gorgeous house. After a while, she found that lifestyle investment was paying her no dividends. People missed her, not just us, and when we toured her absence loomed large. Whenever any of us did an interview we'd be asked about her. All of us in our way would paraphrase what we knew: 'Chris is living the life she wants to live and we all wish she were here with us but she doesn't want to be.'

I'd be open about saying that I didn't understand how she was okay with not writing or performing music. Truthfully, I didn't know how that was possible for someone like Chris. She didn't have to rejoin us, but I couldn't comprehend how someone so connected to her musicality could simply turn that off. I thought she'd miss it and though it was none of my business, I didn't think it was good for her. Now that she's come round, Chris agrees with me. She's basically said, 'What was I thinking?'

She came back to herself through a deep desire to travel and only by confronting her fear was she able to find herself again.

After a few years fulfilling her idyllic English country dream, Chris began to fantasise about visiting China and other places, all of them feasibly accessible only by plane. At that time, she was like a fly in a wine glass, buzzing around, hitting the four walls of her house. Over the years her world had grown increasingly small, so much so that she finally sought help. She got a therapist who specialised in the fear of flying and they began to go to work. In one of their early sessions he asked her where she would like to go first.

'I'd like to go to Maui,' she said. 'I'd like to visit Mick and John.'

'Well, book a ticket, then,' he said.

'I can't do that.'

'You can't do that now and I don't want you to book a ticket to go tomorrow. I want you to book a ticket for six months from now.'

She worked every day to be able to get on that flight, because it had been a long time coming. She'd been bullshitting me for years that she was going to come and visit John and me, so when she referred to it again during our conversations I tried not to get my hopes up; by then I knew how hard it was for her to even contemplate boarding a plane.

Time wore on and just before the date for her promised trip to Hawaii, I flew to London to do some press in advance of our shows at the O2 arena. I was there for a week, and I saw Chris and asked her if she'd rather move her holiday forward and come back with me to Hawaii. I was well aware that this would be her first flight in over fifteen years, and England to Hawaii is a long haul, so I told her we'd make it fun and I'd be her roadie. I'd sit with her, tend to her, and do whatever it took to make the journey a smooth one for her. I wasn't sure she'd go for it, but she did and we had a ball. She'd done the work for all those months and though she wasn't without apprehension, she was mentally prepared to face the fear that had held her landlocked for over a decade.

She had the greatest time in Hawaii, I mean, she really fucking loved it. She stayed down in Lahaina at a great hotel and she came up to my farm to hang out while I rehearsed with Rick Vito and my blues band for an annual fundraiser that I do. I knew Steven Tyler was off tour, relaxing at his house on the island at the time, so I'd called him in to join us. Chris hadn't seen Rick in years and they had a proper reunion and she and Steven got on smashingly.

I would be a liar if I said I didn't hope that Chris would play with us but I honoured my vow to her and never brought it up. The main room at my farm has high, vaulted ceilings and is acoustically a dream to play in; it has been my music retreat for many years and where I always rehearse. At the back of it is a quiet sitting room, where you can watch the proceedings without being in the thick of it. That's where Chris sat, with the splendour of Maui Harbor laid out behind her through the big bay windows. She didn't once approach the grand piano, sitting there just a few feet away, although it begged for her.

After one rehearsal, Rick joked to me that he was going to play 'I'd Rather Go Blind', the Etta James tune that Chris covered in Chicken Shack, earning them a Top 20 hit in England back in the day. He did and launched into it without warning, thinking that surely that siren song would draw Chris to the piano. No such luck. She sat there unfazed. Unbeknownst to me, when I was out of the room, Steven and Rick even asked Chris flat out if she'd like to do a song or two at the gig, and from what I understand now, she replied with an unconvincing 'yes'.

With four days to go before the gig, I was up in my bedroom, lying there early in the morning, when the house phone rang. That was uncommon, because not many people have that line. I picked it up thinking something was wrong.

'Hello, Mick? It's Chris.'

There is no other way to describe this than to say she sounded *tiny*. Tiny like a nervous schoolgirl asking to use the toilet.

'Chris? Is everything okay?'

'Yeah, yeah sure,' she said. 'Um, I've been thinking, um, would you like me to play at this gig?'

'What? *Yes!* Sweetheart! Of course I would! Are you kidding me?'

'I thought it might be fun.'

I had no words – I was overjoyed.

We've spoken about it since, and everything she's done in terms of playing music again hinged on that moment; it literally all started there. I've known Chris a long time and played with her for over forty years so I can say without a doubt that the timbre of her voice expressed just how tentatively she took that first step.

Once she did, she was on her way. She did the gig with us, but to allow her the comfort of backing out at any point up until the last minute, I didn't announce that she would be performing with us. Rick and I brought a piano round to her hotel suite that day and sat with her and rehearsed the songs she wanted to do. We played 'Rattlesnake Shake' and 'Don't Stop' and I could barely contain myself thinking about how the audience was going to go bananas. On the day of the gig I alluded to a special guest, knowing that I could always say it was Steven Tyler, but Chris came through. She did more than any of us expected – in addition to 'Rattlesnake' and 'Don't Stop' she did one of her old ones, 'Get Like You Used to Be', and even stayed on stage for 'World Turning'. She'd flown six thousand miles and got on stage for the first time in seventeen years and she wasn't fucking frightened, in fact, she was amazing.

Her next step was in London at the O2 arena. You can imagine how excited I was to tell Lindsey about what had gone on in Hawaii, but both of us knew that this didn't mean Chris was ready or willing to come back completely.

Lindsey kept me in check, reminding me that we should find out whether Chris was coming back for good or not. We were all fine with her coming out and doing a song, maybe two, but until we knew she was serious, we had to be sceptical. As she had before, Chris started phoning us, and we started phoning each other.

'Linds, have you spoken to Chris?'

'I have, what's going on? She's talking about doing the European tour and playing music again.'

'I know. What do you think?'

'She's talked about doing this before.'

'I know. Maybe she's reconnecting. This really could be it.'

'Yeah, but she can't mess around.'

'I know, Lindsey. No, she can't.'

'Yeah, but what if?'

'I know!'

Our worry was that Chris might not want to commit to the degree of work we were talking about. We had a three year plan for the band so before we got our hopes up, we had to be sure she understood what coming back meant.

'Mick, do you think she realises what we're looking at if we do this?' Lindsey asked.

'Sort of.' It was the best I could do.

A day or so later each of us got a call from Stevie, who had just spoken to Chris.

'Is she kidding?' Stevie asked. 'Is this some fantasy she has, about what this is?'

'No, I don't think so,' I said. "I believe she's really thinking about it.'

After that Stevie spoke to her again and said unabashedly that she wanted Chris back. 'Please,' she said, 'it would make life easier for me!'

Chris had tremendous deference about coming back to the band and when she'd call me to talk about it, she had that same humble, little girl tone to her voice. She wanted to be sure everyone wanted her and that she wouldn't be taking away from what we'd done in her absence because she'd been gone nearly fifteen years.

We flew Chris to Ireland to rehearse with us and it was a lot of fun, as if no time had passed. We decided she'd make an appearance in London and do another few gigs and then we'd address the situation again. We had practised a handful of songs, but in the end we thought it best that Chris come out and do just one, which is what we did. We waited even longer, after the tour had ended, to let the cat out of the bag and announce that she was back for good. But the truth was that after London, in our minds, the band was back together.

During the European shows that Chris came out for, we started exchanging song ideas, and watching her and Lindsey reactivated as a creative pair was invigorating. We started talking about getting into the studio and working on a new record and discussing how we would – and should – give it another go together.

At the end of that tour, I went to her room in Amsterdam and told her the news that John had cancer. She was devastated, no matter how much I assured her that the prognosis was good. We had one last dinner together and the next time I saw Chris was in the studio in Los Angeles in April 2014. She has transformed from the fly trapped in a wine glass of her own design to a world traveller. After that first trip, she went on a huge safari in Africa, flying all over the continent in single-engine Cessnas. She went straight from there to live in LA with us for two months. After we're done with the last date of our next tour, she's going to South Africa on holiday because she was there once and loved it so. She'll be away from home for seven months! I'd say she has faced her fears and then some. It's amazing how much she's changed her life. I might have worried about her considering all the road work we have in store, but she's already done it. She's ready to go.

Chris, Lindsey and I spent two months working on what will be the next Fleetwood Mac album this spring, with John, Chris and me sharing a gorgeous house in Santa Monica and all of us recording in Studio D at the Village Recorder where we did *Tusk*. Chris and I were like the odd couple sitting around the pool, joking that there would be a new rumour that we were emotionally involved. We had the greatest time. It was rock-and-roll boot camp; for two months we'd get up at 7 a.m. and do yoga and exercise, then head to the studio for the day. Quite a different routine to the way we used to prepare to record.

I say without hesitation that this has been altogether different and altogether wonderful. The chemistry between us has never been better and it's all coming together so easily and enjoyably. I'm not alone. Chris has been saying lately that it all feels like a dream, and I know exactly what she means. It is a dream. It's the same one we've been having, all of us, apart and together. But now we're having it together again.

We will start rehearsing for an extensive tour in August 2014. By then we will have the makings of what I hope will be a new album by Fleetwood Mac written by all of us, as it should be. Our tour is already sold out and we've just sold another forty dates well into 2015. That will probably become sixty shows. And that is all before we go overseas.

We have no intention of running our ensemble into the ground the way we used to do; we've learned to look after ourselves. Stevie takes great care of her voice and for the first time Chris is using Stevie's voice coach to take care of hers, as well. Lindsey is a unique creature; he sounds perfect whether he's just finished a tour or hasn't sung in months. I think he could not sing for fifteen years and get on stage and still sound flawless out of the gate. John is a perfectionist and he was back up to speed in no time, cancer be damned. As for me, my job is pretty physical and I've learned my lesson. I need to stick to a healthy regime or none of this will be possible.

Sometimes I think about how I used to carry on and it amazes me that I'm still here. Back then, most of my days off were spent repairing myself. If I knew I had two days off, after the gig I would stay up, organise a party, then go round to some other hotel where another band might be in town. Before I knew it, my days off were gone and I'd been up the whole time. I'd end up backstage pretending to sleep for two hours before our next show, but I wouldn't be sleeping. I'd be way too wired. So then I'd have to really do myself in by drinking heavily just to get through the gig.

As fun as some of those memories are, it's not a healthy business model, and the romance for me is gone. I used to find the lunacy of it electrifying, but now the thought of those scenarios coming to life again makes me feel physically ill. There is a real sense among us all that this is our victory lap, and though we haven't said as much, I've known all of these people long enough to know they feel it too. The mood in the studio – the vibe that John hit upon in that email – is tangible. It's just so wonderful that we're all together again and making such great music that even Lindsey's generally aloof demeanour has been challenged. I'm the first one to shed a tear and bear-hug everyone, but this time around that's been Mr Buckingham! He's been more available emotionally than I've ever seen him. I found myself walking around the studio snapping photos like a tourist: 'Oh look, there's Lindsey and Chris riffing on the couch, happy as two pigs in shit!' This rebooting of our relationship with Chris has brought us all back and reminded us from whence we have come – and it's been awesome.

All of this, of course, is in preparation for Stevie, who will join us in the studio later this year after she finishes her last solo album for Warner Brothers. She won't be distant from the process; rather, we will be ready for her. The truth is that Stevie is a vocalist, while the rest of us are musicians, so we will set the stage for her entrance, and together we will work out what I believe will be a fitting return for this line-up of the band.

One thing I do know is that whenever this band ends, no matter what, that won't be the end for Stevie. I believe she will perform until her very last breath, much like Edith Piaf, whom she reminded me of the first time I heard her sing. The first gift I ever gave Stevie was a boxed set of albums by Edith Piaf, because those two are one and the same in many ways. Edith was on stage only twenty hours before she dropped dead and I think Stevie will go in much the same way, because as much as she claims she'd love some time off, the girl never stops. I picture Stevie in her eighties, writing gorgeous romance novels and finally telling her incredible life story. Like Edith's, Stevie's fans will be there because they are devoted and they will follow their Gypsy wherever she goes.

And me, perhaps I'll be the same.

I SOLD MY SOUL TO THE COMPANY STORE

Looking back, that is truly what I've done – I sold my soul to the company store. I have to accept that reality and make peace with it. For the most part I have, because I've realised that I am the store and the store is me, but there is a sadness in truly understanding the collateral damage that caused, from the emotional suffering brought upon my children, to the lifestyle that inadvertently injured people I loved. Reflecting on my life has helped me to understand how all of that happened, as it has made me realise that I probably wouldn't have done anything differently; mostly because I was truthfully, and somewhat bliss-fully, unaware. I've done all that I can to repair that damage with my children and I've tried to be the best father and grand-father that I can be. My daughter Lucy lives with me in Hawaii and we spend more time together now than we did during the first twenty years of her life. I'm so happy I get to share her life with her, at this stage in mine. Her sister Amelia and I are also closer now than ever. We write a weekly column for an English newspaper and are very much connected. I'm glad that I'm able to give them real time now, since I didn't when they were young.

I have a new partner in my life now, Chelsea Hill, who has a wonderful daughter, and I love the both of them very much. My relationship with Chelsea is a reality that I am learning to integrate properly into my life and my children's lives. Chelsea and I were friends for a few years during the final days of my marriage to Lynn and when Lynn and I parted, I began to spend more time with Chelsea and fell completely in love with her.

I'm a different man than I used to be but often I feel that I'm still the same soul I was as a child; the young boy who adopted the simplistic philosophy that in order to survive he would do the only thing he thought he was good at. I still have the same sense of adventure that urged me to leave home and follow my dream. For better and for worse I've chased that muse around the world and back again, somehow knowing in my heart that it would all turn out alright.

As a young chap, sitting in my sister's garage playing drums, I'd sometimes ask myself, 'What are you doing? How are your parents going to feel?' But I had no answer. I didn't understand then that it had ramifications. I did realise that if I ran away and disappeared into the countryside, it would be the worst thing I could ever do to my parents, because they'd think I was either dead or in danger, and I didn't want to make them suffer. But short of running away, I was only going to play drums, come what may.

I'm sure my mother did suffer, and worry, and I'm lucky that I still have her here with me at my age so that I can make it up to her. She's got a great perspective on my life because she's seen the little drummer boy grow up and make his dream a reality. She's seen the entire Fleetwood Mac drama, every single bit of the whole story. Her comment when I told her that we were getting back together? It was priceless. There she was, ninety-seven years old, sitting on her veranda in Maui, the day I went to say goodbye before flying to LA to meet the others. We had a lovely lunch and as I got ready to go, she called me back.

'Son,' she said, 'good luck out there, and play well. Make a great album. There's nothing like the songs you did when you were all together.'

'I will make you proud, Mum, I promise.'

'But one more thing,' she said, and her eyes lit up.

'Yes, Mum.'

'Now Mick, you must listen to me. This time, they're going to behave themselves, aren't they?'

ACKNOWLEDGEMENTS

It is with a great-full heart that I thank every one of the players, family and friends, past and present, and acknowledge, with deep gratitude, every person who took part in this wonderful journey by my side.

Sincerely,

Mick Fleetwood

Three years ago I had the pleasure of meeting Anthony Bozza when he interviewed me for a Playboy article at a very pivotal point in my life. I invited Anthony to stay with me at my Maui hill top farm and from there, while we talked, a firm bond of mutual understanding and respect was established. It was the first time for me, that I so openly admitted my abandoned hope for the continuation of Fleetwood Mac. What he witnessed was my quest, my holy grail, which has really been my driving force my entire adult life, fading away into the distance. In the end, the article proved to be a catalyst for the next chapter of the play. When deciding to write my memoirs Anthony was naturally my first choice as a partner in crime. With his easy cadence and parallel sense of humour we unravelled, pieced, knocked and strung together the adventures that constitute my life.

Most of the photographs are from the author's collection.

Additional photographs:

© Richard Aaron: 18 (above left and right, and middle). © Alamy: 4 (below right) and 5 (middle right)/ photos Pictorial Press, 21 (below right)/ photo AF Archive, 29 (below right). © Joe Bangay: 18 (below left). © Corbis: 8 (above right)/ photo Jeff Albertson, 15 (above left)/ photo Aaron Rapoport, 15 (below)/ photo Neal Preston, 25 (below)/ Barbara Kinney, 29 (above left)/ photo Bob King. Photography by Danny Clinch: 32 (top). © Sam Emerson: 9, 13 (middle and below), 23 (middle right). © Eyevine: 11 (above)/ photo Sam Emerson. © Fairfax Media New Zealand: 14 (above)/ photo Evening Post Collection. © Getty Images: 3 (below) and 13 (above)/ photos Michael Ochs, 4 (above)/ photo Jan Persson/ Redferns, 10 (above left)/ photo Michael Montfort/ Michael Ochs Archive, 11 (below)/ photo Richard Creamer/ Michael Ochs Archive, 15 (right)/ photo David Montgomery, 20 (middle)/ photo Richard Aaron/ Redferns, 23 (below)/ photo Ron Galella/ WireImage, 25 (right)/ photo Hulton Archive, 26 (above right) and 31 (above)/ photos Dave Benett, 29 (below left)/ photo Michael Kovac. © Randall Hagadorn Photographer: 14 (below), 19 (below right). © Sean M. Hower 2013: 30 (middle left). Jenny Boyd Collection: 7 (below right and left), 8 (above left), 12 (above left). © Jadran Lazic www.jadranlazic.net: 18 (below right), 23 (above). © Mirrorpix: 21 (above). © Dominique Pandolfi: 30 (below right). © Photoshot: 5 (above)/ photo Michael Putland/ Retna UK, 12 (below)/ Paul Cox/ LFI, 20 (below)/ photo Scott Downie/ LFI. © Neal Preston: 22. © Rex Features: 5 (below right)/ Alan Messer, 10 (middle left)/ photo James Fortune, 25 (above left)/photo Dave Lewis, 25 (middle left)/ photo Sipa Press, 27 (above left)/ photo Lannon Harley/ Newspix, 28 (above left), 29 (above right)/ photo Richard Young. © Richard Saputo: 24 (above). © Rob Shanahan: 32 (below). © Jamie Talbot: 26 (below left), 27 (above right). © Über The Archive Agency: 4 (below left)/ photo Alec Byrne. © Sharon Weisz: 20 (above).

Every reasonable effort has been made to contact the copyright holders, but if there are any errors or omissions, the publisher will be pleased to insert the appropriate acknowledgement any subsequent printing of this publication.

INDEX